Planning Lessons and Courses

PUBLISHED BY THE PRESS SYNDICATE OF THE UNIVERSITY OF CAMBRIDGE
The Pitt Building, Trumpington Street, Cambridge, United Kingdom

CAMBRIDGE UNIVERSITY PRESS
The Edinburgh Building, Cambridge CB2 2RU, UK
40 West 20th Street, New York, NY 10011–4211, USA
477 Williamstown Road, Port Melbourne, VIC 3207, Australia
Ruiz de Alarcón 13, 28014 Madrid, Spain
Dock House, The Waterfront, Cape Town 8001, South Africa

http://www.cambridge.org

First published 2001
Third printing 2002

Printed in the United Kingdom at the University Press, Cambridge

Typeset in Sabon 10/12pt

A catalogue record for this book is available from the British Library

Library of Congress Cataloging-in-Publication Data

Woodward, Tessa.
  Planning lessons and courses: designing sequences of work for the language classroom/
Tessa Woodward.
    p. cm. -- (Cambridge handbooks for language teachers)
    Includes bibliographical references and index.
    ISBN 0-521-63354-0 (pb)
    1. Language and languages--Study and teaching. 2. Lesson planning. I. Title. II.
Series.

P53.47 .W66 2000
418'.0071--dc21   00-048625

ISBN 0 521 63354 0 paperback

Planning Lessons and Courses

Designing sequences of work
for the language classroom

Tessa Woodward

CAMBRIDGE
UNIVERSITY PRESS

CAMBRIDGE HANDBOOKS FOR LANGUAGE TEACHERS

This is a series of practical guides for teachers of English and other languages. Illustrative examples are usually drawn from the field of English as a foreign or second language, but the ideas and techniques described can equally well be used in the teaching of any language.

Recent titles in this series:

Using Newspapers in the Classroom *by Paul Sanderson*

Teaching Adult Second Language Learners *by Heather McKay and Abigail Tom*

Using Folktales *by Eric Taylor*

Teaching English Spelling – A practical guide *by Ruth Shemesh and Sheila Waller*

Personalizing Language Learning – Personalized language learning activities *by Griff Griffiths and Kathryn Keohane*

Teach Business English – A comprehensive introduction to business English *by Sylvie Donna*

Learner Autonomy – A guide to activities which encourage learner responsibility *by Ágota Scharle and Anita Szabó*

The Internet and the Language Classroom – Practical classroom activities *by Gavin Dudeney*

Planning Lessons and Courses – Designing sequences of work for the language classroom *by Tessa Woodward*

Using the Board in the Language Classroom *by Jeannine Dobbs*

Learner English (second edition) *by Michael Swan and Bernard Smith*

Contents

To Pat and Robin, all their offspring and to Grandma Lil

Thanks

To Seth for listening to chapters read out loud and for taking over the typing when my fingers gave out!

To Penny Ur for inviting me to contribute to this series and for her helpful, indefatigable and swift responses to my drafts.

To Alison Silver for her patience and humanity while editing the typescript.

To Jane Clifford for all her support.

To Christine Frank for commenting so charitably on my first draft chapter.

To the two anonymous readers who gave comments on a very early draft.

To Phillip Burrows for his beautiful illustrations.

To Ruth Carim for her meticulous proof-reading.

Acknowledgements

The author and publishers are grateful to the authors, publishers and others who have given permission for the use of copyright material identified in the text. In the cases where it has not been possible to identify the source of material used the publishers would welcome information from copyright owners.

Text on p. 53 from *Teacher Cognition in Language Teaching* by Devon Woods, Cambridge University Press; poem on p. 191 'London Airport' from *Selected Poems* by Christopher Logue, Faber and Faber Ltd; text on p. 200 from *Cambridge English for Schools* by Andrew Littlejohn and Diana Hicks, Cambridge University Press. Illustrations on pp. 46, 72, 109, 130, 161, 179, 211, 242 by Phillip Burrows.

Map of the book

A = Activity

Map of the book

Introduction

What do I mean by planning?

The title of this book is *Planning Lessons and Courses* so I'd like to define right away what I mean by it. By 'planning', I mean what most working teachers do when they *say* they're planning their lessons and courses. Thus I take planning to include the following: considering the students, thinking of the content, materials and activities that could go into a course or lesson, jotting these down, having a quiet ponder, cutting things out of magazines and anything else that you feel will help you to teach well and the students to learn a lot, i.e. to ensure our lessons and courses are good. I do NOT mean the writing of pages of notes with headings such as 'Aims' and 'Anticipated problems' to be given in to an observer before they watch you teach.

I also take it as given that plans are just plans. They're not legally binding. We don't have to stick to them come hell or high water. They are to help us shape the space, time and learning we share with students. We can depart from them or stick to them as we, the students and the circumstances seem to need.

What do I mean by a 'good' lesson or course?

I've said above that planning is something we do to ensure our lessons and courses are good ones. But what is 'good'?

When busy and tired, we often regard the variables of our classes (such as the type of class, the prescribed syllabus, the schedule) as constraints blocking the achievement of a 'good' lesson or course. 'If only ...,' we think. 'If only my class were smaller or I had more resources or I had more time to plan. Then I could teach really well.'

We have perhaps too a view of other people's classes, small ones or big ones or homogeneous ones, as being 'normal' and our own as being exceptional or inferior in some way. We might hear laughter through a classroom wall or watch a teacher preparing bits of paper for an interesting activity and we may feel, 'Gosh! I wish I could do that!' We may assume that 'good' lies outside our own work, outside ourselves.

1

If we have the definition above, of a 'good' lesson or course being one that other people experience or that goes exactly to plan or one that is exactly what we've been told is good or one that's only achievable if we have hours of planning time available, then we are setting ourselves up for failure every time a class is bigger or smaller or worse resourced than it's 'supposed' to be, every time students act like real people and do something unpredictable. We can look at the variables of the classroom differently though, regarding them instead as part of the description of our situation. 'I have a largish class,' we can think, 'with not many resources. So some things are not possible and other things are possible. I'll have to create what I can, given my situation. This is my setting and my design problem and this is how I'm going to set about solving it. I'm going to do the best I can and THAT is what I'm going to call "good"!'

We need to have robust, personal criteria for what we consider good work. Granted, we will inevitably have absorbed notions of what 'good' is from outside ourselves, perhaps from our training, from our favourite teachers from school, or from colleagues, authors or conference presenters that we happen to like. But we need to ponder our own definitions of 'good' to make sure they're realistic and set us up for success.

I'll state my own criteria for a good language course or lesson now. A good lesson or course, to me, is one where there's *plenty of language learning going on* and where the students and I:

- feel comfortable physically, socially and psychologically
- know a little about each other, why we are together and what we want to get out of the experience. (We also know these things may keep shifting slightly as we go through the course.)
- are aware of some of what there is to learn
- are aware of some of the things we have learned
- have a notion about how we learn best
- accept that language is a mixture of things (part instinct, motor skill, system, cultural artefact, music, part vehicle for content and part content itself), that it changes all the time and thus that we need to teach and learn it in a variety of ways
- know why we're doing the activities we're doing
- do things in class that would be worth doing and learn things that are worth learning for their own sake outside the language classroom
- become more capable of taking the initiative, making decisions and judging what is good and useful
- start useful habits which will continue after we have left each other
- follow our course and lesson plans or depart from them when necessary in order to bring about the criteria above.

These are some of the things that are necessary for me to consider a course or lesson good, for me to consider my work good!

What are teachers' concerns about lesson and course planning?

Our concerns about preparing lessons and courses tend to differ according to the amount of experience we have.

A beginner teacher's concern: 'Planning takes too long'

'It just doesn't seem right! I stay up till one in the morning preparing for a 45 minute lesson the next day! I can't see how I can keep this up. What happens when I start a real job and have to teach six hours a day? I mean ... does it get any better?'

This is what a beginner teacher asked me recently. I remembered when I started my first teaching job. I used to spend all evening planning lessons for the next day. Why does lesson preparation take inexperienced teachers so long?

I think it's partly because there are so many variables for a starter teacher to consider as they think about the time they will spend with a class. Starter teachers may think:

- What do I know about the students?
- What will be possible in that physical space with those chairs and that table? How long have I got?
- What shall I teach? Culture, a topic, study skills, listening, vocabulary? Or the next page of the textbook?
- How shall I teach it? How do I interest students and get them working together well and doing something worthwhile?
- How will I know whether things are going well or not?
- What materials shall I use? I hate this page of the textbook. I want a picture of a thirsty woman but I can't find one.
- How will I write my decisions down? My trainer has given me a model plan. I have to write in the timing but I have no idea how long things will take.
- How do I plan a whole series of interesting lessons? On my training course I only did one or two separate ones.
- Will the plan happen? Do I really have the control to make these things happen? Is it OK to change my mind in class and do something I didn't plan? Will the students change things?
- Am I really a teacher? Do I want to be one? Or does it mean being like my old, hated, maths teacher?

- I read the other day that languages are learned and not taught, so am I out of a job anyway?

It's no wonder that beginner teachers wander round their homes making endless cups of tea, staring at books sightlessly, and tearing up sheets of paper. There are a lot of things to consider and to try to get right, *all at the same time*!

An experienced teacher's concern: 'It's getting boring!'

'Oh, that was so boring! Well, actually I don't think THEY were incredibly bored. I mean they were working all right but I bored MYSELF rigid! I've done that lesson too many times.'

Remarks like these, which I've heard in staffrooms or said myself, point to the dilemma of experienced teachers. Planning and teaching have got easier. They don't take up much mental space any more. Experienced teachers can switch onto 'auto-pilot', do things they have done many times before and use their energies in other parts of their lives such as bringing up children, learning fencing or falling in love again.

Auto-pilot is really useful. It can get you through times of fatigue, personal happiness or distress, but it can be boring for the pilot. It's good to be able to cut corners and have more time for yourself but it's not so good to succumb to the temptation of using old ideas and materials again and again.

Ways of getting better at planning

As I said above, I can remember how it felt to spend all evening preparing for one lesson, to stare at paragraphs of explanation in grammar books wondering what anomalous finites were and whether it would be useful for students to learn about them. Here I am 20 years later and sometimes I still feel a bit the same! Now I'm reading about the grammar of speech and wondering if it would help me or my students to learn about it. But one thing IS different now. I can choose how long to take over my planning. I can plan a lot of the next lesson by the time I've finished the present one. I can plan a lesson in about ten minutes, jotting down a few notes on a piece of paper and things still seem to go all right. I can have an outline in my head that is designed to hand most things over to the students. I can spend a long time planning a course or lesson and actually enjoy it!

I'm not alone in this. One experienced colleague writes nothing down but says he does a lot of thinking in the bath in the morning. Another plans out loud to herself on the 45 minute car journey to work.

4

Personally, I'm not one of those people who can 'go in with absolutely nothing and think on my feet'. But then I have met very few such people. Even a colleague of mine who positively rants about the insanity of deciding on Friday night what will happen on Monday morning still admits that he doesn't like going in with absolutely nothing. 'Having a few ideas in your mind is like having banisters at the side of the stairs,' he says. 'When you're running downstairs, you don't necessarily hold on to them but it's nice to know they are there!'

Whatever our ideological position on lesson planning, we have to admit that most students come to class expecting something to happen and most experienced teachers put some thought into how to structure time spent with students. Most experienced teachers can do that thinking a lot more easily than when they started their jobs. What's more they can do it before, during or after lessons. We may not know how we got to be able to do this but most of us, looking back, can sense that a distance has been travelled.

So what *does* happen in between the time when planning takes all night and makes you miserable and the time when you can do it easily and enjoyably while washing or driving or teaching? I'll suggest a number of ways this apparent magic might happen.

The first way: Considering our past learning experiences

Anybody who's attended primary and secondary school, driving lessons, sports training and other learning events has put in thousands of hours in the classroom and consciously or unconsciously will have absorbed a lot of information about what's possible in a lesson or course and what good teaching and learning are. Knowledge of types of group, content, activity, sequences, materials and routines will all have been picked up from the student/observer's angle. Thus any beginner teacher rising to their feet in front of a class for the first time may find past teacher 'ghosts' inhabiting their body (Weintraub 1989). You may hear yourself saying things your teachers said and you may instinctively use activities and routines that your teachers used. A likely pattern here is the initiation, response, feedback (IRF) routine. Here's an example:

> T: What's the time now?   (= I)
> S: It's ten o'clock.   (= R)
> T: Good!   (= F)

When you find yourself saying this for the first time, it can make you chuckle. 'Why is it a good thing that it's ten o'clock?' you might ask yourself. But in fact this routine acknowledges that students and teachers are working on at least two levels at once: the level concerned with comment on target language proficiency and another, the level of personal communication. The IRF routine only becomes pernicious when it's used mechanically and without an additional communicative response such as, 'Gosh! That time already!' Many of the routines we've unwittingly picked up during our hours on the other side of the desk are helpful.

The second way: Using coursebooks

Another way of getting better at preparing is by using coursebooks. A beginner teacher using a coursebook will absorb routines from it, especially if there is a helpful teacher's book to go with it. The tendency to pick up activities, lesson types and course models from coursebooks will be reinforced if the same books are taught several times with different classes and especially if a part of every unit is the same.

The third way: Learning as we teach

There are many other ways that we gradually get more effective at our course and lesson planning as we teach. We do so by:

- Writing plans for different classes and then teaching the plans.
- Teaching lesson plans written for us by more experienced teachers.
- Writing plans for a more experienced teacher and then hearing what they did with them in their class.
- Observing teachers or videos and then writing lesson notes for what we've seen.
- Listening to colleagues talking about their lessons and courses.
- Reading transcripts of recorded lessons.
- Team-teaching, reading training manuals, using resource books that have been written around a particular theme such as creative grammar practice or songs or vocabulary, and finding out what students like and then following their directions on how to teach them that way.

As we do these, we'll start to understand that lessons are composed of lots of different elements that affect each other, all of which can be used as starting points. We'll gain the experience of personal examples of individual students, types of classes, and timings of activities. We'll then be able to call up these examples for comparison in future. We'll also get a repertoire of exercises, sequences of exercises and whole stock lessons and courses. I'll call these learned repertoires 'Chunks' and will say more about them below. Thus by thinking, using coursebooks, planning lessons and then teaching them, and by working with others, we soon start to get a repertoire of chunks.

Using 'Chunks'

What are 'Chunks' ?

Let's step outside our own field for a moment. When learning to type we learn where individual letters are before practising high frequency combinations like, 'tion' and 'the'. When learning to drive, we learn how to depress the clutch, put the gear in neutral, then push the gear into first and slowly let the clutch off before combining all this, plus mirror watching, indicating, playing with the handbrake, keeping time with the accelerator pedal, and sweating, into something called 'moving off into traffic'. The chunk, in both the typing and the driving, is the running together into a smooth sequence all the little steps that we have previously learned. The individual steps need to be learned first. Then we need to learn how to chunk.

A chunk usually has a name of its own. Thus the separate steps, in a primary school class, of 'down, around and fly the flag' soon become a chunk called 'writing the number 5'.

Moving back into foreign language teaching, the individual steps, 'I'll write three questions on the board, then I'll ask students to read them, then I'll explain to students they'll be able to answer them once they have read the text', once practised a couple of times, become the smooth chunk 'setting a pre-reading task'. Later, with a bit more experience, the chunks get bigger or longer, and pretty soon the teacher can say, 'I'll do some pre- and in-reading tasks and then work on language and content.' The individual steps of the larger chunk could be stated in great detail but the experienced teacher no longer needs to do this except when asked to for an advanced exam. The individual steps have been thought about and experienced often enough for them to have become integrated into a bigger, smoother unit.

When are chunks good or bad?

Teachers have to think about individual small units of content, steps, activities and material before being able to work at a broader level. But I believe that as soon as possible we need to start thinking about putting steps together, subsuming them into larger units and thinking about shaping lessons and sets of lessons. This enables us to piece whole lessons and courses together without using up whole evenings and weekends!

I believe that it is also partly this ability to call up practised sequences or 'chunks' that makes lesson planning easy for the experienced teacher. If inexperienced teachers could be helped to acquire these, how much easier their lives would be.

On the darker side, however, it's also partly these same chunks that make trying something new difficult for the experienced teacher. The sight of a text, for example, suggests an almost automatic set of activities that can be applied to it and away the experienced teacher goes, down a useful but rather well-worn path. Useful chunks have been learnt by the experienced teacher over the years and they can now lead to a rather stultifying, routine way of working. If experienced teachers could be helped to wander off these paths, how much more interesting our work might be.

Of course, inexperienced teachers can use well-worn routines in class too. These can have been inherited from past teachers or over-learned on training courses. Wherever they've come from, these sets of routines often need breaking down and rethinking.

If you're a starter teacher, you could probably do with picking up a repertoire of new teaching chunks so that you can piece together lessons and sets of lessons swiftly and effectively. If you're a teacher who's settled into your career, you may be looking for new repertoires to help you make the experiments you want to make. If you're a very experienced teacher, you may need to put some of your well-worn routines to one side and try out new ones in order to keep awake personally and professionally. I hope very much that this book will help you, wherever you are in your career cycle, for it's full of chunks and repertoires of different kinds.

Beliefs, perceptions and assumptions

In this book I'll share ideas that have helped me to solve puzzles set by my own classes and situation. While writing this book, I've had the luxury of a two-year conversation with a fellow professional, Penny Ur, my editor. Through these conversations, I've come to understand more about my own assumptions and beliefs. I've had to think hard about why I have wanted one chapter to come before another, or why I want some things in the book and not other things.

Whether you're reading this book on your own or have the chance, as I've had, for conversations with a critical friend, I offer below an activity that helps you explore your beliefs about people, learning, language and teaching. It's our beliefs about these things that ultimately govern everything about our planning from our choice of content, activity, instructional sequence and course model to our personal style. We need to communicate these beliefs or reasons to our participants too.

The activity is called '*The four-column analysis*' and has been a very popular activity with the teachers and trainers I've worked with over the years. It is a way of getting from classroom tactics to talk of beliefs and values. The activity can be done after you have personally experienced a lesson (whether as a teacher, learner or trainer) or by going through a video, lesson transcript or taped lesson carefully or after listening to someone's verbatim account of their own lesson.

A The four-column analysis

1 Draw four columns. Put the following words at the top of the columns: Steps, Chunks, Assumptions (or Beliefs), Archaeology. Thus:

STEPS	CHUNKS	ASSUMPTIONS / BELIEFS	ARCHAEOLOGY

THE FOUR COLUMNS

2 *Filling in the Steps column*
   Try to remember the individual steps of the lesson without looking directly at your source material, e.g. the lesson plan or video. Note them down in the Steps column in shorthand like this:

STEPS	CHUNKS	ASSUMPTIONS / BELIEFS	ARCHAEOLOGY
• Music as S/S arrive • T writes own first name on B/B and invites S/S to join their names to T's as in a crossword or scrabble game • S/S come up and do it • T asks S/S to turn to p. 10 in textbook and mask top half • etc.			

THE STEPS COLUMN

Introduction

Why? As teachers we spend a lot of our time looking forward to future lessons and much less time thinking back through a lesson we have just taught. So we are usually practised at *pre*-paration but not *post*-paration. Looking back is good memory training. It forces us to look at all that went on and not just the bits that seemed most important. It is interesting later, if you compare your notes with a colleague's, with the lesson plan or other source material, to see what you forgot and to consider why you remembered the bits you did. This prompts a more realistic and detailed discussion of a lesson or session than when just remembering the things that stand out most immediately and vividly. If you are looking at a new activity, sequence or lesson shape in someone else's work, taking these kinds of notes will help you to reproduce the same sequence again yourself later on.

3 *Filling in the Chunks column*
Look at all the steps you noted in the first column. See if you can clump some of them together into phases like this:

STEPS	CHUNKS	ASSUMPTIONS / BELIEFS	ARCHAEOLOGY
• Music as S/S arrive	Setting atmosphere		
• T writes own first name on B/B and invites S/S to join their names to T's as in a crossword or scrabble game	Getting to know you / Warm-up phase		
• S/S come up and do it			
• T asks S/S to turn to p. 10 in textbook and mask top half	Start of main work		
• etc.			

THE CHUNKS COLUMN

Why? If you are doing this work on your own teaching and complete the columns for several lessons, you may be interested to find that you often use similar chunks or lesson phases in a similar order. If you do this work on someone else's lessons, you might be intrigued to see that

10

they structure their lessons in identical or very different ways to you. Either way, this work gets us thinking about sequences of activities and chunks rather than about individual activities.

4 *Filling in the Assumptions (or Beliefs) column*
Next look at the individual steps and chunks listed in the first two columns. Try to get to the assumptions and beliefs behind them. If you are thinking about someone else's lesson, then you can only guess at the teacher's assumptions. If you are thinking about your own lesson, then it would be productive to have a friend working with you, thinking about it individually first before comparing notes. Your friend will see things differently from you. For example, I might believe that playing music relaxes students but my friend might think that it all depends on the type of music, type of student and the volume!

STEPS	CHUNKS	ASSUMPTIONS / BELIEFS	ARCHAEOLOGY
• Music as S/S arrive	Setting atmosphere	• Teacher thinks music creates good atmosphere and that atmosphere is important to learning. Maybe T relaxes too! T assumes S/S will like the music	
• T writes own first name on B/B and invites S/S to join their names to T's as in a crossword or scrabble game	Getting too know you / Warm-up phase	• First names are OK. Name-learning is important. Seeing spelling is important. The B/B belongs to everyone. People can move around. The front of the room is not an inner sanctum. Done this way T must have small group and plenty of room.	

11

• S/S come up and do it • T asks S/S to turn to p. 10 in textbook and mask top half • etc.	Start of main work	• Everyone has a textbook. Using a textbook is good. You don't have to use the textbook page as it is.	

THE ASSUMPTIONS COLUMN

Why?   The steps and chunks or phases of your lesson or session are what you and your participants actually do. These events are practical, physical statements or expressions of self. Regardless of what you MEAN to happen and regardless of what you believe about learning and teaching, this is the reality of events in your classroom. So it is interesting and usually very instructive to see if the assumptions spotted by other people are similar to the assumptions the leader of the session actually holds.

5 *Filling in the Archaeology column*
This column could also be headed 'When, how and why did I learn this way of working?' You can only fill in this column if you either taught the lesson yourself or are able to talk to the teacher who did. The teacher tries to remember where an activity or the idea for a phase came from.

STEPS	CHUNKS	ASSUMPTIONS / BELIEFS	ARCHAEOLOGY
• Music as S/S arrive	Setting atmosphere	• Teacher thinks music creates good atmosphere and that atmosphere is important to learning. Maybe T relaxes too! T assumes S/S will like the music	• I first saw music used at the start when a participant in a session by Elayne Phillips. I liked it, thought S/S might and also thought 'Great! I can use something I love in "real life" at work too!

12

• T writes own first name on B/B and invites S/S to join their names to Ts as in a crossword or scrabble game • S/S come up and do it	Getting to know you / Warm-up phase	• First names are OK. Name-learning is important. Seeing spelling is important. The B/B belongs to everyone. People can move around. The front of the room is not an inner sanctum. Done this way T must have small group and plenty of room.	• I got name crossword or scrabble from Rick Cooper when team-teaching. I liked the way it metaphorically drew the indi-viduals into a group.
• T asks S/S to turn to p. 10 in textbook and mask top half • etc.	Start of main work	• Everyone has a textbook. Using a textbook is good. You don't have to use the textbook page as it is.	• We had text-books at school. My eye always wan-dered all over the page so when my Diploma trainer showed me how to 'mask' to get everyone's attention on one spot, I learnt to do it right away.

THE ARCHAEOLOGY COLUMN

Why? This column helps us to understand how we and other teachers learn, where we get our repertoires from and in what situations we are most likely to pick up new ways of working. We begin to dig out the history of our own improvement as teachers. From the above notes we can see that this teacher seems to learn from people. She has learned from a teacher, a colleague and a trainer. She likes the idea that she can bring things from her outside life into the classroom.

With the four-column analysis we are beginning to investigate what activities, sequences, chunks and phases we use in our lessons and sessions, why we tend to use them and if there is coherence between what we believe, what we actually do and how others see our work. We also find out something about the circumstances in which we have learned some of the aspects of our job. We are, with the analysis, starting with classroom evidence and working backwards to beliefs and assumptions. It's easier to get this kind of conversation going, in my view, if there is something visible, audible and tangible to relate it to. I hope you have some interesting conversations as a result of the activity.

The organisation of this book

Most of the chapters in this book are organised around questions that you might ask when starting to plan a lesson or a course. Each chapter provides answers to the questions posed or implied in the chapter titles. The answers may be illustrated by practical activities signalled by A in the margin (see page 9). Illustrative anecdotes from my own or other people's experience are marked by ![icon]. Chapters usually either include or conclude with a summary based on the metaphor of a garden, indicated by a flower in the margin ![flower]. At the end of Chapters 1–8 there is a thematic mind map or other visual summary that aims to give you some light relief and also to remind you of the essence of the chapter you have just read.

In Chapter 1 *Who are the students?* there are sequences of activities that help you to get to know your students before, during and after they are in your classes. Next, Chapter 2 *How long is the lesson?* looks at chronological chunks and thus at the sorts of activities that can come at the beginning, middle and end of a lesson. Chapter 3 turns to content and the question *What can go into a lesson?* Chapter 4 is about the question *How do people learn and so how can we teach?* Chapter 5 *What can we teach with?* describes the tools of the trade and how they can spark off activity sequences of their own. In Chapter 6 the question is *How can we vary the activities we do?* I take traditional activities and show how you can turn them into something more useful for your own setting. Chapter 7 *Getting down to the preparation* takes the practical, everyday starting points and written formats that people actually use and not the ways of working we have been told on training courses that we OUGHT to use! Chapter 8 *What are our freedoms and constraints?* is about the freedoms and constraints involved in working with different types of organisation, class and personality and also about the totally unpredictable side of our work.

As a child I used to consider gardening a boring chore just for 'grown-ups' even though I did love being in gardens myself playing and walking, looking, touching and sniffing. Over the years, I've learned how to turn the noun 'garden' into the verb 'to garden'. As I've moved jobs and houses, I've temporarily taken over small town patches, suburban yards and overgrown cottage gardens. I've looked through seed catalogues and borrowed tools. I've had some successes, made loads of mistakes and am still learning a lot. Now as I look out of my window with great pleasure into the country garden below, I see the primroses that have done well and the weeds that I should do something about! I realise that I have turned into the 'grown-up' I used to watch weeding and digging. I see now that, although gardening IS a chore and involves unending problem-solving rather than perfect solutions, it's also tremendously rewarding. I feel just the same way about school classrooms. I used to be an observant participant in other people's classrooms and now I have my own. And I now see that the chore of planning and teaching is positively enjoyable and that there's always plenty to learn. I can see many other parallels between working in gardens and working in classrooms. If you'd like to join me in exploring this metaphor, watch for the flower motifs throughout the book.

1 Who are the students?

1.1 Introduction

The students we work with are the real reason for the whole learning/teaching encounter. So the most important thing we can do before, during and after classes is, in my view, to listen to students, watch them and read their work. This will help us to get to know them as individuals and thus will give us invaluable information when choosing topics and types of material including coursebooks, and when selecting activities and shaping lessons and courses. We can also involve students in these decisions. Even if our hands are tied in many matters because, for example, we have to stick to a syllabus or teach a certain coursebook, knowing as much as possible about our students will still help us decide on error correction, testing and homework and respond to them as individuals and as a group. It's perhaps the most natural sequence of all in teaching: finding out about the students and then taking account of this information in our work.

In this chapter I'll look at the things you can find out about learners, who you can find out from, how and when, and what you might use your understanding for.

1.2 Who can you find out from?

If you have been asked to take on a new class or one-to-one student, you can get information from the sending institution (if the students are coming in from somewhere else), past and present teachers, other 'stakeholders' (see below), and the students themselves. Let's look at the institutional level first.

The institution

Students from a different institution

Sometimes students come to our institutions from a different company, school or country from our own.

If the arrangements between your own institution and the sending institution are long term, what procedures are already in place for receiving, testing and teaching?

If a government or company is sending students to you for the first time, there will usually be some anxiety on both sides about getting procedures sorted out. It's vital that the teacher notes any kinks in a programme and makes adjustments fast.

If the relationship between the institutions is relatively new or you are new to the relationship, you will want to know:

- the nature of the sending institution
- its aims for the students
- what demands are made by the institution on the students before, during and after sending them
- whether the students are tested before they come
- whether a representative of the sending institution will be coming too and, if so, what relationship they have to the students. For example, whether they will be expecting to visit classes, or help with discipline while you are teaching.

Students from inside or outside your own institution

The sorts of things we could do well to know at the organisational level, whether students come from inside or outside our institution, are:

- whether the course is described or advertised anywhere and, if so, how
- whether any reports exist on past courses and whether any examples of past student work are available
- who is paying for the students to attend and whether attendance is voluntary or compulsory
- how the students are selected
- the length and frequency of the course, the mode of contact and the prescribed syllabus and materials, since these will affect the students
- why YOU were asked to take the course rather than another teacher. If you are told you were chosen because you were the only teacher who has experience of a particular exam or the target language, this will have a different effect on your work from being told, for example, that 'they want someone very creative'.

Although we might imagine that this kind of essential information would be provided for us, it's not always the case! Sometimes institutions feel these issues are so fundamental that everybody must know them already. Other institutions feel that these are somehow not teachers' but managers' concerns and that teachers should just go ahead and teach the course. Sometimes teachers can't be bothered with this level of enquiry or we are too shy to ask.

Since the teacher is the one who works with the students day to day, it's vital that we know whether our students are forced to be in class, are paying for themselves, have a very specific aim in mind, or, for example, have heard very positive or negative things from past generations of students about our institution or ourselves!

The obvious person to ask about these issues is the person who suggests you take the class on. Ask gently, for it may be that the person has no idea of the answers and has not even thought of asking the questions themselves. Once you have explained how useful the information will be for planning and teaching the course though, most people will see the wisdom of the request. It's a good idea to suggest ways of getting the information or even offering to get it yourself, for example, by finding old files or reports, or phoning the sending institution. This will usually prompt some action.

Past and present teachers

If you are taking over or are going to share a class, it makes sense to talk to past or present teachers about the class (or write to them if they are in another institution). If possible, ask questions, and look at any notes on past work, materials used, test results, files on attendance, behaviour, etc. and any language learner portfolios. If at all possible, watch the students while they are being taught by their present teacher. You may or may not like the teacher's style but at least you will know what the students are used to and whether they seem to like it! You're also bound to pick up some ideas from watching someone else teach. If there is a good relationship between you and the previous teacher, then methods of working, materials and grading queries can all be dovetailed smoothly.

Other stakeholders

Other people from whom you can gain interesting information about the class may be parents and teachers of the same class but in different subjects. Try to talk to them where possible.

1.3 What you can know and why

The students

Your main source of information about a class will be the students themselves. You can get to know them by phone, letter, journal, tape, e-mail or face to face. You can get information before or on first meeting that helps you to do some initial planning. Information you get as you go along will help you to adjust your planning continually. Information gained after classes have left will help you plan for similar future courses. Below is a list of some of the things it is useful to know about students and the reasons why you might want to know.

What	Why
• The number of students	So you can choose a room, plan the seating and materials and know whether one-to-one, pairwork or group work will be possible. Very large (50+) and very small (1–3) classes necessitate even more careful activity planning than usual if you are not used to these numbers.
• Names	So you can get them right!
• Sex ratio	So you know whether teacher and students match, and what the balance will be in your pair and group work.
• Age range	So you can allow for different energy levels, concentration spans and choices of topics. The amount of life experience students have to invest in particular themes such as 'work' or 'pop music' will make a huge difference to how long an activity will last.
• Mother tongue	So you can work out what to do if one or two students are without a mother tongue friend. So you can figure out how to establish an English-speaking community and predict what common strengths and weaknesses in the target language there are there likely to be.
• Nationality	So you can understand more about the politics, cultural conventions, prejudices and expectations of the students. Are there any possible 'enemy' nationalities in the group? Will this affect your seating plan? Are there cultural differences between students in, for example, the time of day they like to study, or the amount of background noise they can study with?
• What other languages do they speak?	So you can know how used to language learning they are, where English comes in individual students' and the school's priorities and thus what difficulties you can predict in their workload.

What	Why
• Target language level	What results are there from any placement tests and outside exams?
• Student perceptions of their own competence	So you can add this information to standard test results and make decisions regarding student placement. A confident student may want to join a challenging class. A less confident student may prefer to go into a class slightly under their own level. If the students are already placed, it's still good to know who might be feeling under- or over-confident, and who you'll need to support or stretch.
• Profession and/or interests	So you can judge what content will support or expand their interests. What is each student an expert in and thus what can they teach others?
• Books and materials already used	So you can avoid duplication.
• Learners' target situation	So you can make decisions about the topics and skills you work on. Do the students need their English for jobs in, e.g. air traffic control or some other specialised use? Are they learning a little at primary level so as to get a head start at secondary level?
• Educational background	So you can judge what basic reading and writing skills they have in their own language. How cognitive and academic are they?
• Other commitments during the course	So you can judge how much time and energy they will be able to devote to classes and homework, how stressed or relaxed they will be and thus what workload and pace they can take.
• View of the course	So you can gauge how realistic their perceptions are and how well you can match their expectations.

Things that take a little longer to find out

What	*Why*
• Group dynamic and personality	So you can predict what attendance will be like and consider what to do about it if it's bad as well as considering who needs to sit next to or apart from whom. Are they often quiet, lively or motivated?
• What learner styles seem to be represented in the group? (You may take one of the frameworks available in the literature here, e.g. 'dominant sensory channel' (learning best by seeing, hearing, touching, tasting, moving), or 'type of intelligence' (musical, kinaesthetic, interpersonal, logical-mathematical, intrapersonal, spatial, naturalist, religious, etc.) or others such as self-concept, students' feelings about being in control of their own learning, or the difference in factors to which students attribute their successes and failures in learning (see Williams and Burden 1997 Ch. 5.3).	So you can choose methods and materials, and consider if your learners' ways of working fit your style and, if not, what compromises will need to be made.
• How learners perceive or mentally organise the language	So you can decide how to move students' understanding on.

These are some of the things it can be helpful to know. Some ideas follow on ways of getting the information from the students.

1.4 How to get information before meeting the class

A **Letter writing**

Depending on the students' language level, age and the resources available, pre-meeting can happen by different means.

- A letter can be sent from you to the new class, addressed to individuals in the group or, if their English is not very proficient, to them care of their teacher, in their mother tongue if necessary. In the letter you can tell them a little about yourself. You can also ask them to write to you telling you a little about themselves.

  If you have liaised with their teacher then she can help them to write individual or group responses to your letter. Alternatively, at higher levels and ages, they can reply on their own or with just a little bit of help. Of course some students won't answer the letter. They may forget, be too busy or shy or may not have the language. Others may give inaccurate information. For example, I have received letters from Norwegian or Swedish students who describe themselves as 'elementary' at English. From the naturalness of their letters, I find them near native in proficiency! In my experience, with pre-meeting letter writing, at least half of the students in their teens and above will answer. So you will gain a useful impression of the class you are about to teach. When you actually meet the class, you can start off by referring to the previous contact. It will make things friendly right from the start.

- If you feel that a letter is too personal for you, a questionnaire can be sent instead (see Scharle and Szabo 2000). If you have a good relationship with the class's present teacher, she may be able to coordinate more than just letters and questionnaires and get the class to send things such as photos or local information.

1.5 How to get information on first meeting

First lesson sequences

Some teachers hate first classes with a new group. Others really enjoy it. Many have a fairly routinised set of 'first lesson chunks' that they can use again and again with different groups. Such sequences mean that first lessons can be enjoyable and informative and therefore less stressful for both teacher and students. Picking up the odd new activity for an otherwise well-established 'first lesson' repertoire ensures that an experienced teacher keeps interested.

The way different teachers put a first lesson sequence together will differ. I prefer to start with names and a little personal information and to build rapport in this way before moving on to serious language work. A colleague of mine likes to get going on language work first using the sequence '*How much can they understand?*' (see page 32), before doing work on names in the middle of the first class, and then giving information on the course and eliciting students' hopes for the class. Of course if you have gained information from letters and questionnaires or from watching the class before the first lesson, or if the class members know each other very well already, you will need to spend much less time on 'getting to know you' activities. Similarly if you know the new class level, perhaps from the results of a test you really trust, you can happily work with texts and tapes in the first class. Otherwise, it may be as well to work either with a selection of short texts at different levels or to plan mostly speaking and listening work with a little writing. Even if you are very skilled at thinking up reading tasks on the spot, when you find out that the level is different from what you expected, using one long text that is 'frozen' in level can be a tricky way for a teacher to start. It can also be a bit of a jolt to student confidence to meet a very difficult text or tape on the very first day, so you want to avoid getting the level wrong if possible.

Name learning

There are scores of activities in coursebooks and teachers' resource books encouraging teachers and students to learn each other's names. This is because, whether you learn first names or family names, you accord a real identity to each human being in the room, you can call on them individually and as a result you can teach individuals rather than just the group. If you are not too good at remembering names and have large classes, here are some techniques to help you.

A **Labels**

Ask students to make a little stand-up sign and to write their names in large dark letters. They add a little drawing connected to themselves as a mnemonic, for example, a pair of glasses or some tennis balls (see page 24). Take the signs in at the end of the first class and put a rubber band around them. Next time, using the students' mnemonics to help you, see if you can hand the labels back to the right people.

STUDENT NAME CARD FOR 'LABELS'

A Register mnemonics

Using the class register, call out names one by one. Ask each student to say 'Yes!' and to do something easy in English, for example, say two words they can remember or introduce their best friend. While each student is doing this, note down a way of remembering that student. Use any mnemonic you can think of including hair length, posture, colour of clothes or wordplay on their names (for instance, if you have a student with the name Regina, imagine her with a queen's crown on her head). Make a note of these mnemonics on a piece of paper next to the name of the student. Don't forget to cover these notes up immediately, as a student glancing at your notes might see the helpful but potentially embarrassing mnemonics you have for them!

A Settled places

If you have a large class with fixed seats and students who don't change places much, and you have no time for the mnemonics activity above, ask students to call out their names. Mark these on a seating plan as they do this so that you have a map of who sits where. Then as students do noteworthy things throughout subsequent lessons, mark these next to their name. It may take longer this way and you may not remember the quieter students for a long time but in the end you should have a mnemonic by most people's names.

A Testing yourself

While the students are writing or engaged in group tasks, I spend long spells in the first few lessons with a new class trying to commit their names to memory. I memorise them by rote learning from left to right, from right to left, row by row. I test myself on all the students who have the same name, and all the ones that start with 'S' or 'B'. I continue this self-testing after class by taking a piece of paper and drawing two horizontal lines across it so that I have three sections on the paper. In the top section I write the names of the students that come to mind easily. When I start to slow down and search mentally for names, I move down to the middle section and start recording names there. After a while, I get stuck. I'll know there are, say, 30 students in the class and I've only got 25 names recorded. So then I go to the register to see who I have forgotten. This will give me names of people whose faces or personalities I can't recall at all. These are the people I make a special effort to call on and remember in class next time. I repeat the exercise over the next few weeks until I have all the students well in mind.

(I learnt this from Mario Rinvolucri.)

Building a sense of community

You need to get the individual students in your classes working together as a cooperative unit. Here are some ideas to help you do this.

A Drawing yourself

1 Showing by quick lines on the board that you are no artist and that the drawing part of the exercise is the least important part, do a quick sketch of yourself, just head and shoulders.
2 Next, start labelling easy bits of yourself. For example, draw a line from the part of the picture showing your hair and write the word 'Hair' by it. Sign the picture as if you were an artist, using a flashy signature across one corner.
3 Now give out pieces of paper and ask students to sketch themselves, head and shoulders. Call it a 'vocabulary' exercise as this will take the students' attention off the potentially embarrassing fact that they are required to make a quick drawing of themselves. At higher levels encourage labelling of more difficult parts of the face such as eyebrow or freckle and ask for adjectives as well as nouns, so students write 'Oval face' and 'Pale complexion' rather than just 'face' and 'complexion'.
4 Provide any vocabulary that individual students are curious about. In a smallish class (up to 30), you can call yourself the vocabulary waiter and ask students to call you over when they want to order a word. In a large class (50+), store the requests for extra vocabulary and either teach them to the whole class or suggest that they look the words up for homework. They can bring the words they couldn't find to the next class.

Variation
A variation on this exercise involves students sitting in pairs drawing each other, and then interviewing their partners and writing sentences about their partners under their picture. Done either way, the students will peep at each other's drawings. There'll be plenty of fun and laughter and this

will draw the group together. If you take the work in 'to check the spelling of the vocabulary', you then have a 'rogue's gallery' that you can study, linking faces to the names, at your leisure.

Group profile

 This activity can be done in the target language or mother tongue.

1 Explain that you are going to ask the group a question to find out more about them.
2 Ask something simple, such as 'How many of you live just five minutes from school on foot?' Ask students to put their hands up if they do.
3 Count the hands and make a sentence about the result, such as 'Nobody lives near the school' or 'Most people live near the school', depending on how many hands went up.
4 Everybody writes the sentence down.
5 Ask a couple more simple questions. They should be appropriate for the group and things that you really want to know, such as 'How many of you have a relative or friend who can speak English quite well?' or 'How many of you like doing English homework?'
6 As soon as students have got the idea of listening to a question about the composition of the group, raising their hands and then writing a summary sentence, encourage them to ask questions about things they want to know the answer to. If the people in the group don't know each other very well, there will be natural curiosity about who lives where, what sports, hobbies and jobs people do. If the students have been together for quite a while or are not naturally curious, they may need to be prompted to ask other useful questions, such as who has finished what school work or what homework was set for a class that somebody missed. (See box opposite for possible questions.)
7 Depending on the level of the class, you can gradually build a scale of expressions of quantity such as the one below, being careful about the following verb and whether it is singular or plural.

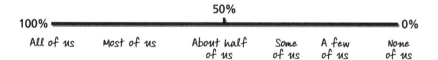

THE SCALE

8 Once everyone has asked something, everybody should have a list of sentences about the group. This is the group profile. It can be stored in people's notebooks or on a poster on the wall, and can be added to

later when more is found out about the group. The language can gradually be expanded too so that expressions such as 'several of us' and 'quite a few' are added to the scale above. The profile can give a sense of community and identity to the group. It may even contain answers to questions such as 'Why is this group different from other groups we belong to?'

Possible starter questions

Teacher

- How many of you live just five minutes away from school on foot?
- How many have a relative who speaks some English?
- How many of you like doing some English homework?
- How many of you enjoy listening to music with English lyrics?

Students

- Who likes playing basketball?
- Does anyone here want to go for a walk next weekend?
- How many of us feel happy in our jobs?
- Who has finished the second assignment for Miss X?
- Does anyone have a big tablecloth we can borrow for the end of term play?
- Did anyone write down the Biology homework?
- Why is this group different from any of the other groups we belong to?

Student expectations

Whatever you have been told about a group, I feel it's wise to spend time on first meeting trying to find out what their preconceptions and expectations of the course are. You need to know what they expect. You can then choose whether to harmonise with or challenge their preconceptions. Here are some ideas for finding out the way students are thinking.

A Why are we here?

In school, students are in class mainly because they have to be. In non-compulsory classes, it's a good idea to find out why people have decided to attend.

- You can ask students to spend 30 seconds each, round the class, telling everybody why they are there.

- Another way, at lower levels, either in mother tongue or in very simple language supplemented by mime, translation and picture dictionaries is to prepare a sheet of paper on which you have written reasons for attending, such as 'JOB', 'INTERNET', 'MEET PEOPLE', 'EXAM', 'GOOD FOR MY BRAIN', etc. Make sure students understand all the words, then ask them to circle the ones that are relevant to them.

Whatever method you use, I feel it's important for the whole class to hear or to read other people's reasons so students know whether their own reasons are unusual or in line with others'.

A Unfinished sentences

Another way of guiding students to let you know what they like or expect is to provide them with stem sentences to complete.

- On the board or on a handout, provide the beginnings of some sentences and ask the students to finish the sentences off any way they like. Here are some example sentence starters that you might want to choose from:

By the end of this week/term/course I want to be able to ...
I learn best when ...
I don't like it when the teacher ...
We use a book and ...
When we do group work ...
When I'm doing English homework I ...
I can understand ...
I can't understand ...
I really hope I learn ...
In class I don't really want ...
The whole point of coming to class is to ...
Once in my life I'd like to ...

Just as in the group profile activity above, it's important to make sentence starters that will tell you something you really want to know. Again I feel it's important for students to hear or read all the responses so that they can gauge if they are unusual in the group or not. Students can also write sentence starters for you to finish. Examples here might be:

I give A grades to students who ...
The best grammar book for students to use at home is ...
I put people into pairs because ...

- You will probably need to help students to phrase their starter sentences unless you are doing the exercise in mother tongue or with a higher level group. As well as being a first lesson exercise you can encourage students to let you know OFTEN what they like and don't like in class.

If you want more ideas on how to elicit feedback in a sustained way and how to use the feedback gained to alter your classes, see Murphey and Woo (1998).

A The graph

The development graph can be used with adult intermediate learners.

1 Give out sheets of A3 (or large) paper and explain to the students that you will soon ask them to draw a line or graph representing their development in English so far. Give an example on the board. It's important that the board work is not too neat as this may intimidate people and make them feel they have to be good at drawing in order to do the activity. They don't! Personal graph lines can go up to represent times when students felt they were learning a lot or when they were enjoying themselves in English, they can go down if they failed an exam or didn't make much progress at a certain period, they can go round in circles for times of confusion, or be split into different paths for periods of choices, etc.
2 Ask students to spend a few minutes drawing their graph. Provide coloured pens and background music to make the activity enjoyable.
3 While they are drawing, ask them to label the high or low points with dates or notes so that later when they talk the graph through with a partner, it will be easier for the partner to understand. Inserting notes also provides the activity with face validity since it involves using the target language and not 'just drawing'.
4 If a particular student can't represent their path in graph form, invite them to try notes and dates instead.
5 After most people have finished drawing, suggest they take their graphs to another student and explain in English their career thus far in life. Set a time limit of, say, ten minutes for people to explain their graphs to each other.
6 When you draw people back together again you can ask them, as a whole group, what they feel is necessary in order to have a sense of progress in language learning.

A Bartering

Here's a lively activity that enables you and the group to find out what they expect of the course. The students can tell whether their own expectations are the same as other people's or not. If people know that they are not in the majority with a particular request, they can understand more readily that you may only get to it if all else has been taken care of.

1 You might like to start this activity off with some music that reminds the class of an oriental bazaar or perhaps ask how many people have experienced some sort of bartering system.

2 Give out one sheet of paper per student and ask them to fold it into three so that they can then tear off three separate strips to write on.

3 Ask students to write something different on each strip. They should write what they want from the class. This could be social, such as 'I want to be with my friends', or academic, such as 'I want to learn the way to ask for things when I travel', or any other wish, such as 'I hope we don't go too slowly. Last year this class was slow and boring.'

4 Give time for everyone to write down two or three things on their strips of paper. Students should sign each strip with their name.
   The next step will depend on how much space you have. If you don't have much room in your classroom, see the *Variation*.

5 Students keep their own strips of paper and stand up and walk around.

6 When they meet someone they read out one of their strips. If the listener feels that the comment is also true of their own feelings, they take the strip. When they 'buy' a strip in this way they sign their name to it. That way when the strips are taken in at the end of the activity, you can see by the number of signatures on a strip how popular an idea it was.

7 Students who have been listening then read out one of their own original strips and see if their partner is happy enough with the comment to take it as their own. If they are not, the reader keeps it.

8 Students keep walking around meeting new people and reading out and listening to what is on their partner's strips. The aim is to get rid of as many of the original strips of paper as possible.

9 You then ask people to sit down again.

10 Finish by asking people to read out the strips they ended up with.

Variation
If you have very little space, once students have written their three strips, continue as here:

5 Take in all the strips of paper, mix them up in a box and then go round

so that each student takes three strips that are not their own.

6 One student starts by reading out what is written on one of the strips they have taken. Everyone else listens.

7 They then look at the strips they have taken and if one has something written on it that seems to relate to what has just been read out, then they read it out. So if someone has just read out 'I want to have a nice time with my friends', then someone else might choose to read out 'I hope the lessons will have some breaks so that I have time to talk to my friends.' If there are no connections after a particular strip has been read out, then someone reads out a strip on a new subject.

8 Continue until all the strips have been read out.

You can also check against these expectations at the end of the course to make sure they have been met (see page 206).

(I learnt this activity from Richard Baudains.)

A 'What we are used to' sentences

If your new students have all come from the same institution or country, and are elementary level or above you can try this activity.

1 Ask each person to say one sentence about their previous class, school or institution. The sentence can be as short as they like, but it must be true. Here are some examples of things the students can say about their previous class: 'There were 32 students in our class. We were all 14 years old. Most of us lived in Kiev. Our English teacher was a woman. Our classroom was warm. The lessons were 50 minutes long. We had a video machine in our classroom.'

2 When students get stuck for something to say, give them a prompt such as 'Classroom … colour?' or 'How much homework?' It should be possible to get scores of simple sentences about the students' past setting which will let you know what they are used to. If you are planning something very different, you can show this by looking surprised at what they say or by discussing differences with them later on after the activity.

Variation
Ask students to arrange the furniture as it would have looked in their previous classroom and for them to behave as they would have done there. One student pretends to be the class teacher and they all replay a lesson. Students spend hours watching and listening to teachers and are usually excellent at noting their patterns of speech and mannerisms. There is usually instant mirth at this exercise but it also gives you a real feel for what the students are used to. Discussion can ensue on their feelings about

the methods and materials used and on what they feel they have learned in their past class.

Level

You may be lucky enough to have a clear idea of the level of the class you are going to take because you have, for example, administered a test of your own making or liking. If you are less certain of what the students can do, then all the exercises so far will give you important clues. You can also try some of the following activities.

A How much can they understand?

1 At the beginning of class, in a natural way, give the students some simple commands in English. Ask them, for example, to move their chairs a little or open their notebooks. See how much they seem to be able to understand and how much of a real language English is to them.
2 Draw a simple picture on the board, one connected to a story you plan to tell, and see how much in the way of vocabulary and ideas you can elicit from students.
3 Tell the story. Use mime, pictures and sound effects, anything to get the meaning across. In the story, leave gaps in your telling before any repeated words or phrases and see if the students can fill in any of the gaps for you.
4 Check their comprehension after telling the story.
5 Ask the students to write down any words or sentences they can from or about the story. If all this is done in a natural, gentle way you can end up after half an hour having a fair idea of who in your class can do what in English, and without the stress of a test. This might be a good time to tell students anything you feel they need to know about the course. For example, whether there is a coursebook and how they get it, times, breaks, where the toilets are, if there are any exams, and so on. It is unwise to give out this kind of information before you are really sure how much students can understand in English.

A One thing I know about English

Ask students to tell you one thing they know about English. If their level is low, they should tell you in their mother tongue, if you share it. Put some ideas on the board, for example, 'I know that the word for ... in English is ...' or 'The sound ... is difficult for me ...' or 'If I want to talk about ... in English I can say ...' You can prompt the students if they run out of things to say by asking them whatever you think they should know, for example, 'What question words do you know beginning with W?' or 'Can you give me an example of a verb?' or 'How do you spell ...?' or 'How can I talk about yesterday in English?'

This is an extremely interesting exercise for a teacher since it will tell you not what a past teacher has 'done' with a class but what student perceptions are of what has been done. Of course this activity can be used not just on first meeting but at the end of your own lessons and after other people's asking, for example, 'Well, what did you learn this morning?' It's important not to ask questions about the teacher but to ask about the students' learning. Another good reason for asking students to tell you what they understand about something is that it raises student awareness of what they are learning and why.

For more ideas on this, see *'Probing thinking to see what students understand'* on page 39.

A   Class dictionary

This activity will give you a very good idea of your students' active vocabulary. I'll describe the activity first for a small group of, say, 7–15 students.

1 Give each student a piece of paper and say that they will write a topic area at the top.
2 Give them the topic areas. For example, one student can write 'FOOD' at the top of their paper, another can write 'SPORTS'. Choose the topics from ones you know they should have covered. (For examples, see the box below.)
3 Explain that they will soon be writing English words down under the heading. Give or elicit examples for each category. So, for example, the 'FOOD' person gets the starter word 'Bread' and the 'COLOUR' person thinks of 'Blue'. Each student writes down one starter word.
4 Now give the students time to write down all the words they know in their category. They can use a dictionary to check spelling. If students have problems with the alphabet, you can help by finding the correct page in their dictionary and then letting them do the rest of the search themselves. It's important to make sure they are trying to recall words they have met before and not trying to find new words. You can be part of the circle too.
5 When the first rush of words onto paper has subsided, ask everyone to pass their paper one person to the left.
6 Students read through the new piece of paper in front of them to check the spelling of the words already written by their neighbour, make a private note of any words new to them, and then add more words in the same category. You stroll around the room checking and helping.

7 Once the students have added as many words as they know to this new category, they pass their papers to the left once more.
8 The activity continues in this way. As more words are added to the list on each piece of paper, there is more recording and checking, more thinking and less writing. The papers should be circulated, always at the same time and in the same direction until each student eventually ends up with the paper he or she first started with. With ten categories at elementary level this takes about 45 minutes.
9 Each student can be responsible for taking home one piece of paper, checking the spelling and bringing it back for the next lesson. You can then make copies so the class has a record of the words they know as a group.

Variation
If you have large classes from, say, 15 students upwards, either put students into pairs so that two students can work together on each sheet of paper and topic, or with much bigger classes of, say, 30 or 40, put students into groups of ten. Get them to designate numbers so that everyone in each group knows who is number one, number two, etc. Then when calling out topics give, for example, all student ones 'Food' and all student twos 'Sports' and so on, as above.

This is the start of a class dictionary. It not only tells you student knowledge of lexical items in certain categories, but can be added to as new words come up in class. Students who made a private note during the activity of new words can look them up at home.

The class dictionary encourages an awareness of word groupings. When one particular group becomes too large, students can suggest new sub-divisions. For example, if the 'Food' category has too many words in it, the class could decide to break the category into 'Dairy', 'Meat' and 'Vegetables'. Students generally like this activity because it gives them the chance to recall and review words without the tension of a test. It encourages cooperation, dictionary use, word grouping awareness and individual responsibility. The end result is self-made and can be taken home, added to, stored and rearranged.

Categories for elementary level
Food, sports, colours, animals, places to go, numbers, days and months, jobs, verbs, adjectives, drinks, clothes, household objects.

Categories for intermediate level
Names of countries, languages, things found in the kitchen, in the bedroom, in the lounge, in the garden, hobbies, vegetables, fruit,

---

vehicles, special clothes for special jobs, adjectives of size, texture, shape, adverbs of frequency.

Categories for advanced level
Raw food, proteins, types of industry, types of government, special tools, expensive hobbies, cheap hobbies, indoor interests, outdoor interests, clothes for special occasions, phrasal verbs with 'get' together with an example sentence for each meaning, art forms, adjectives for weather temperature, ways of expressing vagueness.

1.6 How to get information during subsequent lessons

We can find out some things about our students (e.g. that they are very tired), by looking at their faces and body posture. We can then react quickly to the information (e.g. I'll do the idea I didn't have time to finish yesterday. That'll make them feel brighter.). At other times things are more complex. There is no instant way, for example, that we can find out that one particular student is hard of hearing but doesn't want to admit it or that a class is always out of sorts in Tuesday's third lesson because they are having trouble in the lesson just before ours. This kind of knowledge will normally come to us informally, over time and via a number of different sources. Similarly, there is no one quick, organised activity that will show us how our students are constructing their understanding of English. Sometimes a particular teaching style or a whole working method is necessary to bring this kind of information out. We thus need to keep our own antennae out all the time to pick up information informally through body language, casual discussion or by noticing repeated behaviour.

We can also plan into our work some deliberate elicitative techniques. Some ideas follow, first in medium to large classes, then, later on, in small groups or one to one.

A **Name review – Chair swap**

It takes me ages to learn people's names and so I always assume that students will need chances to review them too.

- If you have enough space in your classroom and up to about 20 students, try the chair swap game. Start by demonstrating it. Ask the students to sit in a circle. Call out the name of a student you remember. If they remember your name too, the pair of you swap seats. Call out someone else's name and, again, if they remember your name, swap chairs. Encourage all the students to do this at once. When they get going there should be lots of name-calling and swapping going on. Encourage students to do this faster and faster and to keep going until they have swapped seats with everyone. The result, in all the noise and confusion, is that those who are uncertain of other students' names will be able to ask people without this being noticed!

(I learnt this from Mario Rinvolucri.)

A 50-second talks

If you have a class that is lower intermediate or above you can take it in turns over a number of lessons for different students to give either prepared or unprepared '50-second talks'. You should explain the guidelines for these talks and can help with or correct talks prepared by the students. You may want to give one yourself first.

- Guidance for the speaker could include ideas for topics (such as hobbies, pets, what I like to eat, the thing I'm best at), starting and finishing phrases (such as 'I'd like to tell you a bit about …', 'That's all', 'Any questions?'), or hesitation devices (such as 'Just a minute, I'm thinking').
- Guidance for listeners could be to provide good non-verbal support, to listen as well as possible and to try to ask one question at the end.
- If you start things off by giving a 50-second talk yourself, use language that is below the level of the class, make the talk fairly prosaic and only talk for 50 seconds, so that students will not be daunted.
- When it's the students' turn to speak, don't cut them off after 50 seconds unless they completely dry up. Most students can talk for much longer than 50 seconds, and are able to do so because they are not too daunted by the task, their peers are being supportive and they are being asked the odd interesting or funny question by their peers.
- While the talks are being given, you can note down information the students share and things that are well-expressed as well as information on what the students can and can't do in English.

A Learner style

Even students of nine or ten years old will have experienced enough learning situations of different kinds (such as bike-riding, word-processing, sports, school, etc.) for them to be able to write or talk about the learning situations they most enjoy and in which they feel they learn most. Once you have got the basic information on names, level, and so on from some of the activities above and once you have settled into some teaching for a couple of lessons so that students know what you normally do in your lessons, have a discussion on learner style, even if a very basic one, based on a questionnaire and conducted in part or in whole in mother tongue. See Ellis and Sinclair (1989) for more ideas in this direction.

1 Make a simple questionnaire like the one below.
2 Make sure students understand the vocabulary and let them add categories and concrete examples.
3 Give students time to answer the questions alone, in pairs or in groups.
4 Discuss the answers.

Questionnaire
1 Are you a thinker or a mover?
Which of the following do you most enjoy learning to do better?

A language / A sport / A school subject / Making something nice to eat / A hobby / Puzzles, crosswords and quizzes / *something else*

Why?

2 What resources do you enjoy using?

A room of your own / A desk of your own / A radio / A TV / A video recorder / A computer / A library / A language lab / A self-access centre / A dictionary / A grammar book / An English club / English newspapers, magazines, books / Someone else's class file with notes in it

Take the resource you like most and describe it.

3 How do you like to study?
Which of the following do you like doing in class or at home?

Learning grammar rules and vocabulary by heart
Being corrected by the teacher
Solving puzzles
Taking risks and making mistakes
Doing tests and getting good results
Reading simple stories
Trying to speak English
Listening to English sounds, speech and songs

> Writing in English
> Picking up English easily without trying hard to study
> Doing exercises in the book
> Working alone
> Working in pairs or small groups
> Working in a big class all together
> Doing regular homework

A Teacher style

Here is a quick idea for checking how students are getting on with your teaching style.

1 Give out a sheet of paper at the end of a unit of work. The sheet has adjectives written on it. These can be in the mother tongue or English. If in English, the adjectives can be taught previously over a number of lessons on other topics. Write the adjectives in random array on the paper as shown.

patient	strict	unfriendly
relaxed	serious	
		friendly
slow happy	impatient	speedy

EXAMPLE ADJECTIVES

Make sure that for every positive adjective there is a negative one and that the students have also learned other words that could go on the paper, such as 'organised', 'late' or 'busy'. Before handing out the paper, remind the students of the other words they know to describe people.

2 Ask the students all to take the same colour pen and to circle the words that they think apply to you. They can circle more than one or circle an important one twice or add new words.

3 If possible, either leave the room or turn away and work on something else while they are busy reading, checking dictionaries and circling words.

4 When they have finished, ask them to gather all the papers together without your help so that the activity is anonymous.

Variation

If you feel shy about eliciting feedback so directly on your personal style, you can adapt the basic idea. You could take the topic of 'Classroom atmosphere' instead.

- On one side of the paper, students write adjectives describing the kind of atmosphere they like in class. On the other side of the paper, they write the words that apply to what they feel is the reality of the classroom.

    Other possible topics for this two-sided approach are 'Student participation', 'Our class' or 'Our coursebook'.
- Whatever topic you choose, you should end up with a sheaf of papers which you can glance at quickly to get an overall picture of how the students perceive the class they are in.

Probing thinking to see what students understand

Conventionally, course planning starts with an analysis of the 'subject matter', in our case the language. We look at the coursebook or at the language and try to sort out which are the most important things to teach, and which things are 'easier' or 'more difficult', and then build our course from there. Secondary school science education as well as TESOL, however, now argues that it is essential to recognise that students have already constructed their own ideas about the subject matter, in this case, about the language they are learning. These ideas may be very different from the analyses in the coursebook or in our teaching. We need therefore to take into account learners' ideas or there may be a complete mismatch between teacher attempts at explaining and student perception. We may need to reconsider the starting points in our teaching and the ideas that we assume the students have available to them. If we know how our students are thinking as well as what they can produce and understand, we can also suggest activities that challenge or extend the range of their own ideas. So, how can we find out how our students are thinking about English? A simple start was described in the activity, '*One thing I know about English*' on page 32. As you get to know your class better, however, you can make student ideas more explicit and sustained by using whole or small group discussion, written explanations by students, student drawings or diagrams as representations of how the students are thinking about English. At the end of classes you can ask 'What did we do today?' allowing students to come up with their own significant categories and it will also be useful to add 'Why do you think we did that?'

1 Who are the students?

A Learning contracts

Learning contracts are written agreements between learners and teachers about what a learner will try to learn and how this will be measured. Although mostly used in adult work-based learning, they can be adapted for most settings. They are designed with the learner rather than the teacher or the subject in mind. They help students to take more responsibility for organising resources, and making the most of learning opportunities. They can make learning more meaningful and democratic since they are partly tailored to the students' own needs and interests and partly to the formal requirements of a course. They require a new skill of the teacher, that of a resource person working with students. (For more on all aspects of learning contracts see Anderson et al 1996 and Boak 1998.)

1 Using course materials and group discussion, explain to the students what is negotiable and what is not. You may want to use contracts for the whole of your course or, if using the idea for the first time, just for a part or for one topic. Students will also need to know what the roles, responsibilities and expectations of all parties are. For students used to a top-down, passive role in their own learning, you will need to go very slowly and give lots of ideas, guidance and support.
2 Explore with the learners what there is to learn, what they want to learn and what they should learn.
3 Show them a simple draft contract like this:

Name of student:

● Topic, skill or knowledge area:

● Start date:

● End date:

● Learning objectives:

● Assessment criteria:

Signatures:

A DRAFT TEACHING CONTRACT

There should be a space at the bottom of the contract, since when this is filled in it will be a working document. As such it may need to be discussed and any renegotiated points noted and signed by both parties in this space.

Learning objectives can be products, processes or reflective evaluations. You will need to get straight in your own mind which is most appropriate for your course and give students appropriate examples of the kinds of things that would be possible.

4 Next, ask students to fill in a draft contract and discuss it with a group of peers. In my experience peers will be a lot tougher on students than teachers ever are!

5 The next part takes a little time. You need to make sure the objectives the students have specified are genuine and not teacher-pleasing, appropriate for the stage of the course, the level of the learner, the time available and the assessment criteria and are likely to result in real learning for the students. Rather than accepting the first suggestion immediately, you may have to refine the objectives with the students.

6 Leave a few days for students to think about their contracts and whether they really can commit themselves to them and to the criteria for assessment that you have worked out between you as being fair.

7 Once you have finalised the contracts and signed them, the next part is for the students to try to fulfil them with your help and support. You will need to have ongoing discussions and adjust the contracts and initial them as necessary when circumstances change.

A Tutorials

Having talks with sub-groups or one to one with members of your class may be a complete luxury in your setting but if it is ever possible (owing to student absence, or other students working on some private task), I would, personally, jump at the chance for this more private channel of communication.

In settings where students are doing a lot of studying on their own it's essential to have regular meetings to check how students are getting on. It's important to talk through with students beforehand such basics as the number and regularity of meetings, the overall aims, confidentiality and preparation tasks for both teacher and student. It's important to be clear about time too. Obviously the ideal might be not to put a time limit on the meeting so that the student can feel free to unwind and open up but this is totally unrealistic in most settings. It's important then that students know how long they have got. Once the logistics of time and place have been sorted out, an inexperienced teacher may be glad of a plan to give a tutorial the best chance of running effectively. Here is a possible sequence.

1 Welcome. Make sure the student is greeted and comfortable and that any small talk necessary to relax the student takes place.
2 'Trauma, trivia or joy' (TTJ). Spend time on what is uppermost in the student's mind on that particular day. If you don't allow time for this, the student will be less likely to be able to free the mind from pressing concerns and attend to the tutorial. You can start each meeting by discussing something particularly good that has happened to the student (a joy such as a good exam result or a visit from a friend), something that has not gone very well (a trauma such as a bad mark or an unfortunate encounter) or something else that is on the student's mind (trivia).
3 Main business. Topics here might be: progress, class participation, attitudes to host country, course methods and materials, study problems, recent or future assignments.
4 Student recap. In this phase the student restates what they think has happened in the tutorial, ensuring that important points don't get lost in the heat of conversation or in the inevitable busy-ness of life after the tutorial. Allow time for you both to make notes here.
5 Arrangements. The last few minutes can be devoted to setting the topic, pre-tasks, date, time, place and method of the next meeting.

It's a good idea, if you plan to have a series of tutorials with your students to ring the changes in the way of working as well as the topic. Here are some alternatives:

• Teacher directs the tutorial.
• Student chooses the topic and starts the discussion off.
• Extracts from learning logs are chosen and read out by students for discussion.
• Student and teacher write some notes before the tutorial. These are looked at during the tutorial and only the differences discussed.
• Student and teacher map the work done so far in class using key words.
• Student sets personal goals and works backwards to establish what needs to be done to achieve them.
• Previous assignments are brought in and discussed.
• Student prepares three questions to ask the teacher. Teacher prepares one question to ask the student. In the tutorial the student asks the first question. If one of the student questions covers the same ground as the teacher question, the teacher scraps their own question.

(See Jeanrenaud and Woodward 1997.)

Other ideas

There are some tactics and methodologies which are especially rich in terms of the amount of information sharing that they encourage. Some of these will be mentioned later in this book. You might like to look at 'Dialogue journals' (see page 67). See also Woo and Murphey (1999). If you would like to read an account of a teacher getting to know individual students, try Hess (1998).

1.7 How to get information after the students have gone

Although it may be tempting to feel that once the course is over and the students have gone that's the end of the matter, there is in fact something you can do to gain further information, that is a 'Tracer study'.

A Tracer study

A tracer study helps you to find out what happens to students after they leave your class. It can give you information about which parts of your course were most or least helpful, whether students are using what they learned, in what contexts, and generally charts their pathways. If you carry out your own tracer study and take heed of the findings, it can extend your professional vista past the rather limited conveyer belt view normally available to a teacher teaching 'generations' of students. It can help you to see where you fit into the students' overall career as well as helping you to retune the course in future.

The basic sequence for a tracer study is as follows:

- Keep an up-to-date record of student names and addresses.
- Mention to students that you may well contact them after the course to ask them how they are getting on and so that you can fine-tune future courses.
- Prepare a questionnaire (see the example below) and photocopy it onto the back of a friendly letter, making sure that responding is made as easy as possible for the students by, for example, providing a stamped addressed return envelope.
- Make sure the student receives all this long enough after leaving your class to have settled into their new course, job or activity, but not so long afterwards that they have forgotten all about your course.
- Wait for the replies to come in and chivvy the slow ones with letters, phone calls or personal chats where possible.

Once the replies are in, you can select a few students for further in-depth interviews or scan the replies for useful information, fine-tuning your next course where appropriate and making sure that you don't over-generalise the results if your reply rate is low. (For more information on tracer studies see Chapman and Fisher 1995.)

The idea of tracer studies can be extended to talking to those in the position of hiring or teaching your ex-students. Without mentioning any particular student by name it should be possible to find out whether the students seemed to be particularly well- or under-prepared in any subject area or skill.

Sample tracer study questionnaire suitable for art and design students who have completed a pre-university induction course

1 What is the name of the course you are studying on now?
2 Where are you doing the course?
3 Which of the components of the pre-university induction course you did in the summer was most helpful? (To remind you of the main components I have listed some of them below.)

  – lectures
  – seminars
  – studio work
  – portfolio construction and assembly
  – understanding project briefs, presenting briefs
  – withstanding the criticism phase
  – study skills
  – writing assignments
  – tutorials
  – outside visits
  – meeting study colleagues and setting up study groups
  – reading
  – other …

4 Which of the components above were not very useful?

5 Of all the things you have to do on your course now which do you find most difficult?

Thank you for answering the questionnaire. Are there any comments you would like to make?

1.8 Conclusion

In this chapter we've looked at ways that we can find out about students before, during and after the time you spend with them. It is a very natural sequence in teaching to find out about the students and then to take account of this information in your work. It would be a very perverse sequence to find out and then ignore the information ... although I have seen this done! Finding out about your students can help you to increase your own confidence and sense of professional competence, can increase rapport with the students because they know you have them in mind, will help you to get started on your first few lessons, will help you to make choices in topics, materials, activities and to determine the overall objectives for your course. This should help students to learn more effectively.

Once you have settled in with a group or at least have got to know them a bit, normal standard teaching and learning begins. That is the subject of the next chapter.

Who are the students?

1 Who can you find out from?

2 What can you know and why?

3 How can you get information before meeting the class?

4 How to get information on first meeting?

5 How to get information in subsequent lessons?

6 How to get information after the students have gone?

7 What can you do with the information?

CHAPTER 1: WHO ARE THE STUDENTS?

2 How long is the lesson?

2.1 Introduction

Once you've met the students and found out something about them, the race is usually on! There are courses to be sketched out and lessons to be planned. While considering the long term you also have to get started on the shorter term. So to get things started realistically and quickly and because the most basic lesson shape of all is perhaps the one that is simply based on the flow of time, this chapter will be about the chronological lesson shape. Everyone, whether student, starter teacher or old lag, works easily with the concept of 'a beginning, a middle and an end'. So the lesson shape in this chapter is the one most likely to be familiar to you. Most experienced teachers have favourite ways of opening and closing classes and favourite ways of doing 'the main bit' too. So even with a beginning, a middle and an end we still have plenty of options. In this chapter I'll detail some of the options you have at the start, in the middle, around break time and at the end of lessons, and I'll work through these options chronologically.

2.2 Beginnings

Beginning before the beginning

If you feel that first impressions are very important and also want to have your attention free once the students arrive, you may well start your own work BEFORE the beginning of the lesson. You'll get into the classroom before the students do. You'll open windows, clean boards, move chairs, turn on music, pin things on the wall, put things on chairs, and generally take over the space and make it your own. There may be a few students in the room but most students will turn up to find you there already. Of course not all teachers have this choice since in many schools the classrooms are occupied by another lesson up to the moment when your lesson starts and you may be teaching elsewhere up to the last minute. However, regardless of when you get into the classroom, whether you show up half an hour early or slide in dead on time, there is still, theoretically, the choice of whether to respect the time boundary at the start of class accurately or to have instead a fluid, organic start.

Clear boundaries

If you and your students feel, quite reasonably, that a 9 o'clock lesson should start at 9 o'clock sharp, you'll probably do some of the following:

- engage the students in eye contact
- shake hands
- ask students to stand up
- shut the door
- greet the class and expect a greeting in return
- call the register
- have a procedure for late students (e.g. asking for an apology and a reason for lateness or conversely expecting a quiet, unobtrusive tiptoe to a chair)
- introduce yourself and the first activity

I feel that if you want students to be punctual, you need to be so yourself.

 I have to admit that with a group of adult students whose culture allowed for many absences, early leave-takings and late arrivals, my resolve faltered and I found myself getting very relaxed about time. However, the more relaxed I became each day, the later the students arrived. I solved my own problem by arriving early, as I like to do, but taking in some marking, reports and other work. I had usually achieved quite a bit before the students deigned to turn up!

Fluid boundaries

In some institutional settings, the feeling may be that time boundaries can be more fluid and organic. You may come in a little late. You may stay a little late after class too. You may leave the door open so as not to create a feeling of lateness in students. You may not say 'Hello!' in a clear and definite way. Rather than drawing attention to yourself, you may hand something out to students instead so that the students look at the text and not at you. You may draw attention to what is left on the blackboard from the last class and discuss what mystery lies behind it. You may start up a conversation with one or two students rather than with the whole group. Whichever means is used, the feeling is that somehow the lesson has got going without a definite start. Culture clashes there are, albeit deep down, unconscious ones, between those who respect time boundaries clearly, and those who take them more casually. The sort of students you teach will greatly affect the way you begin class too. With primary and secondary students, brisk control of energy and enthusiasm will be necessary. If you are working with busy students who are highly motivated and paying for themselves, then saunter in 'organically' at your peril! They will think you lazy and unprofessional.

Working starts

If you are on a tight schedule and keen to create a time-efficient working atmosphere, then you are likely to get cracking on administrative tasks such as having students hand in their homework, checking past homework, calling roll or asking students to get out certain books. You may well socialise later in the lesson but may need to have the feeling that a substantial body of work has been completed satisfactorily before things can lighten up.

 The son of a friend of mine says that if a teacher doesn't generally check homework at the beginning of a lesson, then the majority of the students will spend the class with their heads down, ignoring the teaching and actually doing the homework under their desks, knowing it won't be checked until later.

Other possible working starts are:
- linking back to a past lesson to review things
- explaining the aim of the current lesson and how it fits into the lesson and course
- zooming in immediately on the main work of the lesson, for example, 'Here is your task. Please get into groups now. You have 15 minutes to complete stages 1, 2 and 3.'

If you are a brisk 'let's get going' type of teacher or teach classes who have no time at all for non work-related activities, then skip the rest of this section and go straight to the 'middles' section.

Taking care of the atmosphere

You may be the kind of teacher who is unable to get into the main work of a lesson until you judge the atmosphere of the class to be just right. It could be that your students come to class from different places and are only together for class once a week, and so need time to gel. It could be that students are physically cold or tired, hot or energetic and so need time to get into a constructive mood for working. The time of day too will influence the atmosphere. A class for business people held at 7.30 am will be very different from one held at 4.30 pm after the same people have worked all day. In schools, the difference between the first lesson and the sixth can be even more extreme and most classes and teachers will experience an energy slump after a large lunch.

Class atmosphere can change from day to day, even with the same class and the same teacher for no apparent reason, though there may be links to the weather, time of year and so on. Some teachers will respond to these outside influences by always doing the same things at the start of class trying to induce a working mood out of association and habit. Others will vary their lesson starts from day to day.

Many teachers will spend as much as 10 minutes at the start of a lesson on 'atmospherics'. If you are one of these, you may well argue that it is impossible to do the main part properly until the mood in the class is right or until the students' confidence is built. Atmospheres are very subjective things to create, feel and judge, so 'atmospheric' teachers differ widely in the sorts of atmospheres they try to create and the ways they go about creating them.

- If you like students to be quiet and concentrated, you might say, 'With your eyes shut, listen to the sounds and name them mentally in English' or do some guided visualisation exercises. Clem Laroy (1992) asks students to draw a spiral on a piece of paper, starting from the outside of the spiral and working to the inside. It's important that students do this silently and really follow the movement of their pen with their eyes. The concentration involved quietens the students and as they come closer to the centre of their spiral they focus more on the here and now. They are then more collected for the work that follows.

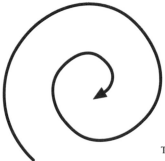

THE CONCENTRATION SPIRAL

- If you like students to be lively and eager to participate, you may tend to choose team games as starters.
- If you need to make a friendly atmosphere, you will tend to socialise, asking students how they got on in the last lesson or whether they have been watching the sport recently. There are lots of warm-up ideas in the first section of Lindstromberg 1990. Below are some ideas for starters that increase learner participation.

Student starts

The fundamental idea here is that students are encouraged to take responsibility for their own learning and for some classroom processes without always needing the teacher to 'crank start' them.

- An example would be if you told your students the topic of the lesson and asked them to recall individually, in pairs or in groups, in note form on paper, everything they know about the topic. They then explain to you what they know before you start to add to this knowledge pool yourself. Other things that can be pooled are ways of learning vocabulary, ways of studying for an exam, and how students make use of teacher comments on homework.

Several colleagues of mine go further than this and arrive in class to find things already happening. They settle in for a few minutes in a fairly passive way, watching and listening to students who have started class on their own. Students can start class not just by taking over administrative tasks such as collecting homework and bringing it to the front desk. They can also:
- start greeting their neighbours and asking them questions in English at the sight of the teacher in the doorway
- give their neighbours an oral summary of something read for homework
- test their neighbours on a list of words from the last lesson
- prepare six to ten review questions to ask the whole class. Have a rota for this and at the end of each class the next student on the rota is reminded of their review question homework for the next day (Bress 1996).

No matter which system you want to get up and running, you obviously have to give clear guidance to the students on what is expected of them and why. If the ideas were not their own, you need to practise several times, expect the students to do the work, and check and praise the work to show your own commitment to it. Careful setting up pays off. It allows you to come into class to the sound of English and the sight of other people working! Some student groups are so lively and cohesive that they will start classes on their own without being prompted or primed by the teacher. I have known students to start class by:

- singing 'Happy Birthday'
- lighting candles and turning the electric lights off
- turning up en masse 20 minutes late on April Fool's Day
- engaging the teacher in a passionate debate on the stupidity of the English
- telling each other personal or international news
- showing photographs and commenting on them in English.

Discussing the menu

In some restaurants there is a fixed menu, in others you can choose from a selection. Either way it's quite nice to know what's coming before it arrives. Menus can work in language classrooms too.

- You can do this by writing a list of planned activities on the same part of the board each day, perhaps the top left-hand corner. You could even detail the possible activities under the headings 'What (we can do)', 'When (we can do it)' and 'Why (we would want to do it)'. Even if students have no choice about what is coming, they can at least decide individually what they don't want to concentrate on and so when they can take some mental relaxation!
- Alternatively, you can list some areas of work and let students decide which order they want to do things in, which things they would like to cross off or add to the list and what personal goals they would like to set for the lesson, week or term.

In order for students to make reasoned choices from your menu they will need information, so you may have to give them a 'preview'. For example, show two texts and state the main differences between them: 'I'd like to do some work today on metaphors. This is a dictionary of metaphors and I can show you how to look up, understand and use some of the entries. And this is a newspaper article about politics, full of sailing metaphors. We can read it and discuss it. We only really have time to do one of these things, so which would you rather do?' You will always have to explain the choices in some way. It's helpful to put notes or mnemonics on the board as you are explaining choices. This will help students by reminding them which option they are voting for later on.

Theoretically the most open choice for students is to be asked 'What shall we do today?' Woods (1996) recounts an incident with his saxophone teacher who preferred this way of structuring lessons and courses:

'My teacher normally greeted me with, "What will we do today?" and I explained what I wanted to do or what I wanted to learn and he either did what I had decided, or he made decisions to help me accomplish what I said I wanted to learn ... The one time I kidded, "You're the teacher, aren't you supposed to decide?" he acted somewhat insulted and put me through an hour of rigorous, repetitive exercises in which I had no say at all.'

Woods's anecdote illustrates the conflict we have here between the principle of student choice on one hand and the principle of professional responsibility on the other. A reasonable compromise would seem to be that: (a) you and the students actually have a choice on hand, (b) you both have enough information to make choices, (c) students are gently introduced to the idea of making choices, and (d) students have the right to delegate decisions back to you if they wish. If students have the right to be consulted about what they wish to learn, they also have the right to delegate such decisions straight back to the teacher!

Using menu starts is not just a way of building learner autonomy, it also gives a sense of structure and progress, keeps you relevant, and inspires confidence in you as a teacher who knows what you're doing.

Whether you're a boundary person or an organic start person, a 'working atmosphere' or a 'friendly atmosphere' person, a self-starter or a student starter, the sooner you work out what is comfortable in your setting for you and your students, the sooner you can take your lesson starts more for granted and stop planning them in so much detail. Once you have some interesting and comfortable routines, they will do for a while. Then, as you change classes or schools, as you and your students evolve and negotiate, you will need to learn new ideas, sequences and lesson shapes. This way you have stability and continuity, interest and flexibility.

2.3 Middles

When you and your students are ready to tackle the main business of the class, you have some choices ahead. Let's imagine that our chronological lesson looks like this:

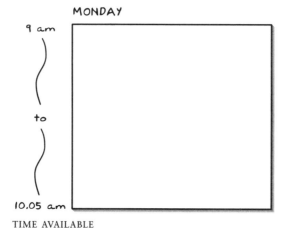

MONDAY

9 am

to

10.05 am

TIME AVAILABLE

If we put in our beginning and breaks and end (see later in this chapter), we get this:

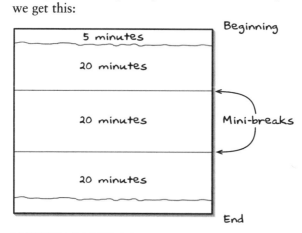

Beginning

5 minutes

20 minutes

20 minutes

Mini-breaks

20 minutes

End

BEGINNING TO DIVIDE UP THE TIME

We are left with blocks of time of, say, 20 minutes, or if we scrap one of the mini-breaks, 40 minutes. These are the main bits or 'middles' of the lesson. I'd like to mention three possible categories of ideas for these middle sections. These are Threads, Middles as stimulus-based blocks, and Generalisable procedures for texts. These three ways of working are not one-off recipes. Once you get the hang of them, and they are all explained in detail below, you will have a large number of moves that you can apply to any activity or piece of material. This will cut down massively on thinking and planning time.

Threads

Some people believe that 'little and often' is the best way to learn. Instead of spending a long time all at one sitting trying to understand something, some teachers feel that it's better to work for a short spell on something, leave it to settle or percolate for a while and then pick it up next time, reviewing and extending understanding a little before leaving it again. It is quite possible that something important happens in learning terms, a kind of 'incubation', in the apparently inactive times between learning sessions. Quite often we have the experience of feeling flustered by something new and then, after a pause, coming back and finding it much easier to deal with. If we want to work with our students in a way that allows for this experience, we can set up activities that do not progress or build 'vertically' down one lesson in connection with other activities done on the same day. Rather, they are threaded through the timetable, so that they build up as they are revisited on subsequent days.

A **An animal a day**

This is one such simple thread idea. This series of activities is designed to work on literal and metaphorical uses of basic vocabulary. The 'animal' can be a cat, fish, bird, horse, snake or frog. The first day, one animal is introduced with its basic vocabulary, e.g. a cat: whiskers, paws, claws, tail. When the thread is revisited in the next class these words are reviewed and new ones added, e.g. tabby, tom, kitten. Your choices each time you revisit the animal in subsequent classes are to:

- review nouns already learned
- add verbs (hiss, scratch, purr)
- add adjectives (furry, soft, playful)
- add strengths and weaknesses (good hunter, kills things, sleeps a lot)
- add metaphors (cat's eyes in the middle of the road, a catty remark, to claw back money in taxes)
- introduce new 'animals' such as birds and snails, discuss the similarities in what they have (feathers versus slimy scaly skin) and where they live (nest, garden)
- ask students to tell you about individual animals of one type that they have known

The 'animal a day' thread can last from 5–20 minutes and can be visited either every class or regularly but at longer intervals. Once students have started work on this thread they will quickly settle into it each time you announce, 'OK, let's go back to our animal a day. Who can give me some cat vocabulary?' Once introduced, threads can be picked up quickly with a minimum of explanation since they are already familiar to everyone. They can be used at the same or different points of the lesson each time. There are many different kinds of threads for speaking, listening, vocabulary, writing, thinking and learning general knowledge. (See Woodward and Lindstromberg 1995.)

If you do the middles of your lessons this way, each class will consist of several 10–30 minute activities that gradually build up over time. These threads do not necessarily have a connection to other activities in the same class (vertically) but do with activities in subsequent classes (horizontally). See page 195. This way of working will minimise planning time and will give the variety and pace necessary to keep students interested and moving along. It will be especially useful with classes who find it difficult to concentrate on one thing for long periods.

For other classes who need more in-depth work, a combination of a block and thread approach will work well (see the next section). Thus, although it is possible to plan entire lessons around threads, it's also possible to use them for just part of a lesson.

Stimulus-based blocks

Another way of looking at the time between the beginning and end of a lesson is as one big block of time that you can use to get a lot of work done on one thing. You may well use this 'block' approach with well-motivated students who can concentrate for long periods. We can take a very open-minded approach to the kind of *stimulus* we can work on in this time. A stimulus, as I'm using the word here, is anything that has the capacity to hold student interest. Thus some example stimuli are a page in a textbook, a listening tape, an object, a visitor, a drawing on the blackboard or a song.

You can apply different kinds of *move* to a stimulus. By this I mean a way of working with a chosen stimulus. Example categories of move are: *meeting the stimulus, analysis, personalisation, alteration and transfer, creation*. A brief definition and example of each category of move follows so that you can see what I mean.

Meeting the stimulus

This stage is when students first encounter the stimulus. Sometimes you will want this to happen immediately for the sake of impact or when the stimulus is extremely rich. However, it can be more productive at other times not to display all the material immediately. If the stimulus is a picture, allow a brief glimpse. If it is a text, cut it into pieces so that

different people have different bits. Not revealing all the stimulus immediately will mean that students can learn language for prediction and
speculation, matching, sorting and reordering.

Analysis

The analysis stage involves studying the stimulus to see what is in it once
it has been totally revealed or pieced together. Examples of analysing
activities are where students comment on the stimulus and compare it
with their speculations, or where students identify and name its parts,
describe it and discuss its natural context and uses, and its past, present
and future.

Personalisation

You can make the stimulus more meaningful and interesting and thus
more memorable to students by establishing a link between the students
and the stimulus. In this stage, students can write or speak about how
the stimulus is similar to or different from them, what the stimulus
reminds them of, if they have ever ..., what they would do if ..., etc. This
encourages oral and written expression of the students' own experience.

Alteration and transfer

Once the stimulus has been dissected and has become more meaningful
to the students through their involvement with it, the alteration and
transfer stage encourages them to work with the material flexibly, thus
improving thinking and language skills. Options here are making new
things from the stimulus, reducing or expanding it, thinking of parallels,
opposites or reversals.

Creation

In the creation stage the students move on from the stimulus, using it as
a springboard to new skills or new products. Example activities are role
plays or letter writing activities connected with the stimulus.

In order to show more clearly how these moves actually work in the
classroom, here's an example from Woodward and Lindstromberg
(1995). The application assumes, and this is very important, that you
have introduced or worked with some of the vocabulary and structures
implied below, as appropriate to your students' level.

USING AN APPLE AS THE STIMULUS

Meeting the stimulus
1 Have the apple thickly wrapped with newspaper in a bag.
2 Write some sentence starters on the board:
> I think …
> It's …, definitely.
> It's probably …
> It could be …
> It can't be …
3 Students feel the object through the bag and speculate about what it is, using the language.
4 Elicit words for its shape. Write them on the board.
5 Elicit words for its texture. Write them on the board.
6 Keeping the apple in the bag, remove the newspaper. Let the students feel again. Write the following sentence on the board:
> If it was a …, it'd be …-er.
7 Students make sentences like these:
> If it was a potato, it'd be longer.
> If it was a grapefruit, it'd be bigger.
> If it was a kiwi fruit, it'd be smaller/rougher.

Analysis
1 Take the apple out of the bag and let everyone see it.
2 Elicit or teach names for its parts (*peel, stem, core, flesh, pips,* etc.)
3 Ask how apples 'happen' and where they come from.
> Nouns: *apple tree, blossom, pollen, bees*
> Verbs: *grow, pollinate, pick*
> Time expressions: *in the beginning, then*
> Ask how apples get to our homes.
> Structures: *People/They* (verb) *them, The apples/They are* (verb)*ed*
> Verbs: *pick, put, load, transport*
> Nouns: *buckets, boxes, lorries, storage shed*
4 Everyone examines the apple carefully.
> Vocabulary: *stem, freckles, bruise, worm hole, red, yellow, waxy, dull, shiny, blotchy*

Analysis activities can also involve thinking of all the stories and metaphors that are connected with the stimulus, e.g. Adam and Eve, William Tell, 'the apple of her eye', in this instance.

Personalisation
Each student writes at least three sentences saying what they and the apple have in common, and at least three saying how they and it differ. Students then share their sentences in pairs or groups.

Alteration and transformation
This can be literal, for example, if you have an apple each:

1 You and your students each peel your apple in one long strip. Toss the whole peel over your right shoulder onto the floor behind. See what letter of the alphabet the shape of the peel most resembles. Say that it's the first letter of the name of your future husband/wife/first child (or whatever seems appropriate).
2 Then elicit or teach vocabulary for the steps of eating (*take a bite, chew, taste, swallow*) adding optional words for fun (*burp, choke*). Then eat the apples.

Or the alteration can be figurative, for example:

1 Ask everyone to close their eyes.
2 Ask them to picture the apple in their mind's eye.
3 Lead a guided visualisation by asking them to imagine it with yellow and blue stripes, covered in fur, gigantic with themselves sitting on top of it, etc.

Creation
Give the students writing or speaking tasks, for example: 'Suppose the apple told its life story, what would it say? What would it say were the high and low points of its life?' Or: 'What do the pips feel? Are they comfortable? What plans do they have?'

In stimulus-based teaching, you can go through all of these moves with one stimulus in one lesson. In this way you and your students will work with the stimulus in a very thorough and sustained way. Or you can go through some moves in one lesson and some another time, thus making a stimulus-based thread. You can use different moves with different stimuli depending on which ones the stimuli seem to lend themselves to best. They don't have to be done in a fixed order. They don't all have to be used each time. The five categories of moves are 'generalisable procedures' which, once you have tried them out and learned how to do them, can be applied to any stimulus at all for the rest of your teaching life.

As well as using one or more stages as a catalyst to help you think of ideas for working with texts, pictures, taped dialogues, etc., you can use the stages to find the patterns in your own work or in your textbook. Consider either a couple of lessons you have recently taught or a couple of units in your textbook. Think of all the activities used and see if you can place them in one or more of the five stages. You may well find that, for example, you or your coursebook do plenty of work in the analysis and alteration categories but very little in the personalisation or creation categories. Knowing this gives you the option of starting to balance things up a bit.

Generalisable procedures for texts

Alan Maley's book *Short and Sweet* was published in the same year as Woodward and Lindstromberg's (1995). We had obviously been working along very similar lines, since in *Short and Sweet*, Maley gives 12 generalisable procedures that he suggests can be applied to short texts. The procedures are: *expansion, reduction, media transfer, matching, selection and ranking, comparison and contrast, reconstruction, reformulation, interpretation, creation, analysis, project work.* Let's take a one-sentence text and swiftly apply each of the categories of move to it. The text (taken from a car sticker) is:
'I've done so much with so little for so long that now I can do anything with nothing!'
   This text is for you the reader rather than for use in your class. Let's take it through the categories in order to gain familiarity and flexibility with them.

Expansion
We can add, say, adverbs to this text (e.g. *usually, sometimes, never*), or sentences before, after or within it, or comments within it, or new characters to it. Here is an example:
'After years of teaching different types of classes in different settings I feel I've done so much with so little for so long now that, given a fair wind behind me, I can do pretty well anything with almost nothing!'

Reduction
We can shorten the text by removing specified items (say, adjectives, sentences or conjunctions), turning it into note form or combining parts of it. This is obviously hard to do with a one-sentence text but here's an example:
'Have done much with little for long. Now can do anything with nothing.'

Media transfer
We can transfer the message into pictures, maps, graphs, or into a poem, a headline, an advertising slogan, etc.
'Experienced teachers! Have you put up with photocopier breakdowns, electricity cuts and shortages of equipment? Do you sometimes feel you can create magic from just one pair of shoelaces and a pair of scissors? Then this is the product for you!'

Matching
We can find a correspondence between the text and a title, a visual, another text or some music. For example, here are some sayings to match the one liner. Which one fits the best?
    An empty pot makes most noise.
    A rolling stone gathers no moss.
    It's easier for a camel to pass through the eye of a needle than for a rich man to enter the kingdom of heaven.
    You can't make a silk purse out of a sow's ear.
    All that glitters is not gold.

Selection and ranking
Who would be most likely to say the one liner, for example,
a car mechanic, a school teacher or a conjurer?

Comparison and contrast
Discuss, say, news snippets. Here is one from a local paper:
'Patrick Jones, a 38 year-old electrician from Maidstone in Kent, was fined £250 yesterday for wiring up his tumble dryer to the street lamp outside his house. The magistrate said that though his action was enterprising, it was also dangerous and unlawful.'

Reconstruction
When jumbled up, sentences can be surprisingly difficult to put back together. Try this!
/now so so so I've I done do much little long with with for that can anything nothing/ Gulp!

Reformulation
Rewrite the one liner as a newspaper headline, poem, recipe or bible story. How about: 'There were once five loaves and three fishes ...'

Interpretation
Discuss what the text really means. For example, is the author proud or grumpy?

Creation

Use the text as a kind of template for making others. Assuming the basic pattern is: 'I've ... so ... that now I can ...', here are two examples:

'I've bought so many bananas so cheaply since I discovered late night Saturday shopping at Sainsbury's that now I can make anything with them ... cakes, pancakes, fruit salads.'

'I've typed for so long that now I can hardly move my neck!'

Analysis

Analyse the text. For example, 'so much', 'so little ' and 'so long' are interestingly vague expressions of quantity. Other similar ones are 'quite', 'rather' and 'a bit'. In what situations do we tend to use these rather approximate quantifiers? Does it have anything to do with written versus spoken style? Is it more of a cultural difference?

Project work

Make a collection of sayings for car stickers. Here are a few I like:

'Practise senseless acts of beauty and random acts of kindness.'

'It's hard to soar with the eagles when you work with turkeys!'

'Dumb sign on board!'

We have worked through the 12 categories in a light-hearted way just for practice. Next, you might like to take a text that you regularly use, perhaps one from a coursebook and think how you could apply Maley's categories to it.

2.4 Break time

If you accept that most people can't concentrate or work fruitfully for more than an hour at a time without some sort of change or rest, and if your classes go on for $1\frac{1}{2}$ or 2 or 3 hours then you will need to think about transitions between different phases of work and about mini-breaks at the very least. Some ideas follow.

A Rounding off

As you and your students emerge from one piece of work, you need to round things off. Rounding off activities come as a welcome rest from periods of intense concentration. They signal the end of a chunk of work and can be used to review what's just been done, as a bridge to the next block of work, to add interest and variety or to activate different learning styles and intelligences. Here are some ideas to choose from:

- After doing as much on a piece of work as you feel is fruitful for the time being, spend a minute just playing with the letters of one long word connected with the subject you have just dealt with. So if you have just been discussing penal systems, a long word like IMPRISONMENT will do. If you have been working on verbs, PARTICIPLE is a nice long word to use. Whatever long word you have which sums up what you have been working on, you now have some choices:
  - Clap out the stress of the word and see if students can guess the word, e.g. ANIMAL. Once they have guessed, see if they can call out other words that have the same stress profile, e.g. BEAUTIFUL and HORRIBLE (stress: Ooo).
  - Scramble the letters of the word on the blackboard in anagram form. See if students can unscramble the letters to find the original word and then see if they can make funnier anagrams. For example, once they have made 'anagram' from 'ngaamar', let them have fun making 'nag a ram' and 'am a gran'.
  - See how many new words they can make from the old one using each letter only once. So, from 'generalisable' you can get 'gene', 'able', 'lean', etc.
  - See how many connected words they can build onto the letters of your chosen word, for example:

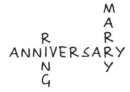

BUILDING FROM A WORD

Other ideas are:

- Ask the students to tell you one thing they have understood, one thing they haven't and one thing they found interesting or surprising in the work just done.
- Ask the students to write down four new words they think they will forget.
- Tell the students what is coming up in the next part of the lesson and ask them what they know about it already.

A Complete break in class

Even if you have to stay in class, you can still give yourself and your students a change.

- If students have been listening, let them talk ('... mother tongue time ... you have two minutes to say anything you want in your own language').
- If they have been talking, let them stop talking and spend one minute thinking of a beautiful sight they once saw or say, 'Bet you can't stay silent for a whole minute!' (see Appel 1995 p. 115).
- If they have been facing the front, let them face the back.
- Give them a two minute 'window break', where they can look out of the window and give you a running commentary on what they can see.
- If they have been sitting still, ask them to stand up, stretch, rub their palms together, rub their faces, their forearms, their upper arms, wriggle their feet, bend and stretch their knees, touch the ceiling, touch the floor.
- If you have been doing 'dry' work, read them a lovely poem, or play some music.

All these breaks work because they are a complete change from what went before. They are also useful if you want to either 'stir' and build energy or 'settle' and quieten energy in your class ready for the next activity (see Maclennan 1987). Break activities can act as smooth transitions to the next phase if you choose them carefully. If you have taught a class with new students in, you can give time for students to help each other to learn the names of everyone in the class. You can also declare a 'one-minute holiday'!

A Complete break outside class

Some students will need to run off somewhere, make phone calls or go to the bank in break time. Others will want to read letters or work on something in class. Most are usually quite happy to have a break. But some students regard breaks as a waste of time and some teachers do too. You can use break time by giving little tasks like these.

- Ask your students to come back from the break with one of the following:
  - the names in English of all the colours that have caught their eye
  - the name of the thing that made the loudest or quietest noise during the break
  - a description of one of the pictures in the hall

- one unusual but repeatable thing they learned about a classmate
- a verbal list of ten words learnt in the first part of the lesson
- a summary of the first part of the lesson
- information on what to do if there is a fire in the building
- the names of some of the books on a certain shelf in the library or book cupboard
- the names and job titles of all the staff on the staff photo board

As people file back into class after the break, check their 'break work'. Your choice of break work needs to be considered in how far it supports the work done in the previous or following part of the lesson. If you have a large class, for example, spending a long time after the break listening to the results of break work could disturb the flow of the lesson and lead to an ebbing of energy you could use more productively to tackle something that needs lots of concentration.

2.5 Ends

Ends of lessons need to start long before the bell goes or finishing time arrives, as the students will start packing up, people will run for buses or physically and mentally drift away. If you are a 'fluid boundary' person, maybe that won't concern you. But there are a lot of important things that can comprise an end. Here are some of them:

- review the lesson
- give back old homework or set and explain new homework
- write dialogue journals (see page 67)
- make plans for the next lesson
- tidy up the classroom for the next teacher

So maybe it is best to think about whether you want to teach right up to the last minute, teach over time and so cut into the students' break, or have a careful, controlled 'touch-down' that has the students cheering at the miracle of being back on the ground again on time, or finish off with a fun exercise.

A Homework

Often the students who have done homework will want to give it to you as soon as they get to class. However, for the forgetful and for those who came late, have a last call for homework that hasn't come in yet. Doing this by name, if you have a small enough class, also underlines your seriousness about the issue.

Giving back homework that you have marked and commented on can obviously be done at any point in the lesson, but for new homework relating to the lesson in progress it's a good idea to sort it out towards the end of the lesson, well before you are trampled in the rush for the door when the bell goes.

In order to set homework properly you need to know what other teachers have set for the students, whether they have any school outings or sports events coming up, and so on. This allows you to negotiate with them the amount and timing of homework. Then you need to:

1 Write up the tasks on the board.
2 Mark clearly which ones are essential, which are for which students and when the different tasks need to be completed. Encourage the students to set their own homework goals too, e.g. 'I'm going to learn five new words tonight.'
3 Check all this is understood.
4 Tell students what will happen to the homework (e.g. Will you mark it or will they read it out in class? What will constitute good work?).
5 While the students are copying this into their notebooks, make a note of it yourself. This will help you to collect the right pieces on the right days and thus build future lesson plans.

- If you have trouble filling in lesson plans, ask the students to do tasks which will contribute to future lessons. Examples here are:
  – prepare a one minute talk on ...
  – bring in three new words on topic x and be prepared to teach them to your neighbour
  – prepare review questions for the class (see page 51 and Bress 1996)
  – read anything you like in any language but be prepared to give a verbal summary of what you have read to a small group
  – bring in a favourite object from home and be prepared to talk about it
  – draw a diagram of your room and label what you can in English
  – copy down the label of any product imported from an English-speaking country
  – bring in an object that has a characteristic in common with the objects brought in by classmates, e.g. it is blue, circular, or made of wool, etc.
  – name five words in a number of lexical fields and check these in a dictionary
  – categorise all the words from the last week into three clear categories of your choice
  – do a matching exercise (match phrases to pictures, summary sentences to paragraphs, pictures to vocabulary, words to their antonyms)

- do some imaginative copying, such as only copying out from a menu those foods that you actually like to eat
- do a word search puzzle
- read something below your level, then write true/false questions about it
- write notes for and against something
- talk to yourself about x in the target language
- If you have too much material for lessons and too little time for marking, then you will need to give tasks for homework which don't require marking, for example:
  - review work done in class
  - prepare work for the next lesson
  - do exercises which have a key you can give out to the students
  - write to pen pals or companies (for leaflets) so that the response to the homework comes from someone other than the teacher
- For students who are doing free writing, ask them to select one or two categories only that they want corrected, e.g. only content, spelling, verbs, style, etc.
- If you work with translation in your classroom this makes excellent homework. You and your students write a questionnaire in English in class (about, say, the TV viewing habits of the older generation, for example). The students take this down in English. For homework they ask their families. This will need to be in their mother tongue as some relatives may not speak English. Students bring back the results with the answers in the mother tongue, and these can be translated and discussed in class, in English, thus involving another translation. (Thanks to Christine Frank for this idea.)

A Dialogue journals

If you want your students to have practice reading and writing natural English for real purposes on a regular basis and you are also keen on getting to know your students a lot better individually, then dialogue journals may be the thing for you.

Dialogue journals are conversations between a teacher and an individual student that are written down confidentially in a notebook that passes between them at regular intervals throughout a course. Students write what they want in the notebooks and teachers write back, not grading or correcting but REALLY writing back, as a partner in the conversation.(For more on the basics of dialogue journals, see Peyton and Reed 1990 and Peyton and Staton 1991.)

It makes sense for students to do the writing towards the end of the lesson as the high social energy period may be over. The work in the lesson can be mentioned in the journal, and as the students write they can mentally disentangle themselves from the group and prepare to leave the class.

- If students tell you that they don't know what to write about, give them ideas, for example:
  Tell me something about your family (or your room, your best friend or your pet). What did you do yesterday? Tell me about something really nice that happened to you this week. If you have a little time, what do you most like to do? What did you think about the topic we discussed today? Just choose one of these topics. If you start writing and think of something else you'd rather write about, then that is OK too.

Variations
If you have large classes, people who write a lot or you are very busy, try these variations:

- Different students write on different days so you don't get all the dialogue journals in on the same day.
- Allow students who don't particularly take to the idea to drop out naturally.
- Allow time in class for dialogue journal writing. You can be reading and responding to dialogue journal entries written by another class while your present class works on their entries.
- Encourage students to write dialogue journals to each other and only drop you a line when they have a query they can't answer themselves.
- Deal with pleas for correction by using reformulation techniques.

A What have we done today and why?

Class time can be full of people's remarks, the content of texts, interruptions, questions and explanations. By the end it can be hard to remember what happened. Students can feel as if they have been on a magic carpet ride involving parrots (in a text), fever (the reason why a student didn't turn up), Wimbledon (mentioned on the tape), flies (buzzing on the window pane) as well as their own images and memories that popped up unbidden. What the teacher thinks has been 'covered' may not have registered at all in the students' minds as the main point of the lesson. So it is useful feedback for the teacher and useful clarification for the students to restate things. There are many ways of doing this:

- The teacher, perhaps referring to a menu previously negotiated with the class, can recap on which points were covered: 'We started with the hot seat activity. Hanna was in the hot seat and talked about all the different wheeled objects she has had since she was little. Now,

what new vocabulary came out of that?' 'Roller skates' and ...?' ...
'Why do you think we did this exercise?'

- The students can in turn state what they think have been the main
points of the lesson. This can go topic by topic, for example, all the
students state what they have learned about, say, 'signpost words' first
before going on to state what they feel they have learned about
Maori culture from the text and the discussion that followed.
- The students can write the ends of sentences that the teacher starts,
for example: In this lesson I found out ...

> liked ...
> learned ...
> began to understand ...
> wanted to ...
> didn't understand ...
Next lesson I'd like to ...

(For a sustained written version of this kind of work using action logs,
see Woo and Murphey 1999.)

A Plans for next time

Give yourself a minute towards the end of a lesson to get some help planning your next one. You may already have written down some tasks that
students will be doing for homework and that will lead to them doing
something (e.g. presentations in the next class). You may well have your
students' views on what they have done this lesson and what they would
like to do next time, you may have items from an unfinished menu and
may need to allow time in class for students to write their dialogue journals. Share these points with your students and run by them any other
ideas you are thinking of for next time. For example, 'Now, when we meet
next, Rifat you will start by asking the class six to ten review questions,
right? We will finish the second reading that we didn't have time to do
today. I'll allow 15 minutes for writing dialogue journals, and many of you
have said that you would like an interview practice for your oral exam. We
can do the animals thread that you like. Anything else?' Students may
come up with other things and you may think of other things once you
hear yourself ask the question. The end result is that you have some ideas
jotted down on a piece of paper to start you off when you get down to
finalising your planning later on.

A Filling up the last remaining moments

There are days when your students have come to the end of a useful section of work, you've set the homework, it feels right to stop and yet they
are supposed to stay in class for another five or ten minutes before the bell

goes or before they cross the magic, invisible line between work and play. Even simple fillers like vocabulary review scrabble can while away a couple of minutes fruitfully.

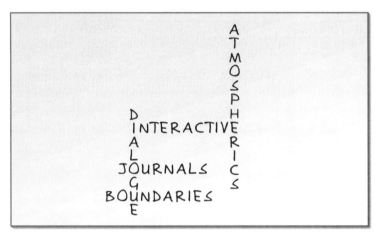

VOCABULARY REVIEW SCRABBLE

A trainer once suggested I keep a list of 20 filler ideas in my bag so that whenever I had a little time left at the end of a lesson I could whip out my list and do something useful. It pays to note down the name of the class by the filler you use so that another time you don't do the same one with the same class. If you write the filler ideas in the list in different colours and drag out the list often enough, you will soon have it memorised. Here are some ideas from my 'fillers' list.

- Name in English all the contents of someone's bag or pencil case.
- Suggest 20 things an ordinary object can be used for apart from its normal purpose.
- Choose a category, e.g. countries, and then go round the class starting the new word with the last letter of the word before (Iran, Nigeria, America, Australia ...).
- I spy with my little eye something beginning with 'J'.
- Give a sneak preview of what you will deal with in the next lesson.
- Tell a joke (of course you have to collect a few before you can do this one!).
- Collect some simple, funny cartoons for people to describe to each other and explain in English.
- Do the reverse of the warm-up ideas used at the start of the lesson. Thus the spiral (see page 50) would now be drawn outwards from the centre, encouraging students to unwind and open up by use of a visual metaphor and become more ready for a change of subject and room.

Other opening ideas that can be used as fillers are:

- Start a discussion about what is now written up on the board from the point of view of the next class. What would they make of it?
- If you moved the furniture, you can now ask the class to put the chairs and tables back where they were before the start of the lesson. For example, in a whisper, 'Ssssssh! I want you all to be silent. Turn to your chair. Imagine it is a delicate crystal vase. You have to pick it up in a minute. Very slowly and carefully. You mustn't drop it or knock it in case it breaks ... Now ... sssh ... slowly ... move your vase!' If you prefer, change the image to a big mound of jelly or a baby bird needing to go back to its nest.

For more ideas on how to while away five minutes usefully, see Ur and Wright (1992) and Stricherz (1982).

2.6 Conclusion

In this chapter we have looked at the simplest lesson shape of all, the chronological or 'beginning, middle and end' sort of lesson and at the sort of ideas that, once set up, will run and run. The activities described in this chapter are not designed to kill time. They're all expressions of concern with cultural, affective, organisational, conceptual or methodological aims. For example, a teacher who likes to get into class before the students do, may be doing this to gain a sense of control over space and resources. This in turn may help them feel organised and competent. Thus we find here the time has been used here for affective and organisational reasons. A teacher who creates mini-breaks in class (see page 62) may do this because of a belief that alternations between times of high concentration and relaxation enhance student learning. Thus she is using time for sincere pedagogical reasons. For more ideas on changing energies, see Agosta 1988.

If you are an inexperienced teacher, then just learning how to do a couple of different beginnings taken from this chapter, depending which ones suit you, your students and your aims, a couple of different break activities, a few different endings, a little suite of threads, and two or three generalisable procedures (that can be applied to any text, tape or other teaching aid) will give you enough to start with. You're away!

If you are an experienced teacher with a repertoire of your own, then you might like to pick up a few extra ideas from this chapter.

 If you'd like a gardening metaphor, then this chapter has been about planting hedges and putting in lots of perennials so that, apart from weeding, feeding and watering, you will have a low-maintenance garden that you and your students can enjoy for many seasons.

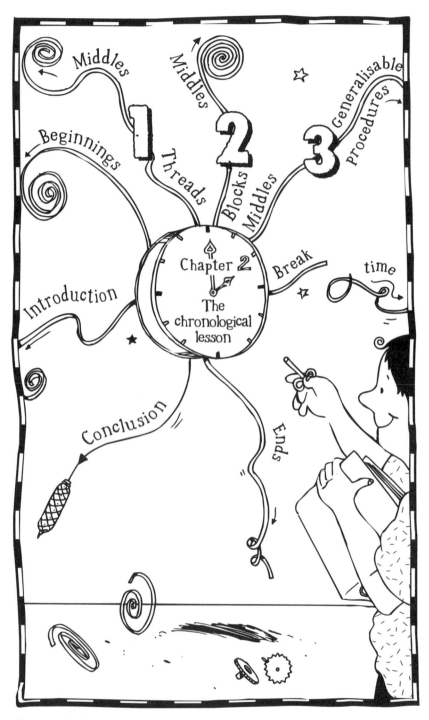

CHAPTER 2: HOW LONG IS THE LESSON?

3 What can go into a lesson?

3.1 Introduction

 In this chapter I'll look at a wide choice of content to put into a lesson or course. If the last chapter was the garden, metaphorically speaking, then this chapter is the seed catalogue where lots of different possibilities are briefly described just to get you thinking about your choices of what to teach. Just as you don't normally read a seed catalogue from cover to cover, I'd suggest you dip in to this chapter as and when you need to.

I'll deal in separate sections with classes and people, language patterns, language skills, and combinations of these in situations, topics and themes, literature, culture, study skills (or what we could call the learning curriculum), and other subjects. I'll explain what I mean by each of these categories and give some examples and practical principles to bear in mind when working with each of them. But first I'll explain how I came to realise that this chapter was necessary in a book about shaping lessons and courses.

When I first started learning how to be an EFL teacher, I attended a course where there were lectures with names like 'The Present Tenses' as well as talks on clarifying the meaning of vocabulary. I attended a lecture entitled 'The Anomalous Finites' where I waited for an hour for it to become clear what these were. After an hour, seeing everyone else scribbling away, I somehow couldn't pluck up the courage to ask. So I came away with some notes such as 'Able to form questions without using an auxiliary' but no real understanding of what anomalous finites were, or how they fitted in with the things I had learned in other lectures.

Apart from this, on my course, I learned that I could while away time in classes with texts. I could clarify the meanings of words with mime and pictures. I could activate role plays and build dialogues, and when it came to teaching the language itself head on, this mostly meant teaching the verb tenses, the 'three conditionals', active and passive, reported speech, and, yes, those anomalous finite things. This is one of the main drawbacks of being a native speaker of the language you teach. You can speak the language but have rarely been required to describe it or talk about it and thus have little idea about how it works as a system.

Over the years since my initial training I have learned a great deal, given the deep ignorance of my starting point, about the way teachers and students divide up the matter of language courses. In case you have the feeling that your own personal categories of 'what there is to teach' are either limited, repetitive or disconnected, you might like to stand back with me and take stock of the potentially huge variety of 'items' there are to put into a foreign language lesson and the many things there are to know about them.

What there is to teach and learn

I've divided all the things I can think of that could go into a lesson or course into the following areas:

- classes and people
- language patterns
- language skills
- combinations
- literature
- culture
- study skills
- other subjects

Everyone in the classroom – whether teacher, teacher assistant or language student – needs to learn about these things in order to be able to teach them, or to refine their own understanding of them. I state this rather obvious fact since I think we forget sometimes that teachers can learn and learners can teach. Teachers need to learn how students are thinking about something already before they can settle on the best starting point and way to proceed. We also need to continue to refine our own understanding of what we teach and how we learn. Students can help us to understand more about their language, literature and culture if it is different from our own, as well as about their professions, interests and views on the world. By having a fresh 'beginner's mind' (a Zen concept), students will notice, categorise and connect information in unusual ways that can enhance our own rather more fixed ways of looking at what we teach.

3.2 Classes and people

I visited some nursery schools recently and watched children from ages three to six learning the basics of school life. They sat rapt during story time, thus unconsciously learning to sit still and attend for longer periods. They laughed or blushed when they called the teacher 'Mum' by mistake and so learned about a new type of distance in relationships. They held scissors with the blades closed together pointing downwards and covered carefully by their fists as they walked across the room from the scissor pot to their desks. This, plus taking care of class reading books, constituted first lessons on looking after resources. In their first six months at school they learn a lot about what is expected of a human being in a group learning setting.

The learning doesn't just happen at nursery school. It goes on at all ages. Every time a student or teacher changes groups, institutions or countries, there is always a lot to learn about dress codes, punctuality, turn-taking and the routines and rules of the new setting. There is also a lot to learn about individuals, their memories, projects and personalities.

Some of the points below will be made explicit by the institution or by teachers, perhaps in pre-arrival information or in a group meeting on the first day. Some may be negotiated continually throughout the course. Others we may be less conscious of. They may remain largely unspoken. If we try to become aware of them, however, we can check that they are allowed for, implicitly or explicitly in our planning and teaching and so minimise causes of misunderstanding. The list that follows thus gives some areas that are legitimate subject matter for a lesson or part of one.

- *Time* Examples in this category are how long a lesson, a break, a day, a week is in the place you work in, how long students are used to spending on classroom tasks and homework, how late and how early it is normal for teachers and students to arrive, what happens to students and staff if they're too late or too early, and how fast the pace of the teaching usually is.
- *Territory* Questions of interest here are where staff and students are allowed to go, whether you have a place to store your clothes or books, and what areas of rooms people are allowed to decorate.
- *Clothing* There may be differences between schools and countries in how much it is normal to cover or reveal, how different from other people you or your students may look, and how status is marked by clothing.
- *Conduct* Issues here can be how noisy students are allowed to be, whether physical contact is accepted, who you can talk to and look at, and whether students can help, cooperate, compete, laugh, turn round, ask questions.
- *Resources* Things to learn about resources are: what belongs to whom, what you can touch or use with or without permission, whether anything is dangerous and what happens if someone breaks

something. You need to know who has the keys and which of the following are available or acceptable at work: word processors, newspapers, digital dictionaries, puppets, masks, mobile phones, internet access.

- *Student behaviour alone and in groups* Issues here are whether students are expected to regulate their own behaviour, whether they work well alone, in pairs, or groups, how much they are allowed to be physically or mentally present or absent, what the level of each student's participation is and how students can improve their own memory and confidence. Other issues worth considering are how you and your students can put yourselves into a resourceful frame of mind and actually enjoy classes. There is the issue too of how students prefer to learn.
- *Spoken or unspoken ground rules* Classes operate differently in terms of confidentiality, making decisions, commenting on attitudes and behaviour, and supporting others.
- *The people in the class as the subject matter* I have mentioned issues above about people and their behaviour in classes. The people in the classroom, the teachers and students, also form part of the content of lessons in their own right. Students draw on their own interests, jobs and projects, they express things they really want to say, and find out real things about each other. Teachers use stories and examples from their own life experience. The group process (i.e. what is happening in terms of interaction, attitudes and behaviour between people in the group) can itself become one of the central topics. Some teachers and students who are used to working with language as an external subject distanced from themselves will not like the 'unmasking' that is involved in using the people in the room as human, personal subject matter. Others may feel that at last things are becoming interesting and relevant to them and that this is the only way to work with language, itself a social venture.

Where to go for help on classes and people
If you're interested in classroom routines I'd recommend you look at Wragg (1993). Written about the primary classroom, it discusses philosophies and approaches to class management as well as suggesting activities designed to help with first encounters, rules, relationships and decision making in a way relevant to all teaching situations. Blum (1998) is a marvellously honest and concrete book about classroom culture.

For more on using people as the real content of the language lesson, see Dufeu (1994) and Davis et al (1998).

3.3 Language patterns

The next main topic that can be included in a language lesson is, predictably enough, language! I'll start this section by looking at language as an 'out-there' subject that can be divided up for study. There are some linguistic definitions coming up. If you're comfortable with this side of your work, then skip these sections. If you're not a great linguistics expert, then take it slowly. There are useful practical principles and ideas coming up at the end of each section to reward your patience!

Since there are many different possible levels and systems of language to mention, I'll start with the simple, organising principle of length. The individual letter or sound is the shortest item, but I will start with the word, a combination of letters and sounds, since I think most students can relate to words more easily at first than tinier fragments. When learning a new language, people often want to start translating and collecting names for things (What's 'bread' in Swahili? How do you say 'Hello'?). Learning words, the names for things in a new language, is very important and very natural. Words are instantly useful for making friends, getting enough to eat, avoiding accidents and thus are a natural place to start.

Individual words

Students often berate themselves for not being able to learn words the first time they meet them. But there is a lot to learn about a new word. It may well take many meetings before you know most of the following things about a new word. Let's take a few words, for example, 'responsibility', 'plump', 'horse', 'free' and 'to run' to see what there is to know about them.

Learning about words

Students need to learn the following:

- *What a word means* There are several different sorts of word meaning to know about, such as a word's closest translations in your own language, and its metaphorical meaning (e.g. 'horsing around'). Part of meaning also comprises what the opposites are (is the opposite of 'plump', 'thin', 'skinny' or 'scrawny'?), what the synonyms are (does 'free' mean 'at liberty', 'independent', 'uncontrolled'?), and the hyponyms ('horse' and 'dog' are hyponyms if 'mammal' is the superordinate). Meaning is also about how the word is the same and different from other words in the same semantic field (e.g. how does 'to run' differ from 'to jog', 'to sprint' and 'to race'?). Meaning also involves considering other words that look or sound the same (such as 'free' meaning 'independent' and 'free' meaning 'no charge'), and what the connotations of the word are ('she's a bit horsey'). Knowing about meaning includes understanding what the range of a word is (e.g. 'A parent can be responsible. Can a member of parliament, a government, a country, a continent be responsible too?').

- *How to say a word* How to say the individual sounds, how to say the word in rhythm, with the right mouth setting, and with the correct intonation in a number of moods and voices, e.g. lovingly or angrily.
- *How to write it* How to shape the individual letters and join them up and whether to use capital or small letters or a hyphen.
- *Morphology* What are the word's constituent building blocks (ir + respons + ible) and its grammar or patterns? For example, how to add prefixes (he was unhorsed) or suffixes, (run + ny), how to pluralise it (one horse, two horses, a herd of horses), what its word class is (noun, adjective or verb, for instance) and how to change this ('runner', 'runny', 'to run'), how to make plausible new words from it ('I'm tired of the anti-horse attitude around here'), and where it and its parts come from.
- *Its use in context* What order it can be used in with other words ('free and easy' or 'easy and free'?, 'to be responsible to someone for something'). What its function is in a chain of words (e.g. can it act as a subject or object of a verb as in 'horse bit man' and 'man bit horse'?), how fixed or free it is in combining with other words (what words can 'to run' combine with easily apart from 'a mile' and 'like crazy'?). See the section below on groups of words for more detail on this. How you can recognise it when listening or reading. How you can produce it in speaking or writing fast, accurately, naturally and at will.

Where to go for help on words
I'd suggest you look at a corpus based English language dictionary for learners such as the *Collins COBUILD English Dictionary* (1995) because it has natural up-to-date examples of usage and learner-friendly definitions. Use a normal English dictionary for your own purposes, something like the *Concise Oxford Dictionary* (1999), since it will carry more erudite words which you will need when reading poems, plays or other authentic material. See Underhill (1980) to learn how to get the best out of a dictionary. Look at the *Longman Language Activator* (1993) so that you can teach intermediate students how to use it and thus how to

go from a restricted word store to new words within the same semantic categories. For your own background reading try Gairns and Redman (1986).

I have gone into detail over the different things there are to learn about words. This is to show how much there is to know about a piece of language if you decide to teach or learn it. Of course the teaching and learning will usually need to be done bit by bit. You can't usually understand and use all this at once. I'll go on now to mention, more briefly, other language that can go into a lesson, things such as lexical phrases and grammatical patterns including sentence types and stretches of discourse. It is important to remember that, at some stage, we may need to go into the kind of detail above with regard to whatever content we plan to include in our lessons.

Groups of words

Since a language is made up of thousands of individual words, it might theoretically be possible to learn a language by learning thousands of individual words, just as it may be possible to become a teacher by learning thousands of individual teaching steps. 'Chunking up', or enjoying sequences and patterns, starts happening naturally and very quickly, however. Students will pick up multi-word chunks like 'It's the real thing', 'Well, basically' or 'Turn it on' from ads, songs, teacher talk and other places. These word groups can be noted, recognised and produced by learners as whole meaningful units which are simply reeled off as if they were just a single word. These groups can include quite long phrases, such as, 'One thing that really drives me crazy is ...'

As long as they are helped with a meaningful setting and all the information and practice they need, students can pick up these lexical phrases as easily in class as if they were single words. They are thus a very useful thing to include in language lessons.

Although we're now dealing with groups of words as a possible thing to teach, instead of single words, some of the same things can be learned about them as can be learned about individual words. For example, if we take the word group 'fish and chips', we still need to know how to pluralise it ('I got two fish and chipses' or 'I got two bags of fish and chips'). If we take the phrase, 'an overwhelming response', we still need to learn about meaning and use, range and register, since 'I got an overwhelming response to my birthday' sounds rather strange.

Where to go for help on groups of words
For theoretical background on lexical phrases, see Nattinger and De Carrico (1992) and for some practical activities, see Lewis (1993).

Grammatical patterns

So far, I've taken words and groups of words as the starting place for things to include in a language lesson. It's time now to think about longer stretches of language and thus, about grammar. For although it can be useful to learn 'milky coffee' or 'a little bit' as word groups, it takes you a lot further in life if you can pop these word groups into fuller sentences or utterances such as 'I hate milky coffee!' or 'I'd like a little bit, please!' The form and meaning of individual words, groups of words, sentences and utterances are affected by their environment in longer chains of words or stretches of discourse. It's similar to the way flowers in a garden are affected by soil type, temperature and rainfall. We could say that grammar is to utterances and sentences as nature is to flowers. It is the patterning influence or rule-maker. It says which flowers can bloom at Christmas, and which adjectives can take the suffix '-en' and still stay adjectives. Students will often start noticing these patterns and rules pretty soon themselves. They'll start noticing similarity in:

- form, by which I mean look and sound (e.g. do<u>n't</u>, wo<u>n't</u>, ca<u>n't</u>, did<u>n't</u> or princ<u>esses</u>, dr<u>esses</u>) or indented first lines of new paragraphs and word order ('A large, brown envelope', 'A small, white dog') and
- meaning ('A <u>sort of</u> redd<u>ish</u>, brown<u>y</u> <u>stuff</u>') and generalisability ('I ... + ed and then I ... + ed')

As a learner looks through a transcription of a conversation or other kind of text, or listens to target language talk, patterns or similarities of this kind will readily be noticed. This is useful because the patterns can act rather like templates from which we can turn out lots of similar versions for our own use. So, for example, when we learn the basic meaning and form of the word group 'too ... to ...', we can use it to express 'too hot to handle', 'too fast to dance to', 'too mouldy to eat', and so on.

We need to select for teaching and learning the most generative, usable patterns, structures or 'rules' we can find. Finding them used to be a matter of one's own intuition and recollection plus the invention of examples, or of looking in the textbooks and coursebooks to see what the authors, also working from intuition, memory or habit suggested. These days, people interested in describing and categorising language and seeing how language works, can run huge numbers of texts (samples of natural writing and speaking known as a 'corpus') through a computer program (known as a 'concordancer') to see which patterns are most widespread in samples of actual native speaker data. From these we can gather patterns which are really of proven use. Of course, intuition is still useful as we need to consider how current and widespread a pattern is in the speech community that our particular learners are destined for. There follow a few brief ideas on the kinds of patterns that can be included in language lessons:

- Normal word order (Subject, Verb, Object) as well as marked English word order. This is so that students whose language has a different normal word order can express their thoughts clearly in English.
- Working on the SVO pattern entails dealing with noun phrases every bit as much as verb phrases, so it's important not to spend a disproportionate amount of time on the latter.
- Work on four basic sentence types, e.g. declarative ('My husband told me that it was true'), interrogative ('Is it true?'), imperative ('Say it's true!)' and exclamative ('It's true!'). Work on the form of these sentence types needs to be coupled with work on meaning and use, since we can use a declarative not just to declare some information but also to complain, request or ask for information depending on the circumstance and according to the speaker or writer's intention and the listener or reader's perception. As always, concentrating on form cannot be divorced for long from meaning and use.
- There are a number of reasons why it is useful to study language in sentences. Sentences are short, easy to write up on the board, well-described in grammar books and provide a secure framework for teachers and learners. Sentence level work also has disadvantages though. Sentences treat language as if it was a selection of discrete units almost divorced from language user meaning. Working with separate sentences doesn't help learners to string discourse together. It's important therefore to supplement work on patterning or grammar at the level of the individual sentence with work on stretches of language, also known as discourse or text. Apart from all the patterning that is already happening inside words and lexical phrases, and in sentences or single utterances, stretches of discourse or text have their own patterns too. When talking or writing, for example, there are acceptable and non-acceptable ways in every language of doing the following:
  - Indicating the topic of discourse, e.g. in speaking, 'Erm, about this money you mentioned ...', or in writing, 'This article sets out to ...'
  - Indicating a block of ideas that hang together, e.g. in speaking, 'Yes, but you also have to remember ...', or in writing, 'Not only is ... but it is ...'

- Indicating change, e.g. in speaking, 'Oh, by the way ...', or in writing, 'An interesting digression here is ...'
- Suspension, e.g. in speaking, 'Just a sec', or continuation, e.g. 'Anyway, as I was saying ...', or in writing, 'To return to the main argument ...'
- Hanging things together physically using changes of vocabulary or pronoun, e.g. 'This money', 'the cash', 'the loan', 'that amount', 'it'.
- Hanging ideas together intellectually by putting them in an interesting, logical or chronological order, e.g. in speaking, 'Would you like a lift in to town? There's something I want to ask you and I'm going that way anyway', or in writing, 'First', 'Secondly', 'It thus follows'.
- Taking turns, pausing and winding up, e.g. 'Gosh! Look at the time!'

Discourse or text is thus a perfectly respectable thing to choose to work on with your students and can be started at beginner level with the introduction of the word, 'and'!

Where to go for help on grammatical patterns or rules
You may pre-select language patterns within or beyond the level of the word, phrase, sentence or text. The selection may be done for you by your coursebook. Alternatively, you and your students may tease out the patterns that pop up in the texts and activities you happen to be working with. Whichever way you arrive at them you will eventually need to know quite a bit about their form, meaning and use. If you feel slightly at sea when it comes to grammar or if you're just interested to know more about the language you plan to work with in the classroom, there are a lot of books around to help you. There are grammar books especially written for language students and others mainly for teachers. There are reference books that try to describe just about everything that occurs in the English language. These books are for different purposes, have different points of view and include different divisions and terminology. For example, if you read a book written by a functional grammarian, you will meet terms such as ideational, interpersonal and textual function. If you read a book by someone in the Chomsky school, you will read about transformational grammar, and deep and surface structure. If you read books from other schools you will come across subject, verb, object, complement and adverbial. If you read a pragmatics book, you will read about speech acts and relevance theories. Each school of thought will be better at describing some things than others. And each will give you different ideas for things to teach in your language lessons.

My personal recommendations are ... first the *Collins COBUILD English Grammar* (1990) because it takes its main patterns and examples from a corpus, is concerned with language function and meaning and not just form, it includes discourse and is easy to find your way around. For high speed work I often use Swan (1995) as it lists about 600 grammatical items in alphabetical order so you can go directly to 'as ... as' or 'would' or 'articles' as fast as you could use a dictionary. An accessible book on discourse is Cook (1989).

Functions

Another category of language we can work on in class is functional language, i.e. language grouped by what it's used for. The 'functions' selected for study in EFL coursebooks are often clusters of language different in form but similar in purpose. Coursebook functions often end in *-ing*, e.g. thanking or inviting. We can invite someone with any of the following pieces of language, which are known as 'exponents of the function': Would you like a ...?, Fancy a ...?, X requests the pleasure of ..., How about ...? and more. There may be literally hundreds of ways of inviting someone, depending on factors such as the situation and role relationship. We need to know just as much about the exponents of a function as we do about other pieces of language. We need to know their form, meaning and use, at sentence and utterance level and when embedded in discourse. Below are a few guidelines if you are thinking of including functional language in your classes:

- Don't just teach positive functions such as accepting, thanking and complimenting, but also teach functions such as turning down an invitation and expressing displeasure.
- Keep teaching plenty of vocabulary to go with the functional exponents and help students to sort all the functional phrases into learnable groups whether by using formal similarity, style, register or range.
- Don't just teach 'short' functions like blessing someone when they sneeze or the initial exchanges involved in a conversation, but remember to include larger, longer functional areas. Work on natural combinations of functions, such as greeting someone and then going on to enquire about health and recent adventures.
- Choose functional areas that help students to combat their expressive limitations by, for example, helping them to hesitate or draw someone else out in conversation.
- Do more than just intuit examples of language which will fit each functional area. If we take a topic such as disagreeing, for example,

and a setting such as a meeting of colleagues at work, we may dream up phrases such as, 'I'm awfully sorry but I can't really agree with you there' or 'I think you're right to a certain extent'. If we taped some real meetings and noted down the actual phrases used, we might find that 'Yeah, but ...' is the most common exponent of disagreement in a particular meeting. Again, corpora and concordances can inform our work here.

Functions, as met and discussed in some EFL coursebooks, can seem a rather narrow way of working on language if the exponents are displayed as brief, decontextualised phrases. But if we are careful to include the kind of work above, setting them in time, place and role relationship, this can be an interesting and useful category of language to include in language lessons.

The original meaning of the term function is 'purpose or use'. Thus we can ask the 'function' of any unit of language, e.g. What is the function of this word in this dialogue? or What is the function of this paragraph in this essay? or What is the function of this letter, seen from the newspaper editor's point of view? We can look not just at coursebook functions and not just at what is said or written in any conversation or text, but at what is done with what is said or written.

Where to go for help on functions
Lists of functions and their exponents can be found in Blundell et al (1982). Van Ek (1990) is a well-known example of a functional syllabus in use.

Practical principles for teaching words, word groups, grammatical patterns and functions

Teachers and students will decide to teach and learn some words and patterns perhaps because they appear in the coursebook, they occur frequently in an exam students are to sit soon or are of special interest to students' academic, business or leisure pursuits. Other words and patterns will be picked up or acquired without special study. If we want to plan for the first kind of learning, we need to work through the following stages in our lessons: exposure, noticing, remembering, and use and refinement of language. I'll take these four types of work one by one, explaining what they mean and suggesting guidelines or activities for each.

Stage 1: Exposure to language

To ensure that students have the chance to meet new language, whether it consists of individual words, word groups, patterns within sentences or texts and talks, we need to plan plenty of exposure so that students can encounter it in any or all of the following places:

- in mini-contexts such as lists (e.g. in dictionaries), at the back of coursebooks and their units, on the board taken from texts that will be read later, in their notebooks, spoken by the teacher or by fellow students
- in short constructed spoken or written texts including one short meaningful sentence or exchange, or other short texts deliberately under or just at the level of the students
- in elaborated or supported texts, i.e. original authentic texts containing paraphrases, synonyms and other supplements such as glossaries and pictures to aid understanding
- in longer and in increasingly unsupported stretches of discourse
- in a variety of channels such as radio, TV, teacher or other language user talk including peer talk, faxes, e-mail, films, letters, and in a range of graded and unsupported text types such as readers, unabridged stories, dialogue journals and oral presentations

I will say more about the way the exposure to language can be handled in the next chapter.

There are many potential language items and patterns to meet while learning a language. Once met, however, rather than trying to arrange for prolonged and detailed focus on each of thousands of words, phrases, patterns, functions and sentence and discourse types, the main idea in many classes is for the teacher to help students to adopt useful strategies for working with the language they are exposed to. This involves encouraging students to notice, learn, use and refine language. I will explain what I mean by each of these below.

Stage 2: Noticing

While working on words, groups of words, grammatical patterns and functions, plan to teach students how to notice their form, meaning and use. This will reinforce what is already happening at an unconscious level and also encourages students to branch out and do more learning on their own. It starts a useful habit.

When planning your work on 'noticing', you'll need to include how things look, how they sound, what they mean and how they work in context. I'll deal with these separately below even though of course they overlap in reality.

Noticing form – The look
Once students have encountered a new item of language, they will need to notice what it looks like, i.e. its spelling, capitals, hyphens, word order, punctuation or layout, what stays the same and what changes as the language is used. They need to get strong images of these forms. These ideas will help:

- Associating the target language with a similar form or feature in the mother tongue.
- Pulling the item out of its context and demonstrating, perhaps by using a table, which parts of it are fixed and what sorts of words and patterns go before and after the target language at phrase and sentence level or discourse level.
- Transforming the item back and forth, for example, from mother tongue to target language (see Laufer and Shmueli 1997), formal to informal language, active to passive, interlanguage to reformulated natural English, or other appropriate states so that similarities and differences in visual form are thrown up and shown up.

Noticing form – The sound
In order to be able to say new language, students will need to notice the number of spoken syllables, initial and final sounds, contractions, stress patterns, pauses, intonation and so on. This can be helped by:

- Associating the new language with similar sounds in the mother tongue.
- Writing out the sounds of the new items with sound symbols from the mother tongue.
- Using rhymes, chants and songs, colours, mime and symbols.
- Forward-chaining (i.e. saying things bit by bit starting from the front end, as in 'I know, I know it, I know it sounds, I know it sounds barmy, I know it sounds barmy but …').
- Back-chaining (i.e. saying things bit by bit starting from the back, as in 'but, barmy but, sounds barmy but, it sounds barmy but, know it sounds barmy but, I know it sounds barmy but …'). Back-chaining gets rid of fears about managing to get through to the end of a difficult utterance since … you've already got there!
- Again, transformation and reformulation as above.

Noticing meaning
Some students will want to hear or see language clearly at length and in context before they work on meaning. Others will need to notice the precise meaning closely before they want to focus on form. Yet other students will want to do both simultaneously. Whichever type of work

students want to do first or you plan in first, go to the level of meaning the students require. Don't go too much further as it will confuse and bore many students. The new item or patterns in the target language can be:

- translated verbally into the mother tongue, from mother tongue to target language or back and forward between the two
- defined verbally in the target language
- explained by means of pictures, diagrams, sounds, realia, mime, video, metaphor, flowcharts
- partly guessed from context, layout or genre clues
- distinguished from words or patterns in the mother tongue that look and/or sound the same but actually have a slightly or totally different meaning
- partly guessed from their constituent parts
- explained by reference to the semantic category they belong to, their hyponyms and superordinates, qualities, opposites, synonyms, sequences
- analysed by the components of the meaning
- understood by discussing connotation and association

Ways of aiding noticing: Physical storage
A lot of the 'noticing' mentioned above can happen during work on physical storage since this is when students concentrate on transferring information about a target language item into their notebooks. Example storage systems that you can plan to work with are:

- *Lists* For short items students can write one or two lists of items (with the target item on the left, say, and the translation on the right). Other information can be internalised if, for example, all the items in a certain category (such as nouns or verbs) are stored together in a block, or in a different spatial position, or are written in a certain colour or on different coloured paper. Symbols can be used to record whether patterns are F (formal) or N (neutral), etc.
- *Cards* Students can write down target items on one side of a piece of card and can record information about meaning and use on the other side of the card.
- *Tables* Columns can be provided for, say, word class or item type, meaning, context in which first met, example of use, other possible items built from it, collocations or usual sequences or sequitors, fixed parts and free parts.
- *Mind maps* can record associated topics, words or components of longer discourse types.
- *Scales* can show grades of meaning difference.

- *Posters* can group items that are similar in sound, sight, meaning or use.
- *Flowcharts* can map the order of ideas in a text.
- *Mime, gesture and other physical mnemonics* can be very important for some students.

 I have met some extremely able language learners who have resisted all my attempts to make them record information about new language! One student in particular, a speaker of several languages and a simultaneous interpreter at the UN said, 'If it's important enough, it will keep coming back. I'll start seeing it and reading it everywhere. I won't need to write notes about it.' He was an excellent language learner with his own way of noticing. Most students, however, need to do more to make things stick than just wait for the items to come back. This is possibly because they have very limited exposure to the target language.

Stage 3: Remembering (or mental storage)

If students use the physical storage systems mentioned above this will help most of them to start getting the language into memory. Most remembering is helped by both the frequency of meeting the target items and the quality and depth of processing of the items. More ideas for both of these aids to memory are described below.

Frequency of meeting

Although features of some words, patterns and discourse types are doubtless learnt first time because they are of importance to the learner, other items may need as many as 16 meetings before they are well and truly in the learner's repertoire. This means planning lots of varied practice. Here are some ideas:

- *Grouping* Items can be organised and reorganised into categories, or prioritised lists, according to criteria such as 'things I like', 'things I don't like', 'things I think I'll remember' or 'things I don't think I'll remember'.
- *Ordering* Items can be ordered by letter of the alphabet, chronology, size or other criteria that make sense to students.
- *Rote learning* This can involve simple copying, repeating silently or aloud in different voices (shout/whisper, slow/fast, with different emotions, pitch or intonation) or in different written voices (capitals/lower case, slow/fast, in pencil or on the keyboard). The

rote learning can be made more fun if it involves different activity types such as jazz chants, songs, poems, short talks or writing texts within differently shaped outlines.

- *Reference work* This can involve learners in searches, copying and note taking from dictionaries, grammar books, corpora and other reference sources as well as from magazines, stories and other authentic sources.
- *Serial practice* Examples here are students reading the same text repeatedly and trying to increase their speed each time, or answering increasingly difficult comprehension questions each time or counting instances of the new language as they read or listen. In speaking it could involve students telling the same story to different people and trying to tell it faster or better each time. Teachers can give dictations that feature previously met items in new situations or that feature dictation in, say, the mother tongue, with students writing down in the target language.
- *Matching exercises* Items listed on separate cards can be matched by, for example, putting the cards together. Items in parallel vertical lists can be matched by lines drawn between matching items. Matches can be of various types such as item to meaning, item to collocation, item to picture, item to key word, item to mnemonic (e.g. funny word in own language or funny picture), item to association with a story or text, paragraph to box on discourse chart, summary sentence to appropriate part of talk or text.

  Matching exercises and the games below can be made by students.

- – *Spot the difference exercises* Differences can be spotted between spoken and written texts, between simple and expanded texts, or between the mood or purpose of one dialogue and another.
- – *Games* These can involve hide and reveal, e.g. Kim's game, crossword and word search puzzles, odd one out, gap fill with no words provided, with choices provided or jumbled fillings provided, cloze tests.
- – *Composition* Students can put the new language into sentences, utterances, conversations, a personal example or a story.

Quality of processing

Above I mentioned that the sheer number of meetings with new language is important for remembering. Another important factor is the quality of processing since this will mean that the students gain personal connections with the target language items. Language items gain rich associations as the learners use them more for their own expressive intentions and for reasons of personal, social and cultural identity. The reasoning goes that the deeper the experiences the learner has in the language, the deeper the language will sink in. There follow some ideas for deepening the processing of the target language:

- Engage learners in topics and tasks that have real life force and meaning to them rather than distant topics.
- Give learners a chance to come up with their own examples and explanations in class and encourage them to make their own links and associations with the content.
- Allow students to organise work in ways that are meaningful to them and allow time in class for this.
- Encourage students to make the items to be remembered vivid in some way, perhaps making them bright and colourful or connecting them with crazy stories.
- Use activity types that encourage students to apply new learning to their own situation, e.g. guided dialogue journals.
- Use activities that allow students to get really involved in the language e.g. role play, simulations, personal story telling and discussion.
- Use out of class reality as much as possible by bringing in real objects, pictures, visitors, projects, interviews and surveys.
- Be real yourself, responding to students with human remarks as well as with error correction or grading strategies.
- 'Follow the smoke'. This phrase from psychodramatic language learning implies an ability in the teacher to put their own concerns and plans on hold sometimes and to sense where the students' real passions lie, and allowing time for these to be followed in class.

Stage 4: Use and refinement

The fourth type of work you will need to plan is use and refinement. By trying to recall language and use it, learners will be able to gauge whether they have really noticed and learnt the form, meaning and use. If they find they have not, they can try to get closer on all these points. Use of new language can thus involve all the categories of activity mentioned above as well as:

- tests
- reconstruction of texts from notes followed by comparison with the original
- essay writing, talks and presentations
- reading and listening comprehension
- rewriting or restating events, ideas or arguments in different moods, times, styles, channels or for different purposes

- face-to-face interaction and negotiation on tasks that are designed to help tease out form, meaning and use at ever increasing levels of subtlety
- personal research where students come back to class with examples of language items found in real situations (such as on soup tin labels or in newspaper articles or in the lyrics of pop songs)
- personal reflection where students look back through past work in order to make a list of, for example, 'my favourite mistakes'

The process that is indicated in this phase is recall, generalisation and transfer, followed by further noticing and refinement of understanding. The feedback, so vital for helping students to notice when further refinement is necessary, can come from the students themselves, peers, teachers or other language users. Time must be allowed for this and students should be encouraged to see its importance.

We have looked at four really important elements of learning new language: exposure, noticing, remembering or mental storage, and now, use and refinement. These different elements work together as shown.

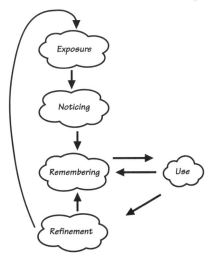

THE FOUR ELEMENTS

In language learning then, first we need some exposure to the language, then we need to do some noticing. Much of the noticing will be at the unconscious level and teachers try to make it conscious. Some fast learners or learners who are highly motivated will be able almost straight away to use the language they have been exposed to. Other students may be exposed to lots of new language and may even notice things about it, both consciously and unconsciously, but because they are tired or unmotivated, or motivated NOT to remember or learn, or because they are working with language they perceive as being difficult, will not be able to remember or use it. They will need lots of motivating and many moves through the noticing, remembering, using and refining cycles before they feel they have got the hang of it. I have put the 'use' stage slightly to one side because it is also possible to use language again and again without noticing much about it or caring that you are using it wrongly, thus without refining it. We have probably met lots of people (ourselves included!) whose target language has fossilised in this way.

Although the order of the stages of exposure and noticing seems logical, learning and refinement and use can happen in many different orders and simultaneously in the experience of the learner. It's highly unlikely that all the stages of work mentioned above can be got through for all the new language in one lesson (!). It is likely, however, that most of the stages are necessary over time for new language to be learned, and thus they need to be planned in.

3.4 Language skills

In order to express yourself in any spoken language and understand other people, you have to be able to read, write, speak and listen in the target language. So time has to be spent practising and using these skills. It's been fashionable in recent years to break down these four skills into 'sub-skills' by considering what a learner has to do in each skill in order to function effectively.

Listening

When listening, one has to be able to:
- recognise sounds, words and phrases
- get the general idea, remember salient points and predict what's coming next
- understand the discourse type or genre you're listening to
- get used to listening to different types of people for differing lengths of time
- screen out what you're not interested in and focus on what you are interested in
- deal with accents and dialects
- interpret a message against a background of expectations and respond accordingly

Speaking

When speaking, you have to be able to:
- use different parts of the mouth and body from those needed in your own language
- make individual sounds and combine them
- produce correct stress on individual words and on longer stretches depending on the meaning you want to convey
- use intonation (including tones across discourse)
- work with appropriate rhythm and pace
- express your own meaning and your own personality by choosing from a range of physical and verbal expressions
- interact with people appropriately, repairing breakdown of messages, taking turns and speaking alone for short and long periods
- describe, agree, beg, plead, insult ... and all as naturally as possible

Naturalness also involves clothing, posture and body orientation, gesture, body contact, facial expression and gaze.

Reading

When reading, we need to be able to:

- recognise different formats such as headlines or faxes and different styles and genres
- know letters, words and phrases
- understand implication and style
- skim, scan, predict, guess and remember
- relate what we've read to our own experience, mentally agree or disagree, criticise or commend; physically turn the pages from right to left, and read the lines from left to right
- survey books; speed read
- read aloud
- pore over what every word means or read for pleasure and the general idea

Writing

When writing we need to be able to:

- form individual letters, both upper and lower case, space them from left to right in relationship to a line and join them up
- think of something to write
- make sentences with punctuation
- indent and know what a paragraph is

- write different kinds of texts such as letters, postcards and summaries, with appropriate choice of layout, vocabulary and logical structure
- read and reread our own work, crossing out, rewriting and reorganising as well as correcting grammar, spelling and punctuation
- write with accuracy, fluency and confidence

Practical principles for working on skills and sub-skills

All of these skills and sub-skills can be dealt with in the language class-room. Here are a few suggestions if you decide to include this type of work:

- Take nothing for granted. Individual students can have very different skill profiles. Just because a student can speak fluently, for example, it doesn't mean they can write well. Groups too can differ wildly in this respect. One 'intermediate' group will have good listening skills, another won't.
- Don't forget the fact that students having problems with skills work may not just be suffering from a lack of facility with the target language. Many students are either short-sighted, hard of hearing, stutter or suffer from weak or severe dyslexia or word blindness.
- Just because you hear of certain things as being 'forbidden' (such as using mother tongue–English dictionaries, asking students to read aloud in class, letting students read transcripts while listening to a tape, etc.), doesn't mean you have to accept this without thinking about it.
- In the same vein, there are good reasons sometimes for using a particular skill order, but there are no hard and fast rules. It's acceptable to do writing before speaking or reading before listening if the work builds that way naturally.
- If you think there may well exist an initial 'silent phase' in language learning, then build in some 'no response necessary' or 'minimal response' activities to your classes.
- The proportion of time you spend on different skills will depend on why your students are learning the language. If they have no chance to listen to or speak to other English language users, don't deny them the chance to stay in touch with the language and gain pleasure from it by reading.
- Skills can be worked on individually and in combinations depending on what students are hoping to use the language for.
- There used to be quite a lot of attention paid to the differences between formal (usually written) and informal (usually spoken) texts. The sorts of differences often mentioned were that written

language was considered densely packed with information, not immediately interactive and lasting. Spoken language was seen as often more spontaneous, full of hesitation and redundancy, usually interactive and often ephemeral. These sorts of differences are still ones you could spend time on in class. But views have changed a bit in the last 10 or 15 years. People now feel that the differences are less hard and fast than they used to be. Much of what we hear on the radio and TV, for example, is unscripted and yet we can't interact with the speakers. Lots of natural speech ends up quoted in writing. New forms of communication such as e-mail are blurring the old distinctions. Differences between speech and writing still exist but they may now be in terms of intricacy and density.

- Be careful in skills classes to sort out your motives at various stages. Are you using a text because it's interesting, because it enables good practice of certain sub-skills to take place, or because it has some useful vocabulary and language patterns in it? Of course you may want to do a little work on all these things in class but, within any one phase, be clear of your reasons and communicate these to students. Otherwise it can be very vexing for students, for example, to be told to 'listen to the gist' and then later to find themselves being quizzed on some minute item contained in a stretch of listening.
- Don't always concentrate your feedback on student speaking and writing at the micro level correcting individual sounds and commas, important though these may be. Spend time on the larger issues such as whether an essay has any real content or fits its title, whether a talk shows enthusiasm and whether a speaker has good eye contact with listeners.
- Work to improve your feedback skills, finding different ways to comment on written work and respond to student talk. Learn something new yourself. It's a good way of reminding yourself how distressing and frustrating it can be to be a beginner or intermediate student.
- Let students learn to write by doing lots of writing, learn to speak by speaking, etc.
- Use plenty of different styles, lengths and genres.

If you would like a useful methodological model for doing skills work in class see the 'pre-, in-, post-' model on page 124.

In order to be able to listen, speak, read and write, learners need to know lots of individual words and lexical phrases and to be able to recognise and use patterns at sentence level and beyond. But also BY listening, speaking, reading and writing learners will pick up and learn more about all these things. We start to see then how language is like air. We can know about the composition of air in terms of molecular components and yet we are breathing it and it is doing things in our body that we have no consciousness of. We can't say that knowing about air is more important than breathing it. We can't say that knowing about bits of language is more important than using language.

Where to go for help on skills
There are plenty of skills books around and everyone has their favourites. Mine are: for listening Rost (1991); for speaking Celce-Murcia et al (1996) and Klippel (1984); for reading Nuttall (1996); for writing Yorkey (1970), Horn (1977), Pincas (1982), Hedge (1988) and Douglas Brown et al (1991).

3.5 Combinations

Everything mentioned so far in this 'What there is to teach and learn' section can be combined. For example, you can learn what behaviour is expected of you in a classroom in terms of punctuality, dress and posture all on one day in the same class. And in terms of language, lexical phrases are combinations of words, and messages are combinations of noun and verb groups. Speaking and listening in a foreign language involve combinations of sub-skills, as well as combining all the previous items mentioned in this chapter and including cultural knowledge such as when to interrupt or take the floor. Everything that we could include in a syllabus is a combination of smaller constituent parts.

The simple nesting of smaller units inside bigger units is not the only combination possible, however. Pronunciation, for example, can be studied, or practised, under 'words' (e.g. how to pronounce the word 'comfortable') or under 'functions' (e.g. how to intone 'Excuse me ...' when you have said it three times already to a shop assistant bent on ignoring you) or, in a speaking skills lesson when you want to sound sure in an argument. Learning about group dynamics can happen in any kind of lesson whether on discourse analysis or prepositions. Different types of unit can be not only nested inside but also mapped onto other units.

With higher level language learners other types of subject combination become possible. We can take issues such as 'gender', 'plurality', 'role' and 'degree of definiteness', issues which cut across all the language items described so far, and look with students at how these are dealt with in the target language. These concepts are hard to define and yet, as native speakers, we know a lot about them intuitively in our own languages. The best way to tackle them is simply to display them at work, in context, in stories, conversations and magazine articles and encourage students to explore positive and negative exemplars of the concept under study. Other issues that cut across individual categories of language item are notions of correctness, language change and the individual coinage of new language.

More standard combinations mentioned in TESOL coursebooks are situations, topics and themes, literature and study skills. Broader combinations still are culture and information subjects. I'll go on to mention these below. All of them can be planned into lessons and courses.

Situations

Many coursebooks have little sections based on the idea of situational English. A situation may be expressed as a place, such as 'at the railway station'. A situation often implies:

- roles, e.g. a ticket seller and a passenger
- relationships, e.g. rather distanced since the seller and passenger don't normally know each other
- attitudes, e.g. polite but perhaps slightly rushed or brisk
- tasks, e.g. getting information, buying a ticket
- vocabulary, e.g. platform, departure
- skills, e.g. talking, listening, reading
- materials, e.g. money, ticket
- structures, e.g. the present simple for timetables (What time does the train leave?)
- functions, e.g. asking for information

A situation creates a fairly meaningful and realistic context and exerts a loose binding force for the choice of vocabulary, skills, grammatical patterns, etc. Of course, almost anything can happen at a railway station. You can buy things and eat things, meet old friends and have arguments and use virtually any vocabulary, structure or function. Even if you take the standard task of asking for a ticket, there are hundreds of different ways of asking for one. We must recognise then that situations are useful contrivances for gathering language together for a particular lesson. We should not take them too seriously or rigidly.

Topics and themes

Real world topics such as 'my family', 'mobile phones', 'how to solve conflicts', 'escape' and 'honesty' (see Grundy 1989 for other interesting themes) are organising devices similar to situations in that they are designed to pull together vocabulary, skills work and so on into larger more integrated contexts. They are potentially more interesting than pure language topics such as 'verbs that take gerund complements' or 'ways of phrasing offers'. See page 226 for an example of a topic-based lesson.

People can thus work in language classes on worthwhile things they wish to accomplish, such as finding out about themselves and others, making plans and decisions, clarifying personal values or effectively commenting on the amount of homework given to them by a range of teachers. Working with topics and themes can thus put the language user's message first and can help learners and teachers to see the target language as the vehicle for messages rather than the central aim in itself.

Practical principles for teaching situations, topics and themes

- If they are to be motivating, situations, topics and themes should not be regarded just as useful contrivances for gathering language together. The emphasis, especially with topics and themes, needs to be more on the content and on conveying messages and expressing opinions than on the study of discrete units of language themselves, otherwise the motivational impact on students can be lost and the whole thing seem very artificial. Thus the content of any material, whether an article, poem, song, story, phone conversation or advert, can be noted and commented on, questioned and discussed, for its content, as well as or instead of the language features the piece contains.
- Negotiate the choice of situations, topics and themes with students so that the choice has maximum relevance.
- Take time to build the background and settings with music, real objects, pictures or other props to get students into the mood of things.
- Topic and theme based lessons can be very useful for reinforcing learning in other subject areas such as history or biology, so don't be afraid to stray outside 'your' patch. At primary level foreign language specialists are often teachers of other subjects too. At secondary level and above, liaison between foreign language and other specialists can be fruitful and interesting.
- When starting a topic or theme ensure that a wide enough range of target aims is included (e.g. culture, vocabulary, skills, language patterns, functions, pronunciation, social skills) so that everyone in the group can meet something new which they wish to learn.
- Use topic-based lesson notes (see page 226) so that you can be flexible once the lesson starts and can follow student interests.

While situations are often used at lower levels as a setting for language functions, topics and themes can be particularly useful as students get better at the target language. Students will have encountered many different words and patterns already. Topics and themes draw these together giving students the chance to recall different items and choose which is appropriate for the occasion. This will enable further refinement of items already met. Topics and themes can get us away from the notion of language being 'out there', something to be studied, and can move it 'in here', inside the person who has something they want to express and understand.

Where to go for help on situations, topics and themes
Unfortunately I can find NO references on using situations, topics or themes in language lessons!

3.6 Literature

Many teachers include literature in their list of things to work with in a foreign language class. By literature I don't just mean poems and plays from the fifteenth century! I would include twentieth-century poems, whether they appear in greetings cards, as part of the 'poems on the underground' movement, as haikus of only seventeen syllables or nonsense rhymes. I'd also include one-act plays, stories whether short, science-fiction or fairy tales, song lyrics and prose from graded readers or talking books. You may want to include even more types of expression such as graffiti or TV adverts.

There are many reasons for working with literature. It constitutes a high point in language usage often representing quality of expression. It takes us beyond the often rather trivial topics of TESOL textbooks filled with their questionnaires on shopping or sport. Literature gives us not just language but cultural background and emotional content. It can speak to the heart and personal experience of the learner encouraging imagination, creativity, personal discovery and increased perspective on life. Because the message and the form are special they can raise the quality of the noticing, which is so important for a true understanding of form, meaning and use. Literature can give us a welcome escape from the classroom situation; it can amuse us, provoke us and be musically pleasing.

If a piece of literature is used as a stimulus, in the same way that a picture or an object or a set of language items can be a stimulus, then we can apply generalisable moves to it such as analysis and personalisation, etc. For more on this way of using literature, see page 60. If the piece of literature is seen as a means of according students practice in a skill or sub-skill, then the 'pre-, in-, post-' lesson frame can be applied to it (see page 124). If you want to build on the special qualities of literature mentioned above, however, there are other ways of working.

Perhaps the most traditional way of treating literature in the classroom goes through some of the following stages:

- The teacher gives background information on the work or the author, etc.
- There is reading at home or reading in class, often out loud.
- Difficult words are explained either orally or by reference to glossaries, dictionaries, pictures, sounds or mime.
- There is detailed comprehension work and perhaps some translation and memorisation of key passages.
- There is some literary criticism or discussion of received opinions on the work. This usually involves discussion and writing.

In this approach the literary work is central and the author's intention is seen as being very important. Many language learners over many years have derived a lot of pleasure from this way of working. Learning off by heart has often given them the pleasure of being able to say long stretches in the target language smoothly for the first time. The remembered passages may also contain lexical phrases or patterns from which learners can generalise. The act of discussing passages may also represent the first time that learners actually use the target language to do something other than just practise it.

There has been a watershed in literature and other forms of art. Previous 'outsiders' (e.g. the untutored, the institutionalised) are now seen as capable of producing works of art. Audience interaction with the work is now also seen as very important. There has inevitably been a shift in current practice too. While I would certainly not suggest that the traditional approach to literature mentioned above should be abandoned, I do feel it can be augmented by the practical guidelines that follow.

Practical principles for teaching literature

- Don't worry that you are not a 'literature teacher', enjoy the literature at any level that you and your students can.
- Start helping students to enjoy the musical and expressive nature of language and literature at beginner and/or primary level even if the work only consists of working on rhymes such as those in 'Bye bye', 'Marks and Sparks', 'Diddy dishy, diddy dishy' (Did he? Did she?).

Some people say that it's at the very beginning of learning a new language that the strangeness and humour in the sound and sights of the new language are most consciously felt. Pretty soon these things are taken for granted and the chance for childlike play and enjoyment is lost.

- Choose pieces to work on because they are short or funny or match student interest rather than because they are on a 'good literature' list.
- Use anything you need to for enjoyment and understanding, including pictures, mime, role play, video clips.
- Provided you have copies of the pieces you are working with, don't treat the work as sacrosanct. So, for example, encourage students to circle, underline or change texts. Work with paraphrases so that learners can understand the message more readily and also see how the original choices made by the author were well chosen.
- Make the piece come alive by helping learners to forge connections between themselves and the piece of literature. Here you can list all the characters or important elements of the work and then ask students to do some of the following:
  - state which they are most like
  - rank them from the most to least likeable
  - choose one and describe the way the character (or element) would dress, behave, speak, shop, sign documents, etc.
  - choose one and state what they can remember about it
  - become one temporarily and state its relationship to one that another learner has chosen, or write a letter to another one in role
- Save time in class by asking students to read or listen out of class. This may involve you in making support materials for home study.
- Treat the students' response to the piece as being as important as the author's intention.
- Allow for criticism, praise, distaste, joy without worrying if this is the response the students 'ought to' have.
- Allow time for students to create work of their own as well as enjoying the work of other people.

Provided you consider working with light and short, relevant and interesting literature as well as with longer pieces for the classes who really love literature and are highly motivated, literature can be very fruitful to work with in the language classroom.

Where to go for help on literature
For an enhanced version of the more standard approach above, see Collie and Slater (1987). For a book based more on participant response, try Bassnett and Grundy (1993).

3.7 Culture

Culture is another broad combination of work that gets past a focus on discrete units and moves towards self and group expression and the comprehension of other people's messages. By culture I mean the features that characterise the way of life of a particular group of people, whether they are young or old, women or men, national, language or ethnic groups. Culture is about difference and variability and thus contains both the potential for opportunity and for conflict. Although this section apparently places culture within a range of optional subjects for the language class, it is, in my view, actually impossible NOT to work with culture in the language class, although the work may be happening unconsciously. First of all, as a good user of the target language, you will show by the way you speak and move and the materials and methods you choose, not just who you are in terms of your own genes, personality and circumstances but also in terms of the amount of target culture that has rubbed off on you. Secondly, the moment the learners hit a difference in the target language, whether this be a sound or sight, a gesture, or a way of expressing a concept, they are exposed to cultural difference. You can consciously choose to treat matters of culture too, of course, whether by discussing differences in the language, the maps, bus tickets or poems of the target culture. The opportunities that open out from this are:

- the chance to meet the new culture and deal with the interest and/or stress that this involves
- the chance to learn about aspects of the new culture, understand its significance for people in that culture and thus, by contrast and comparison, to learn more about the home culture
- the chance to develop the intercultural abilities of getting on with people who are different and learning how to express yourself in a new language with minimum distortion or loss of meaning and expressive power

Whether you choose to deal with cultural differences in music, food, clothing, myths and legends, holidays, taboos, language, knowledge or other matters there follow some practical principles you might like to consider.

Practical principles for working with culture

- Don't forget that cultures change and so things may now be a little different from the time when you had most contact with the target culture. Take time to keep yourself updated.

- Objects and pictures, maps and music are an easy way into the area.
- Another possible way in is to consider the section at the start of this chapter on the culture of the classroom (page 74).
- Comparisons of different cultures can be done via topics the students are interested in (whether sport, food, body language, death rates, attitudes to animals, the treatment of elderly people, the amount of litter) and can be enhanced by, for example, using interviews with people who have cross-cultural experience, visits, or internet connections with groups in other cultures.
- Virtually all resources carry cultural messages, so don't overlook the obvious resources right under your nose, e.g. what entries are excluded and what definitions given in dictionaries, which cities are included in temperature charts in newspapers, what is included in and excluded from the *Longman Dictionary of English Language and Culture* (1992).
- If students have the chance to stay for a while with host families in the target language culture, homework can be given that draws, gently at first, on this rich cultural seam. Possible questions for this kind of homework are:
  - Ask your host family to teach you five new words a day from the following rooms. Take a different room each day. Start from the kitchen, then go to the lounge, bathroom, bedroom, hall, cellar or attic, patio or path, greenhouse or garden shed.
  - Ask your host family if they can remember particular events or changes in their lifetime, e.g. in the UK, the change to the metric system of money, the 'Winter of discontent', the fall of the Thatcher government, the start of local radio stations.
  - Ask your host family what images they have of different parts of the country or different cities, e.g. in the USA, New York, Los Angeles, San Francisco, Chicago, Dallas. (See Rinvolucri 1998b for more ideas on using host families.)
- Ask students to make a list of all the groups they belong to. To help them to remember, mention groups of different size (two people, three people, and so on), and of different type (family, job, club, sport, hobbies). Encourage discussion of what makes each group different from the others (clothing, place, rules, activity, closeness to other members). This will help the class to begin to understand the frameworks that can be applied to cultural difference.
- Start to explore other personal and published frameworks for looking at cultural difference. Here are some example frameworks:
  - Noticing the use of different personal pronouns when discussing different groups. This work can be sparked nicely by using the Kipling poem '*We and They*'.

- Discussing proverbs and sayings. There is of course 'When in Rome do as the Romans' versus 'To thine own self be true'. There are also parallels in different languages for proverbs such as 'Silence is golden' and 'A stitch in time saves nine'.
• Use frameworks (see Trompenaars 1993) which help you to start thinking about where the different cultures stand on variables such as:
  – universalism (there's one right way and it's always right) versus particularism (there are no rights or wrongs, it all depends on the person and the circumstance)
  – collectivism (group and common purposes are more important than the individual) versus individualism (think about what you need first and then negotiate with others to get the best compromise you can for yourself)
  You may need fairly mature students for this kind of work in class. But it can be extremely rewarding to do some private reading for your own benefit, especially if you are finding yourself at odds with the people you are working with or with their attitude to the target culture that you represent.
• As well as dealing with the question of home and target culture, you can introduce the classroom as 'The third place', a place that lies between native and target culture or between all the cultures represented by the participants in your group. This third place, peopled by full beings who may have few words in the target language, is a place where work is done to help participants to discuss and express their own cultures and meanings in 'their' language.

As soon as discussion of similarity and difference starts there will be reactions. You need to be able to deal with them wisely. Here is a suggestion: As soon as you hit the 'OOH aren't they strange!' phenomenon in class, as students stumble upon something they think is odd, apply the 'mirror principle'. I'll explain! The first time I managed to say in German 'Wie geht es dir?' (How are you?) and received the answer 'Danke!' (Thank you!), I felt irritated, if not downright thwarted. I had been thanked but my request for information about my friend's health had been denied. I felt strange. I had crossed some sort of cultural boundary and it didn't feel too good. This is the first step and it doesn't take you very far. The mirror principle makes you take the <u>all important next step</u>. It involves reasoning like this: If I feel denied of information when I get the answer 'Thank you', then how must a German speaker feel when they ask me how I am and I proceed to give them some information such as 'Not too bad apart from my cold' but DON'T thank them? They must feel odd too. They must feel unthanked and in possession of information about my nasal passages that they don't really want! Working with the mirror principle means that there is always a recognition of difference but it is mutual difference. Both sides of the cultural boundary are considered.

Many grammarians and language teachers feel that describing and analysing language as 'out there' subject matter is an unfortunate fate for a cultural property used normally for information and ideas exchange, social bonding and personal expression within a context, culture and society. We need thus at the very least to supplement 'English' as an analytical enquiry with the use and setting of English as a medium and experience in cultural and cross-cultural as well as cross-curricular applications. Also, when deciding to treat matters of culture, we need to do so in terms of how it is externally displayed ... in objects and music, etc. and as it is IN the language.

Where to go for help on culture
Apart from the reading already mentioned above I would recommend Kramsch (1993) as an extremely thought-provoking read in this area. See also Doyé (1999) and Valdes (1986).

3.8 Study skills

While some students will have excellent study skills, know how to prioritise tasks and organise their time and materials, and know many mnemonics methods, many students can feel a bit at sea when learning a language. There are so many words, phrases, patterns, texts and conversations even in just one class. Teachers too differ in how we help students to make sense of the materials and tasks we give them. I feel that it is vital to include a study skills component in courses and lessons. It helps students to take more responsibility for their own learning, become more active, and usually more effective as language learners. The study skills learned within a language teaching programme can be usefully transferred to any other subject too.

The following skills can be taught, learnt and encouraged in a language class and also used by students and teachers when learning any other subject in or out of class:

- organisation of time, place and materials
- ways of consulting reference works, e.g. dictionaries, encyclopedias and ways of using resource rooms and libraries
- knowing what's required of you in a particular task, making decisions about what to work on, when and how

- knowledge of and flexibility with a range of task, activity and information display types
- preview, review and overview
- motivating yourself, improving your own confidence, being active by asking questions, tolerating frustrations and difficulties, improving your own memory, clarifying things, developing and organising your own ideas.

    Nunan and Lamb (1996) see work on areas such as these passing through an optimum set of stages: awareness, involvement, intervention, creation, transcendence.

- practising different kinds of thinking including the purposeful, disciplined, cognitive kind and the slower, more playful, exploratory kind (see Claxton 1998)
- knowing how to study alone, in pairs and with other people and how to get the best out of your teacher and peers
- assessing your own progress, the learning course materials, the methods, etc.

As well as the areas above, the four skills of writing, reading, listening and speaking play a big part in helping students to study better. Work on writing, for instance, can include everything from researching, planning, drafting and rewriting an academic essay to learning when to use capital letters. Reading can involve analysing exam questions or surveying a whole book. Listening can involve understanding spoken briefs given by lecturers on an architecture course or understanding instructions for homework and recording these in a notebook. Speaking work can involve learning how to give a presentation in a seminar or phonological accuracy of the key words from a particular class. Vocabulary development will accompany the skills work above and can involve word building, mining subject texts for useful lexical phrases or learning storage and recall techniques. There is plenty to work on if you choose to include a study skills element to your course. Below are some practical principles for handling this kind of work.

Practical principles for teaching study skills

- Start work on study skills from beginner level even if it just involves, for example, a display of a couple of different ways of storing new words in notebooks and asking students to record the number of words they've learned in the week.
- Be careful not to force particular study strategies onto students. Once alerted to different strategies, let students choose the ones they personally like best. We are all very individual in how we study.

- Think through your own material before you teach it so that you can point out study skill options as you go along by saying, for example, 'You might like to underline this as it's important', or 'This could go into your story folder'.
- Work on the study skills that will have pay-offs for students in both the short and long term. This is known as short-term and long-term practical surrender value. Short-term surrender value could be, for example, showing students how to mark the stress on a particular word that comes up in class. Long-term surrender value, for example, would be displaying several different ways of marking stress on words and encouraging students to choose, stick with and remember to use the system they like best.
- Make sure you keep abreast of new study methods yourself. Practise doing mind maps, brainstorming, circling key words and surveying books yourself as well as learning to appreciate different kinds of thinking (see Claxton 1998).
- If you are preparing students for real study such as an art foundation course abroad, a one-week study break in England or an undergraduate degree in soil sciences in the capital city, familiarise the students with both the content AND methods of the subject they are headed for. If students are headed for an art degree in Britain, they will need exposure not just to art vocabulary but to art course study and assessment methods such as 'the brief', 'the crit' and 'the portfolio' too.
- If you choose a project based approach to your study skills component, requiring students, for example, to produce an essay, you need to keep the project clear and short and provide plenty of guidance and support, possibly by tutorial. Many students are not used to working on their own and need help to get used to it.

I feel that working on study skills gives added value to a course. It shows that the work done in class has been thought about by the teacher, can be stored, previewed and reviewed. Even if you have spent a morning doing light-hearted exercises, it pays to spend a little time helping students to notice what they have been doing in terms of language and content and why and making sure that they have an adequate record somewhere that they can look at again on their own later.

Where to go for help on study skills
My own particular favourites are Yorkey (1970) for those destined for the USA, Buzan (1995a and 1995b), and Jordan (1997) for those headed for study in Britain. For a detailed discussion of how learners deal with the process of learning, see Williams and Burden (1997).

3.9 Other subjects

We have gradually moved from learning about classrooms and groups of people to concentrating on pieces of language and using them in increasingly realistic settings. We can work in English as we help students to improve in any of the following areas: numeracy, computing, pottery and getting to know a new person and new culture. If we are concentrating hard on other content, the language we are using becomes almost incidental. Working in a real life situation in English, we just try to achieve what we want for ourselves and for others, taking part in meetings, sending faxes, listening to records, reading short stories, playing with children, phoning for information. We deal with linguistic problems as we hit them, thus learning the skills of repair, clarification, suspension of task, regaining the thread, and generally coping as we go along. Although we can import visitors into the occasional language class, take students out for visits, do projects from time to time, and generally do real and authentic things in our classrooms, we have mostly come off the end of the spectrum of things we can consider for inclusion in the average language lesson or course. The rest is simply everyday real life!

3.10 Conclusion

Even if I've missed out from this chapter some of the things that you and your students think are very important, we can still see that there is no shortage of things to teach and to learn, from the analytic, micro end (e.g. studying and practising a tiny fragment of language such as the sound /ə/) to the macro end (e.g. using all skills in full flight to get an MSc in bio-chemistry at a university in New Zealand). I hope then that the next time you're stuck before a lesson or course thinking 'What can I teach?', a dip into this chapter will give you lots of alternatives!

CHAPTER 3: WHAT CAN GO INTO A LESSON?

4 How do people learn and so how can we teach?

4.1 Introduction

In the first part of this chapter I'll look at four main ways that people can learn and be taught. These are:

- Finding out for yourself
- Things made plain
- Periphery learning
- Use and refinement

I'll explain what I mean by each of these four, detailing how they might be used outside language lessons. For each of the four ways of learning and being taught I'll then give language class examples, first of functional expressions and then for other content areas. In the second part of the chapter, I'll look at some common instructional sequences found in coursebooks and on teacher training courses. These are:

- Test, teach, test
- Pre-, in-, post- stages for receptive skills
- PPP (Presentation, practice, production)
- TBL (Task-based learning)

Ways of learning and teaching

4.2 Finding out for yourself

What it is and how it works

In this way of learning there is a natural setting for the exposure to the new and the learner does the noticing, pretty much on their own. I'll give an example from country life.

The quickest way to learn about the effect of an electric fence used to keep cattle in or out of an area is to blunder into one by mistake when it's switched on and to get a jolt from it. This teaches you that you are made up of conductive material, that electricity gives you an unpleasant shock, and that wires that tick should be avoided. We often call this process of exposure, noticing and remembering 'trial and error' or 'discovery learning'. We find out things this way by bumping into them or by making slightly more controlled experiments all the time. Not all the things we find out are shocking. We can discover that foot massages feel wonderful, that zabaglioni tastes sublime, or that being with a particular person always makes us feel good. Finding out for yourself can be a powerful, deep way of learning and that's why we try to harness it for use in the classroom.

Going back to that electric fence, it would be possible to learn about its effects more pleasantly if you had someone with you who knew all about electric fences. 'See that wire?' they might say, 'Don't touch it, but put your ear close to it. Can you hear something?' And then, 'Get a blade of grass and put it on the wire. Can you feel a tickling sensation?' You would still find out for yourself that an electric current passes through the wire but your guide could structure the experience for you so that it was pleasant and effective. The guide could be anyone with a little more knowledge about something than you have.

How it works in the language class

When we transfer Finding out for yourself to the language classroom, it's important to include a first stage of establishing what the learners already think and know (see steps 1–3 below). Conventionally, course planning often starts with an analysis of the subject matter, in our case, the language. We look at the language or the coursebook and try to analyse which are the basic ideas, which things are easier or more difficult and build our course from there. Writers in school science teaching as well as language teaching now argue, however, that it is essential to recognise that students have already constructed their own ideas about subject matter and that these may be very different from the analyses contained in our course or coursebook. We need to take into account learners' ideas. This may lead to our revising what we consider to be the starting points in our teaching and the ideas that we assume students have available to them. If we know how our students are thinking, we can suggest activities that challenge or extend their ideas. So first of all, we need to find out how our students are thinking about English. If we believe that English lessons should be about more than just English, then we'll need to find out what our participants think about other things too.

From the teacher's point of view then, the following are necessary for this type of guided learning encounter:

1 Provision of motivating tasks designed to show what learners already know and don't know. This could include small or whole group discussion, written examples, diagrams, drawings, a statement of 'rules'.
2 Provision of interesting materials, data or activities designed to move the learners' understanding on. These could contain unexpected or deliberately discrepant data or examples.
3 Provision of guide questions to foster learning from (2) by helping students to notice where their own thinking is incomplete or inconsistent.
4 Provision of time and space for learners to interact with the stimuli, and the capacity to stand back and let this happen, and to be surprised, since investigations may throw up unexpected results, no matter how carefully the tasks are shaped.
5 The capacity to answer investigatory questions from learners genuinely and flexibly and to allow class sharing of questions and answers.
6 Encouragement for students to observe how their understanding has changed as a result of the investigation and to evaluate their new understanding.

Finding out for yourself will go down well with students who are prepared to take risks in a safe environment. Some students may feel they learn more quickly and at a deeper level by finding things out for themselves. When students 'find out for themselves' in class, we can't take it for granted that learning will take place, that it will always be of the things that the teacher wants the students to notice, or that students will actually change their own language as a result of this guided noticing. With a forgiving atmosphere though and plenty of risk-taking, most students can help each other towards the same shared understanding.

A **Finding out for yourself: Functional expressions**

1 Put the students in pairs for a conversation about a film they've seen recently. Ask them to consider the phrases they know for commenting on the film, e.g. 'It was really interesting.'
2 Play snippets of real conversation on tape and ask students to note down all the phrases used by the speakers to discuss films seen recently.
3 Students note which phrases are the same and different in form, function or meaning from others on the tape and from their own and categorise the phrases according to whether they are positive (e.g. 'It was absolutely ace') or negative (e.g. 'Dreadful!').

4 Students ask any questions they like on, for example, form ('How do you spell "absolutely"?'), application ('Can I use these phrases for books and meals as well?') or distribution ('I noticed the phrase X. Is that common?').

5 Students are then invited to state what they've noticed about what the people say on the recording. For example, 'They often don't make a sentence, they just say "Great"' or 'The range of adjectives was really narrow.'

6 Students choose new words that they feel they'd like to use in a similar conversation in future, e.g. 'I like the word "ace".'

A Finding out for yourself: Discourse structure and lexical phrases

1 Ask the students singly, in pairs or small groups to discuss a minor real life problem one of them has had and has solved, such as repairing a broken hairdryer or soothing a quarrelsome sibling. Once a minor problem has been settled on and discussed, together with its possible and actual solutions, the actual solutions need to be evaluated and the whole thing written up in the past tense. This will show what language and discourse structure is available to the students so far.

2 Next, provide natural examples of 'problem-solution-evaluation' narratives taken from stories, advertising texts and/or personal accounts.

3 Provide guide questions, gapped diagrams, etc. to help students to see the discourse structure and useful lexical items in the supplied examples.

4 Students note similarities and differences between their own work and the supplied materials.

5 Students ask any questions they want.

6 Students comment on anything they feel they have learned about 'problem-solution-evaluation' discourse structure in English and the phrases used to employ the discourse structure in different genres.

4.3 Things made plain

What it is and how it works

Things are plain when something is explained successfully. The explanation may be prompted by a question, e.g. 'What is voicemail?', or it may just happen in a conversation when someone tells us about their job when we hadn't even asked about it.

How it works in the language class

In a language class, a teacher making something plain to students could, for example, successfully explain the difference between 'so' and 'because'. Whether a learner has or hasn't prompted the explanation, we could break down the explaining process into the following stages:

1 *Opening* In this stage interest is aroused, links are made to past and future learning, the general purpose is made clear, what is already known is discovered and, if necessary, terminology is dealt with.

2 *Exposition* In this stage the matter is explained clearly with words, metaphors, analogies, demonstration, visual methods, or joint brainstorming. The explanations are broken down into clear sections using the students' own ideas where possible, with examples and illustrations relevant to the students. You need to emphasise key points, pause, repeat, link and summarise as you go along, changing the pace to suit the learners.

3 *Recap* Paraphrase the main ideas and emphasise key points, e.g. using colour or movement so that they are consciously noticed.

4 *Question and answer dialogue* This is to ensure that new ideas are truly meaningful. You need to be able to pose good questions; then wait; then listen to the responses, which will be correct, incorrect and unexpected; then wait again; and then finally discuss them. Elicit concrete examples of principles and concepts and, if possible, develop a desire to learn more.

5 *Summary* Given by the teacher or students or both.

6 *Closing* This may be a joke, some questions for next time, or a link forward. From the point of view of lesson design, this part is important since it rounds things off nicely. From the point of view of learning, however, this stage is less essential than the ones above.

This type of encounter is 'explaining'. This approach used by itself suits students who prefer to be told rather than to find out for themselves. Some students feel that being told what to notice and remember is quicker than finding out for themselves. Of course they may be confusing the time spent on something in the classroom with the time it actually takes to learn it. Some students prefer an initial encounter this way as a first introduction and then the personal experimentation later.

Let's see what this type of encounter looks like translated into a language lesson.

A **Things made plain: Functional expressions**

1 Ask students what phrases they know to discuss a film they've just seen. After they've made some suggestions, explain that you'll teach them several new ways of commenting on a film.
2 Ask students what films they've seen recently and put titles up on the board. Put a plus sign by a popular title and a minus sign by one that students don't seem to have liked. Introduce phrases such as 'It was absolutely great/awful' by the appropriate titles.
3 Ask students to repeat the phrases.
4 Ask students what other films they could apply the phrases to.
5 Together summarise what has been learnt. Students write it up in notebooks.
6 Say that next time you'll discuss films to which they had more mixed reactions.

A **Things made plain: Sentence structure**

1 With a monolingual class that has a different sentence structure from English, ask students to give you an interesting sentence in their own language. Write it on the board and translate it word for word into English so that the words in the English translation, written below, are in the wrong order. Next, take a different interesting sentence in English and write it on the board. Work with the students to provide a word for word translation into the mother tongue. Write the translation underneath the English sentence. If you'd like to see examples of these strange word for word translations, see Swan and Smith (1987).
2 Show students how the word order, word class, etc. are different in the two languages by drawing coloured boxes around words of different types, labelling clearly and drawing arrows.
3 Emphasise the key similarities and differences by summarising and recapping.
4 Pose some questions designed to show that students have understood, e.g. 'Can I put the verb here (*point*) in this English sentence?'
5 Allow time for comments, note taking, student summary, etc.
6 Finish by saying a couple of things in the mother tongue, but with English word order and word class just for fun. With luck students will pick up the game and start talking to each other in anglicised mother tongue, thus ensuring lots of practice and hence memorisation of the salient differences.

Let's look at the main differences between 'finding out for yourself' and 'things made plain'. When students find things out for themselves, a large part of what they find out is probably predictable to the person who shaped the materials, tasks and guide questions, although some things will still be unexpected. When you make it plain, you point out the salient learning points directly and focus more closely on the things you want the students to learn. Less unpredictability is allowed for. In both approaches, you need to be clear and patient, encourage students to ask questions, and understand the degree of learner difficulty. Most teachers use both approaches at will and in combination. In both approaches, students are actively trying to learn something.

4.4 Periphery learning

What it is and how it works

In our third basic type of encounter with new ideas, there is no conscious attempt by students to notice or learn anything. But after being exposed to new material, they find that they know it. We've all experienced this apparent magic. We all absorb music or lyrics without trying or remember advertising slogans and jingles without wanting to. While reading, we may unconsciously note the position on a page of a particularly interesting section, or we may find that we know the colour of the wallpaper in our dentist's waiting room.

How it works in the language class

The stages of this type of encounter with new material in the classroom are:

* Unconscious exposure to the material
* A time of relaxation or concentration on something else
* A situation where we're asked about the material and to our surprise find that we can use it or answer questions on it effortlessly

Periphery learning is also known as '(unconscious) acquisition', 'natural learning' and 'learning by osmosis'. Periphery learning has three very important features:

1 While relaxing or enjoying yourself or concentrating (on, say, a film, a song, a cartoon or a story), new words, patterns, cultural information, etc. are absorbed without your needing to work hard.
2 Periphery learning involves the unconscious consolidation or familiarisation with material previously encountered (whether through finding out for yourself, someone making it plain for you or

by periphery learning). When you are listening or reading you are meeting again material that was previously new or difficult for you. It thus becomes easier and more familiar without your noticing this or reflecting upon it.

3 Periphery learning involves the speeding up and general improvement of skills. Thus by reading interesting books you get better at reading, by having the chance to take longer turns at speaking the target language, your speaking fluency improves. Using the four skills in a target language is basically how you get more fluent in them.

A Periphery learning: Functional expressions

In terms of the content we have been dealing with so far (expressions for discussing films), a list of expressions or a dialogue could be put on a poster on the wall, and video clips or film reviews could be available in a self-study centre. Later in a course you could ask students what they thought of a particular film. It's quite possible that different students would have absorbed different ideas from the peripheral material and be able to contribute these to the lessons.

A Periphery learning: Study skills

If you'd like some students in class to improve the legibility and organisation of their work, expose them to legible, well-organised work in the following ways:

- Have examples of clear, clean, intelligent work on display on shelves or on the walls in the classroom, but don't draw attention to it.
- Use different coloured paper or pens for different categories of work, e.g. lists of regular past tense verbs on blue paper and irregular ones on red paper. (The colour may incidentally be remembered by students who review the pages. Students then only have to remember two things, that blue means regular and red means irregular.)
- Team up a disorganised student with a better organised classmate and have them compare individual class notes, or discuss how they are going to tackle making a file of their best work, or ask them to correct each other's homework (for the spelling of certain words or the answers to certain questions but not for presentation or organisation). You may well find that over time the sloppier students (and indeed you too if you are not the world's most organised person!) will pick up ideas from well-organised students, such as underlining titles, using sub-titles, and using colour effectively.

117

- Give positive feedback using grades or comments, publicly and privately, to students who complete work in a legible well-organised way. Don't chastise other students at all.
- Produce legible, well-organised work yourself and show that you are trying hard to do this.

In an attempt to harness periphery learning, teachers can make available a rich diet of materials with no particular agenda or plan. You can also design materials, tasks and activities to dwell on subjects already covered in class. For example, giving people tasks that involve talking about past experiences will provide opportunities for unconscious and conscious consolidation of features of past time including verb phrases which have been met before. This brings me to the third example using periphery learning.

A Periphery learning: Grammatical patterns

If you'd like to provide students with the chance to do some periphery learning of, say, ways of talking about past time, here are some things you might try:

- Have posters on the classroom wall listing, for example, regular past simple verb forms on yellow paper and irregular ones on blue, and also showing, say, short poems and interesting texts containing past tenses copied out in handwriting.
- Have a 'natural listening' thread running through your classes. Perhaps for five minutes a lesson, either talk naturally yourself, bring in an interesting English-speaking colleague or play snippets of home-made recordings of people talking about their driving tests, funniest or most embarrassing moments, sports highlights, recent learning experiences, etc. Students simply have to listen and try to understand. Once the listening is over, they tell you what they understood. Don't correct. Treat it as fluency practice.
- Build in little tasks where students have to interview each other, visitors or their families (in mother tongue if necessary) about similar occurrences to the ones above. They can then write down the gist of the non-confidential bits in their journals. Tell them you're interested in content rather than accuracy.
- Use graded readers with students and let them choose the level and the topic. Encourage them to read for pleasure.

If you choose the materials carefully, students may absorb what you'd like them to but may well pick up something else about the material too, just as they may notice that the poster on the wall where they queue up for coffee has two green drawing pins at the top. We don't really know enough about how periphery learning works to know what kind of students it appeals to. Instinct suggests that the students who gain most are the ones who are mentally active, who like to tune into and out of the class process, have their own mental agenda and are capable of thinking about more than one thing at a time.

4.5 Use and refinement

What it is and how it works

Using and refining what you've started to understand is also called 'conscious practice'. It involves trying out any new understanding in increasingly varied contexts to check what has been learnt, its applicability and whether any fine-tuning or further learning is necessary.

How it works in the language class

New items of language need to be used and refined regardless of how they have been encountered, noticed and remembered. There are three main sequences of stages in the classroom. I'll explain these by using a concrete example. Let's imagine that you have been working in previous lessons on explaining how to do things. You've started off with 'simple' things like how to video a TV programme or how to do a particular piece of homework. You've worked on language such as time sequencers and imperatives (e.g. 'You start by *...ing*. You then ... Next, put ...'). The language has been encountered, noticed and, to some extent, remembered. You're ready for the use and refinement stage.

1 Start by giving the students a statement of the task and time to do any planning necessary. Thus, in our example, students in different groups are given some time to think about or discover how to, for example, make a cup of tea the English way, send an e-mail or use a tricky piece of school equipment. They then plan how they will tell a student in a different group how to do this.

2 While the learner tries out the new understanding, you give guidance and alert them to cues, or ask questions to check that their hypotheses are correct, and draw attention to the range and limits of applicability of the new understanding. In our example then, students in one group try to tell students in another how to do one of the tasks they have thought about and researched while you listen. You make sure the ideas are in a good order and, for example, that the students are correctly surmising that if you can say, 'You start by

...*ing*' you can also say 'You finish by ...*ing*' but NOT 'Next, you ...*ing*'. Guidance can become lighter and lighter as students get more competent. You gradually withdraw support and allow students to make some useful errors.

3 Give feedback on results and encourage the learners to note how this feedback is done so they may do their own in future. The ability to give clear, constructive, informative feedback based on agreed criteria is fundamental. Any gaps between the target and the students' results are noted and further practice planned.

This kind of learning differs from when a learner does some trying out with absolutely NO guidance or help. We could call that 'diagnosis' or 'testing' instead.

A Use and refinement: Functional expressions

If your class has been learning how to discuss films, perhaps using ideas similar to those above, here's how you could use and refine that work by helping students to transfer the language to a new situation.

1 Explain the task in step 2, how it relates to past work on discussing films and give students a few minutes to prepare their thoughts and discuss language with each other so that they are ready to join in step 2.

2 Start writing up on the board a dialogue between friends who've just had a meal together. Students can call out ideas and dictate the parts with positive or negative judgements, and spell newish or more difficult words out loud for you.

3 Next, you can give pairs of students different role cards to do with liking or disliking meals, books, parties, lessons, discos and so on. Students act out their conversations in front of each other.

4 The class gives feedback on all the pairs' role plays, discussing criteria such as: stress on the adjective, energy in the voice, and what they've learned.

A Use and refinement: The listening skill

Let's imagine you have practised with the students the idea of listening to the stressed words in a stretch of conversation. They have noted down as many of these as possible, working alone or in pairs, by listening several times to the same stretch of discourse. Once the main words have been noted down, students have practised reconstructing the passage from their notes, their imaginations and their common sense. You have done this with a few short trial passages. Next you want to give students the chance to use the same strategy but this time transferred to recovering the gist of some short, simple anecdotes on tape or read by you at natural speed.

1 State the task, which is to listen and note down the strongly stressed words. Students are then to pool notes before trying to retell the story to you.
2 Students have a go.
3 Students compare their version of the anecdotes with the original versions either by stopping and starting the tape, reading a transcript or asking you questions. You can guide the students to notice that important words such as negative particles are often missed in this technique, but otherwise as much as 70–80% of material can be recovered satisfactorily given a reasonable amount of shared understanding.
4 Give the students more practice with longer, faster or more difficult stories. Students discuss what information was missed, what misinterpreted, etc. thus evaluating the use of the listening strategy for their own purposes.

Working on use and refinement will appeal to students who want to become more independent in using and monitoring their use of new language.

4.6 Taking stock

In this chapter I've isolated four main ways of meeting and treating new ideas in the classroom. The teacher in all this, is in Vygotsky's and Feuerstein's terms, a mediator who helps learners to acquire the knowledge, skills and strategies they'll need in order to progress. The mediator and the learner are both active participants in the process (Williams and Burden 1997).

It might be tempting to think that the four basic ways of working identified in this chapter always happen separately in certain sequences and in a certain time period. For example, a 'normal' sequence for one reader might be: 'finding out for yourself' and then 'use and refinement'. In fact, though, we probably often use all four types simultaneously. Let's take an everyday example of the combination of these four basic ways of working. Here is a transcript of a first driving lesson:

> Driving Instructor: OK. Start up.
> Learner: I can't. I don't know how to.
> DI: Well, just try.
> L: (*Learner starts car and it jumps forward and stalls.*) Oh!

121

[Finding out for yourself] What shall I do?

DI: Right. This is the gear stick. Waggle it around. It feels free because it's in neutral. [Things made plain]

A little later on, as the learner is driving along with the driving instructor next to her. [Perhaps some periphery learning is going on!]

L: Why is the car slowing down? I'm not doing anything.

DI: No, but I am. I've got over-riding control of the brake. [Making it plain]

L: Oh.

DI: OK. We'll be turning left down there. Check your rear view mirror first. [Making it plain]

L: (*Checks rear view mirror.*)

DI: Good.

L: (*Feels for and successfully locates the indicator, having noticed previously when she has been a passenger where it is on the steering column.*) [Periphery learning]

DI: Good. Now you'll need to slow down and change gear. So remember … mirror, brake, clutch, change down …

L: (*Attempts the manoeuvre and more or less succeeds!*)

DI: Good but don't forget to steer at the same time! It's a good idea to keep your hands on the wheel in the 'Ten to two' position. It gives you more control. [Use and refinement and Making it plain]

Once familiar with the elements of learning and the main ways of working with them in class, we can take any lesson in any field and by listening to or watching what happens in the lesson, we can see what sequences and combinations of the four ways of working are being used.

Let's continue with the gardening metaphor. In Chapter 2 I established the boundaries of the lesson or garden, made its beds and borders and threw in a few easy-care perennials. Chapter 3 acted like a seed catalogue to help you decide what to put in your garden. This chapter discusses how to sow the seed. 'Finding out for yourself' is like sowing on open ground. 'Things made plain' is like sowing in prepared beds and seed trays with clear labels. 'Periphery learning' is like those plants that self-seed. You don't realise the parent plants have sown their seeds until the young plants pop up all over the garden in unexpected places! 'Use and refinement' is like transplanting little seedlings, however and whenever they grew, to new places where they can establish themselves and extend their territory.

Commonly found instructional sequences

I've claimed that there are four main ways of working in the language classroom: helping students to find out for themselves, making things plain to them, allowing for periphery learning and encouraging students to use and refine their understanding. Next, I'd like to look at some of the commonest instructional sequences found in coursebooks and on teacher training courses to see which combinations and sequences of these four ways of working they contain.

4.7 Test, teach, test

The normal sequence here is:

1 Discover what a learner can do in a certain area.
2 Attempt to teach the learner some of the things she apparently can't do.
3 Check to see if learning has in fact taken place.

In terms of our four basic ways of working, the sequence is thus: 'Use', with no help or guidance, then, 'I'll make plain to you what you need to learn', then 'Use' (again with no help or guidance) 'so I can see if there's been an improvement as a result of my teaching.' In terms of opportunities for learning, the first 'test' stage offers students a chance to try to remember and use what they have remembered. The 'teach' stage may offer exposure to new language or some chances to notice features of language. The second 'test' stage could give the chance for use and refinement, if the teacher goes on to support students here.

Here are some notes about a 'Test, teach, test' lesson with advanced students who had asked about differences between American and British English.

> *Level:* Advanced
> *Time:* 20 minutes
> *Language area:* Differences in prepositions in telling the time in British and American English
> *Steps:*
> 1 Students looked at some clock faces showing different times, such as (in British English) 'twenty to four' and 'ten past seven'. They were asked to write down the times shown using American English. They wrote down the times in British English.

2 Students listened to tapes of Americans telling the time. Their attention was drawn to the use of the preposition 'of' before the hour and 'after' after the hour. Students made a note of these differences and practised using their own watches. The teacher corrected where necessary.

3 Students were shown clock faces showing different times. They were asked to write down the times in American English. This time most of them wrote things like 'ten of two' and 'five after six'.

4.8 Pre-, in-, post- stages for receptive skills

The words pre-, in- and post- give us the clue that this is another type of instructional sequence resting on a chronological frame (see Chapter 2).

Pre- stage
Students are prepared for reading or listening by getting them interested in a topic, discussing what words may come up, learning a few key words for later or planning how they may tackle a reading or listening task.

In- stage
Students do the listening or reading and work on the allotted tasks that are designed to make the listening or reading easier.

Post- stage
Here there is evaluation of the work done during the in-stage tasks, discussion of the topic of the text and discussion or practice of the language encountered in the text.

There can be several moves through this cycle, with a different task set each time on the same text or with different parts of the text dealt with each time.

If the 'pre-, in-, post-' frame is used to give students a chance to practise their reading or listening skills, then it involves 'use and refinement' ('Can I recognise the vocabulary I already know when it is embedded in fast speech or natural writing?') and exposure to the new by 'finding out for yourself' ('This Scottish accent is quite different from the Southern English accent of my normal teacher') at the same time. The 'pre-, in-, post-' frame is often used to develop the so-called reading and listening sub-skills such as 'giving students practice in inferring the meaning of unknown lexis from context'. The assumption is that global 'receptive' skills will improve if practice is given in the sub-skills. The pre-, in-, post-lesson shape can also be used when working with a written or recorded text in a topic-based lesson (see page 226) for content purposes or in a stimulus-based lesson (see page 56) to give it a chronological shape.

Here are some notes about a 'pre-, in-, post-' skills lesson.

Level: Intermediate
Time: 60 minutes
Skills: Reading and speaking
Pre- stage: Students were put into groups depending on their position within the family (an only child, the youngest, oldest, or (one of) the middle child(ren)). They discussed the advantages and disadvantages of their position in the family before reporting in plenary to the other groups. They were then told they would be reading a story about a family with two children. The family has had a bit of a tiff and the story is composed of letters to one child from different people (see Richards 1994). Copies of the story were given out and students asked to mask all but the first letter.
In- stage: Students read the first letter. They asked questions about words they weren't sure of.
Post- stage: Students stated their understanding of who the letter was from and to and went on to discuss the attitude of the letter writer. When asked to, they unmasked the next letter.

This basic cycle was repeated for each of the ten letters in the story. Variation was provided in the reading of the letters (some were read silently, some aloud, younger sisters in real life read letters from the little sister, boys read letters from boys), in dealing with vocabulary (students asked, teacher asked, students explained to students), and in the post-stage, where different letters were discussed according to letter writer attitude and strategy, as well as likely outcome.
Post-post- stage: The story was discussed in terms of whether anything similar had happened to students, and whether they thought the family handled the event well, and records of useful words and phrases were made.

The students enjoyed the initial comparison of their own position in the family with others and were amused by the story. The motivation and energy remained high enough for there to be smiles when, in later lessons, the vocabulary and useful phrases were revised.

4.9 PPP (Presentation, Practice, Production)

This teaching sequence involves setting up a situation, eliciting or modelling some language that fits the situation, having students practise the new language in a controlled way and then encouraging students to use the new language in a freer way either for their own purposes and meanings or in differing, artificially constructed contexts. In terms of our four basic ways of working, the presentation stage, with its setting up of the situation, is an opening stage in which the teacher makes the new language plain. The practice and production stages are chances for students to use and refine their understanding. If, during the presentation stage, a student comes up with the target language, then this student is using memory from past learning encounters and may then be used as the person who makes the target items plain to the other students.

Although the PPP sequence could theoretically be used for any type of content from a single new word to whole stretches of language in context, in TESOL classes it has traditionally been applied to small, discrete items of language that are gradually combined over the length of the course. These items should be learnt in a checkable way in a definite time period. All the mistakes or errors are to be got through quickly in a set time, and accuracy is a central aim.

Here are some notes about a PPP lesson.

Level: Intermediate
Time: 75 minutes
Language area: The language of passions
Presentation: Students prepared some questions to ask a visitor coming to their class. They focused their questions so they could get the visitor onto a topic that would set her enthusiasm alight. The visitor arrived. The interview started and the students recorded a lively talk about how much the visitor loved taking her motorbike out at weekends.
Practice: After the visitor left, the students played the tape, noted down and discussed the content and the phrases that particularly conveyed the speaker's enthusiasm.
Production: The students interviewed each other using the focus questions and the language gleaned from the tape while talking about things they really enjoyed doing.

In terms of our four basic ways of learning and teaching, this would compare to an opening stage, followed by exposure to new language either by finding out for yourself or someone making it plain, finished off with some use and refinement.

4.10 TBL (Task-based Learning)

There are many versions of TBL around. I'll take one with the following sequence (see Willis 1994):

1 Introducing the topic or task (by brainstorming, using texts, etc.).
2 Doing the task (in pairs without correction).
3 Planning the reporting back (teacher goes around advising).
4 Reporting back (students speak in front of class; teacher chairs and comments but doesn't correct).
5 Teacher input.
6 Language analysis, review and practice.

In terms of our four ways of working and opportunities for learning, Step 1 offers a chance for use and exposure to new material by someone making it plain. Step 2 is use. Step 3 is use and refinement plus exposure to new material by someone making it plain. Step 4 is use by some students and exposure to the new by periphery learning for other students. Step 5 is exposure to the new by someone making it plain. In Step 6 students find out for themselves, use and refine.

Here are some lesson notes about a TBL lesson.

Level: Intermediate
Time: 60 minutes
Skills: Integrated skills
Steps:
1 Students were divided into groups and given the task of coming up with an everyday problem experienced in or with their host families, suggesting ideas for its solution, thinking of the possible merits and demerits of each solution and then choosing one to try out. They were then to present their 'case study' to the rest of the group.
2 Each group worked on the task.
3 Once the groups had had time to think up a problem, some solutions and a reasoned choice of the best one, they planned their report to other groups. The teacher went round monitoring and helping groups.
4 Amid much laughter, groups reported back on cases involving host families that allowed pets into the kitchen, bathrooms with carpets on the floor, lack of mixer taps and many other cross-cultural delights of living in a family away from home! The teacher chaired and took notes on the good ideas and the language.

> 5 The teacher gave the group feedback on both the cultural background to some of the problems and solutions and the discourse phrases that can be neatly used in this kind of case study.
> 6 The group considered what they had learned overall and, for homework, wrote up one more case study, this time based on a real incident given by the teacher on her travels and troubles in Japan.

(For more on planning classwork based on TBL, see Estaire and Zanon 1994.)

We start to see then that although, theoretically, our four basic ways of learning and teaching can be applied in any combination to any type of content, once people have gathered certain combinations together into a particular sequence and given the combination a name, the combinations quickly gather other assumptions to them such as the type and amount of content selected and the type of learning objectives set.

4.11 Conclusion

In this chapter I've discussed four different ways of learning and teaching and have suggested that most of the instructional sequences found on teacher training courses and in coursebooks, regardless of what they are called, are combinations of these four. In practical terms I have some suggestions as to what to do with this knowledge.

- If you are an inexperienced teacher, try out two basic instructional sequences:
  1 One that involves students finding out for themselves and then using and refining their understanding (see the steps outlined on pages 110 and 119).
  2 One that involves you making something plain to your students and then allowing them to use and refine their understanding (see the steps outlined on pages 113 and 119).
  If you try (1) plus (2) a few times, you will have real experience of most of the fundamental ways of learning and teaching. You could then go on to add in the chance for periphery learning (see the steps outlined on page 116).
- If you are fairly experienced, just teach some lessons as normal. Then consider the lessons in the light of the instructional sequences they have contained. It will be revealed to you, perhaps, that your lessons fall into patterns using only some of the sequences mentioned

above. These may reflect the way you were taught to plan and teach on your training course. Whilst having a routine or established pattern in our work can be relaxing and saves us thinking time, it could also mean that we've got a bit stuck. We may need to become flexible again for our own sense of development and to give the students a change too by using different ways of working and new instructional sequences.

- Whether experienced or not, it's useful, when considering any stage of any lesson, to notice that you can make sense of it by understanding which of the four ways of learning and teaching it contains.

- You'll notice too that some TESOL instructional sequences, despite their different names, are strikingly similar when seen in terms of the ways of learning and teaching they contain although they may emphasise some ways of working more than others or point up *new* distinctions. (An example here, if you do some background reading in TBL, is the distinction made between planned, spontaneous, public and private use of language. This is not usually discussed in other TESOL instructional sequences.)

- Experienced teachers will tend to adapt common instructional sequences. This will mean we either compensate for or compound the different emphases already present in the instructional sequences themselves.

I hope that this chapter will help you to see the wood (i.e. the learning and teaching) for the trees (i.e. the plethora of names of instructional sequences that have recently appeared in TESOL publications).

CHAPTER 4: HOW DO PEOPLE LEARN AND SO
HOW CAN WE TEACH?

5   What can we teach with?

5.1 Introduction

Part of the challenge in becoming better at a job is getting to know the range of tools available, what they're called, how they work, when and how to use them wisely and how to look after them. In this chapter I'll look at some of a teacher's tools of the trade.

I will start by diagramming the sorts of tools normally available in schools or collected privately by experienced teachers. I'll consider what sort of things we need to know about them and run through these with some example teaching aids, such as the dictionary, the board, rods, a pack of pictures and music tapes. I'll next give some tips on how to look after the messier sorts of material, although most teachers' desks are inevitably in a bit of a tangle, in my experience! As the most important teaching and learning aid for many people is the coursebook, I'll devote the second part of this chapter to it, discussing the advantages and disadvantages of using one and suggesting a way of finding out what's really in the coursebook and not just what coursebook writers tell us is in it! I'll finish that section by providing some generic activity types for use with any coursebook. Incidentally, this will provide a review and extension of work done in Chapter 2. Don't worry if you haven't read Chapter 2 though, as this chapter will stand on its own. So let's start by metaphorically sticking our noses into the garden shed and having a good look at what's in there!

Part 1

5.2 What materials and equipment are available and where?

In the figure on page 161 you can see, by peeking in the shed, many of the materials and equipment available in the language teaching trade. You'll notice that I haven't mentioned the students as owners of the standard kinds of equipment. In my experience it's wise to assume that the students will not have anything and will forget to bring anything at all to class including paper, pens, dictionaries or completed homework. If you assume this 'worst case', things can only pleasantly surprise you in reality!

Next I'd like to take a few common tools of the language teaching trade, detail their main uses and give some practical activities for each. I'll take the dictionary, the board, the box of rods, the picture pack and the music tape.

5.3 The dictionary

Main types of dictionary

The dictionary is a very handy tool. Although we may think of it as a standard piece of equipment that rarely alters, there are in fact many types of dictionary available. Dictionaries can be in a small pocket size or in a large enough size to sit down for dinner at! They can be in hard or soft covers, corpus or non-corpus based, in book, pocket computer or CD-ROM form. There are several types, including these:

- Standard dictionaries such as the *Concise Oxford*. Teachers and advanced learners can work with these.
- Learners' dictionaries in both one and two language varieties, e.g. English to English or English to Chinese. Most learners will work with these.
- Picture dictionaries of simple and sophisticated types (that include detailed pictures of computers, tennis courts, cars, etc.). Everyone can make use of these.
- Production dictionaries (see opposite).
- Specialised dictionaries of phrasal verbs, common mistakes, language and culture, twentieth-century biographies, etc.
- Subject specific dictionaries, e.g. for medicine, engineering, etc.

Most dictionaries usually come on their own but a few have a workbook or a 'How to use your dictionary' manual accompanying them (see Underhill 1980).

Uses of dictionaries

Dictionaries, of the kind we have all been using for years, can be helpful in many ways. You can use them, for example, to:

- look up a word or phrase met in listening or reading to find its meaning

- check the spelling or pronunciation of a word or phrase
- check alternate uses and meanings of a known word met in a seemingly different or unusual setting
- check the root, etymology, word class or morphology of a word
- check the use of a word or phrase by studying the examples and noting collocation
- find out about the register, connotation or association of a word or phrase
- find synonyms and compounds from the entry for a headword
- learn about the cultural significance of items looked up, the biography of a famous person or, with a subject specific dictionary, more about, for example, a concept in engineering or science

'Production' dictionaries are similar to a thesaurus but have been written with the second language learner in mind and are much easier to use. An example is the *Longman Language Activator*. It can be used to help students to expand their vocabulary. You look up a general word like 'walk' which you know already, and from it you are taken, via a choice of different semantic areas, to more specific words such as 'stroll', 'saunter' or 'limp'. You can use production dictionaries to:

- find the right words to express an idea
- learn new words in a specific semantic area by going from the known (e.g. 'eat') to the unknown (e.g. 'munch' or 'crunch')
- find out quickly which of two or more words similar in meaning is right in which context (e.g. written or spoken, formal or informal)
- find out which subjects and objects go with particular verbs and vice versa

Students will often ask 'Which dictionary should I buy?' In order to answer this question you obviously have to be familiar with quite a few yourself. You'll need to know which dictionaries are available for beginners, intermediate and advanced students, whether the dictionary gives definitions only or, better, samples of use, whether the dictionary gives phonetic transcriptions, and if it's clearly laid out with an attractive font and size of print. It also pays to discuss with students their preferences as to size and price, appearance (layout, use of colour and pictures, type size) and/or sound (does the computer dictionary have the accent on it that the student wishes to emulate?). Take into consideration the student's level and the look-up situation the student is most often in. You can also discuss any accompanying workbooks and the theoretical underpinning of the dictionary itself, which is often explained in the introduction. My personal recommendations would be:

Beginners: the *Oxford Elementary Learner's Dictionary* and the *Oxford Photo Dictionary*.

Intermediate students: the *Collins COBUILD English Dictionary* (because it's corpus-based, full of natural examples and well laid out), the *Cambridge International Dictionary of English* (because it covers British, American, Australian and other spelling, usage, pronunciation and patterns), and the *Longman Language Activator* (because it helps students to learn words on their own).

Advanced students: if they already have one of the three above, a standard dictionary such as the *Concise Oxford*. This will give them access to a greater word store, and the definitions are written with a wider vocabulary.

A Use dictionaries yourself

If at all possible, have a pile of good sized dictionaries in the classrooms where you work. Use them yourself to check spelling, definitions, word stress, and so on. Students will see you doing this. This reinforces the message that even competent language users need to go to the dictionary to get help.

A Looking up words you know

Here is an idea for helping students to get used to using English–English dictionaries of a reasonable size.

1 Ask students to look up words that are either:
   a) international, e.g. 'Coke' or 'Cola' or 'café' or
   b) false friends, that is the sound and/or spelling is the same or very similar in both the mother tongue and target language but the meaning is different, e.g. 'aktuel'/'actually', 'simpatico'/'sympathetic', 'demander'/'demand', 'sputnik'/'sputnik', or
   c) ones students are sure they know in the target language, e.g. 'table' or 'chair'

2 Whichever category you choose, ask students to look the words up and tell you one thing about them that they didn't know beforehand. The thing they choose may be semantic, phonemic, syntactic or relating to usage. Students will feel safe thinking that they know what they will find in the dictionary. Thus the activity is an unthreatening way of starting to work with a large reference tool. Students are in fact almost guaranteed to find out something new and interesting about the word they look up, such as that 'Coke' is a name for the drug cocaine, that false friends are no friends at all, or that chairs can be jobs at a university.

5.4 The board

Main types of board

The board is another standard piece of equipment that we may feel we know all about but, again, different products abound. There are:

- flannel boards that you can stick towelling or felt shapes to
- black and green boards nailed to walls, sitting on easels or in wooden frames, on which you can write in chalk
- whiteboards (also on walls or easels) of all sizes from scarcely bigger than a poster to those covering an entire wall or constituting a metre high frieze around the middle of a room. (By the way, different whiteboards accept different types of marker pen, so test your pen carefully by drawing a line at the edge of the board before you launch into a central screed. If you can wipe the test line off easily, the pen you're using is the correct type. If you can't rub it off, it's the wrong type. Don't despair if you don't have any spirit or alcohol cleaner with you. Simply retrace the same line exactly with the same pen and wipe it off instantly. It may take two or three attempts but this homeopathic cure does work.)
- whiteboards that print out whatever has been written on them.
- magnetised boards that you can stick things to using small specially manufactured magnets. These boards range from small and portable to very large. You can 'pin up' notices and pictures, etc., with the special small magnets. You can also attach magnetic shapes to these boards. Thus you can store words or ideas and move them around, organising and regrouping them throughout a lesson.

Uses of boards

You can use boards to do many things, including to:

- write up what you need in a lesson before the lesson starts. Don't forget to write 'Please leave!' on your beautiful work somewhere though or some helpful soul might wipe it off for you.
- avoid photocopying
- add visual impact to a lesson, especially if you use colour pictures and icons as well as words
- provide a model for writing
- explain a word
- tell a story, record points in a game, explain a task
- test the mood of the class (see below)
- facilitate thinking by recording brainstorms, mind maps, flowcharts, and so on
- write up homework so there are no excuses!

5 What can we teach with?

Here are two ideas for using the board.

A Group landscape

1 Draw a couple of swift lines on the board to suggest a landscape of some kind, like these:

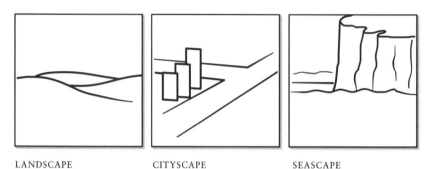

LANDSCAPE   CITYSCAPE   SEASCAPE

Don't draw much or well, or students will feel too daunted to join in with the next step.

2 Stand back and invite students to come up and add anything they like to the drawing. Hold out pens or chalk, coloured if possible, and wait for students to come forward. One or two will probably drift up and add a sun, a river, a bridge, a bird or some stick figures. Often one or two students will wait until everyone else has been to the board. If they join in at all, it will be to add something that changes the mood of the picture. Something like a lightning bolt, an atomic cloud or a space ship.

3 When everyone has added what they want, you can simply enjoy the picture, recognising the kinds of moods people drew in, or use the picture for vocabulary work, story building or teaching spatial prepositions.

(I learnt this from John Morgan.)

A Mapping the lesson

If you wrote up a negotiated menu at the start of the lesson (see page 52), then you can either tick things off as you go through the lesson or, alternatively, at the end of class, you can mark the menu to show what's been covered and what there hasn't been time for. Alternatively, towards the end of class write up on the board the headings for a skeleton lesson record. Students recall what they have done in the lesson and call out while you record these items on the board. Students may get the order of

136

some items wrong, miss things out or even put in extra things from different lessons. Using group discussion you should eventually be able to get most things recorded correctly. Depending on how much time you have left, you can do one of the following:

- have students copy the lesson record down so that they have the overview in their notebooks
- ask more detailed questions about the different stages of the lesson
- ask students whether they understood what each stage of the lesson was for and whether the pace was right or not

5.5 The box of rods

The dictionary and the display board are two tools that every language teacher in the world probably has access to. I'd like to turn now to some slightly more unusual items in the tool box, the rods.

Main types of rods

Manufactured by the Cuisenaire Company and originally used for teaching maths, available in wood or plastic and packed in boxes, rods are little sticks in ten different colours – natural wood (or white, if plastic), red, light green, purple, yellow, dark green, black, brown, blue and orange. They go from rods 1 cm in length increasing by regular proportions to the longest 10 or 15 cm rod. You can get small boxes of just a few and deluxe boxes containing scores of these smooth, colourful objects. They were made popular in language teaching by Caleb Gattegno, the founder of the Silent Way. They are now used by teachers, many of whom are not Silent Way trained, but who have come across these versatile objects somehow and have grown to like them.

Uses of rods

Rods can be used for many things, including to:

- represent what they are, e.g. long or short, blue or orange, two or four
- form part of a physical action in the target language, e.g. 'Anna, please pass two green rods to Stefano'
- demonstrate particular target language items such as prepositions, e.g. 'The red rod is under the black one', comparatives, e.g. 'The red rod is longer than the light green one'
- represent phonological features (see page 138)

- represent things other than themselves, such as the hands of a clock, the floor plan of a room or a family tree, thus helping students to talk about things other than the rods
- tell stories (see below)

Here are two ideas for using rods.

A Marking phonological features

Let's imagine students have trouble saying something in English, such as 'My name is Ozymandias, king of kings' – if they've been working on the Shelley poem – or, 'How come I'm always the last to know stuff' – if they've been watching an American sitcom.

One standard way to help students with their pronunciation is to say 'Listen and repeat after me', but sometimes that doesn't work, as here:

S: Ozy...?
T: Ozymandias.
S: Ozymias.
T: Ozymandias.
S: Ozydemias.

And so on into the darker reaches of the night.

Some teachers think sound will cure everything. But some students need sight and touch, and the rods can help.

1 Lay out five little rods in a row, one rod per syllable of 'Ozymandias'. Say each syllable flatly with equal stress as you touch each rod, 'Oz-y-man-di-as'.
2 Then put the third rod on its end so it's higher than the others. This indicates that the third syllable is stressed.
3 Push the fourth and fifth rods together so they touch. This indicates that they are said almost as one syllable.
4 Encourage the student(s) to touch the rods and repronounce the word slowly, 'Oz-y-MAN-dias'. It usually works.

A Story telling

1 Choose a story that you think your students will like. If you don't know it off by heart in English, write down the key words and phrases on a card that you can keep at hand as a prompt in class. Stories are much better told than read out loud. Work out which of the rods you will use for your main characters and to symbolise places and objects, etc. See the illustration.

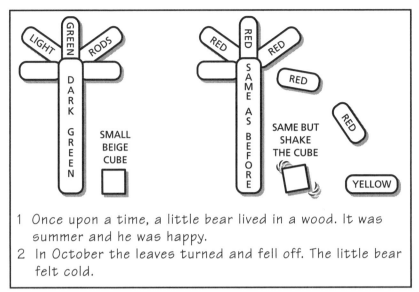

1 Once upon a time, a little bear lived in a wood. It was summer and he was happy.
2 In October the leaves turned and fell off. The little bear felt cold.

ROD STORY

2 Tell the story using the rods as prompts throughout. Students will be so busy looking at the rods and listening to the story that they won't see you glancing at your skeleton story notes.
3 When you've finished the story, sweep the rods gently to one side. You can now elicit vocabulary or whole phrases from the story by silently placing the same rods in the same places as before and indicating to students that they should try to help you with the story. The rods also act as an *aide memoire* when the students retell the story to each other.

5.6 The picture pack

My next two examples of tools of the trade are things you can gather or make for yourself and which, once you have them, can be used again and again with different classes. The first I call a picture pack. I personally wouldn't want to be without it.

Main types of picture pack

Collect about 50 pictures cut from magazines. You can select them for their beauty, strangeness, humour or ambiguity. Some can be no bigger than a playing card and some of A4 size. I made my initial picture pack over a period of two weeks by cutting out anything bright or interesting from magazines. I add to the collection whenever I see a good picture. I have made one deliberate ground rule for myself, in that I try to include a representative selection of different ages and types of people, different climates, flora and fauna, and different degrees of affluence. This means I have to go to *National Geographic*, Greenpeace and UNICEF materials, *Ebony* and other special interest magazines, since the best-selling magazines in northern Europe tend to feature similar looking rich, tall, thin, blond westerners and are thus very bland. The picture pack is lightweight and portable so you can pop it in your teaching bag and use it any time you run out of lesson material. I have even whiled away time in a traffic jam by looking at my favourite pictures!

Uses of picture packs

Here are some things you can use a picture pack to do:

- generate vocabulary
- do mutual picture dictation ('Draw a person up a lamppost')
- play guessing games ('Is there a cabbage in the picture?')
- generate dialogues between the characters in the pictures
- create stories by guessing what would come before and after the picture if it was in a cartoon strip
- help students relax and enjoy themselves
- bring the outside world into the classroom

Here are two ideas for using a picture pack.

A   It reminds me of ...

1 While students are busy, walk around the room laying out pictures on surfaces. You need about three times as many pictures as you have students.
2 Ask them to look at the pictures and choose one to take back to their desks. Explain that they mustn't write on the pictures. While they're selecting their one picture, you do the same. Students will ask if they can select more than one. Tell them they can if they're desperate to.
3 Depending on how good your students' English is, you can move straight to the pairwork below or, alternatively, do this. Hold up your own picture and talk about it naturally and spontaneously. Every time you hear yourself saying something particularly useful to the students, write it up on the board. Thus, after your one minute talk, you might have the following phrases on the board: 'I chose this picture because ...', 'It reminds me of ...', 'When I was ...', 'I'm not

sure what …', 'The atmosphere's quite …', 'At the top …', 'In the
background …', 'On the right …'

4   Students talk to each other about why they chose their picture and
    what's in it. You wander around helping with new vocabulary and
    refining utterances.
    (I learnt this from John Morgan.)

A Standardising practice

These days there are lots of theme calendars available, such as dog or cat
calendars, or calendars full of Welsh or Canadian scenes. They are
wonderful for class since, if you pull them apart and cut the dates off,
you instantly have sets of 12 similar, large, quality pictures.

1   Give each student one picture page from a calendar. If you have a large
    class, use two or three calendars all similar in some way, for example,
    showing outdoor scenes. You need to have a page yourself too.
2   Make sentences about your page which you know the students can
    also truthfully make about theirs, for example:
       T: My picture comes from a calendar.
       S: My picture comes from a calendar.
    (You can teach or elicit 'too' at the end or, at higher levels, 'Mine does
    too.')
3   Start making sentences about things that are identical in all the
    pictures, e.g. 'It's an outdoor scene' or 'The picture is of a foreign
    country.' Then make sentences that students will have to change a
    little when talking about their pictures, e.g. 'It's a hot day' or 'It's
    autumn' or 'I think it's Saudi Arabia.' Then slowly move to statements
    that need more changing, e.g. 'In my picture, in the background, you
    can see a train.' Depending on the level of the students, you can:

    • increase the complexity of your ideas/sentences
    • increase the amount students have to change
    • ask individual students to lead with a sentence of their own that the
      rest of the group shadows with appropriate changes

    (I learnt this from Jim Wingate.)

5.7 The music tape

Main types of music tape

Since I like music very much and find that lots of students do too, I use
several different kinds of music in class. I personally use tapes as I have

a tape recorder with a zero counter that is good for finding my place in class. Of course, if you have access to a CD player you can use that instead.

I mainly use instrumental music. A lot of my colleagues do intensive language practice in song lyrics so I try to complement that by doing something different! I play music that is very distinctive in genre, e.g. jazz, blues, classical, folk and 'world music' from many different countries.

Here are some practical tips for using music in class:

- Make sure that any tape recorder you select or buy has a zero counter so you can find your place quickly.
- Don't have it on all the time. After all you don't want people to feel they're in a supermarket or an airport!
- Don't have it on too loudly.
- Don't turn it off instantly if one person complains, but check how many people like it. If most people are enjoying it, suggest that the one who isn't trades places.
- Let students join in by bringing their music to class.

Uses of music tapes

You can use a music tape for many things including to:

- relax yourself and put yourself in a good mood
- relax students while they're coming into or leaving class
- play quietly in the background to help small, quiet classes to speak out in the target language
- play quietly in the background during group work so that groups are not so conscious of what other groups are saying
- start a musical thread to your lessons. If students suggest bringing in other music, guide them towards instrumental music that doesn't need to be played incredibly loudly.

Here's an idea for using a music tape.

A Mental images

1 Explain to the students that you're going to play a piece of music. Ask them to listen with their eyes closed, and see what mental pictures they get. Suggest that they try to notice the following about the picture in their mind's eye: climate, vegetation, geography, colours, smells, buildings, people and animals.
2 Play them one minute's worth of some music, e.g. 'world music' from the Sahara or by Australian aborigines.

3 Ask students to discuss in pairs what they saw in their imaginations. Tell them there's no right or wrong to this, just what they got from the music personally.

4 After the pairwork, ask students to throw out ideas and record useful vocabulary and phrases on the board, e.g. 'an arid place', 'a dusty brown plateau', 'distant mountains', etc.

If you choose music with a real atmosphere to it, many students will 'see' similar things. Thus you will tend to have words generated around a particular topic.

5.8 How to look after your tools: Maintenance and storage

When dealing with expensive equipment such as computers and photo-copiers, manuals and engineers will give plenty of advice on how to look after them properly. What I have more in mind in this section is a sharing of simple practical tips to help to keep less expensive equipment in some sort of order.

Getting materials ready

- If you're inexperienced and not yet good at thinking on your feet, assume there will be a power cut, photocopy jam, tape break or equivalent disaster on the day of your classes. If at all possible, get copies done beforehand, carry spares of tapes and have a plan B up your sleeve for when the emergency strikes.
- Again if you're inexperienced, prepare too much material rather than too little. You can always use it to save you planning time before your next lesson if you don't use it in this lesson.
- Have a list of five- or ten-minute activities that require no materials or preparation which you can whip out when needed.
- When making materials such as reusable worksheets, cover them to protect them from wear and tear.
- Label and number tapes so you can find your place easily.
- Stick visuals onto card and then label them on the back so that you can display them fast in class the right way up without peering at them. Colour code them so you can file them fast after class.
- Label expensive items with your name and tie extension cords and leads to machines so that they don't get separated.

When you go into class

- Having made a list on your lesson notes of the materials you need to prepare for a particular class, have a last check to make sure you have them all with you.
- Lay out the materials in the order you'll need them.
- Clean the board if necessary and write up anything you need to have there in advance.
- Put up any notices.
- Check your student name list to refresh your memory of who's in your class.

In class

- Once you've finished with materials, you can return tapes and rods to their boxes, cards to packets, photocopies to their piles and clean off display surfaces while students are doing a task. Alternatively, students can do this kind of housekeeping as part of their finishing off routine. Either option will avoid the problem of being left at the end of a lesson with a mammoth mess and no time to get it sorted out.
- If you or a student find that something is missing, broken or has run out, make a note of this. This is so that you or the school can fix it before someone else goes into class and gets stuck with incomplete materials in the middle of an exercise. Many listening, learning, reading and pronunciation centres have a little notebook on the main desk where you can write down any mechanical problems or record which materials have run out.

Between tasks in class or between classes

- Keep your display surfaces up to date. This will mean prowling around the room taking down notices and also allowing students time to add up to date work to already established displays.

On leaving class

- Unless you are the only person who uses your classroom and you can lock it securely, or you are otherwise absolutely sure that things will be safe, take all your materials out with you when you go. It's amazing the sort of items that can 'walk' in some settings.
- Clean the board as a courtesy to the next user.

Filing systems

Find a system of filing that works well for you. You might like to store similar posters or charts in the same colour coded cardboard tube, put materials for one lesson in a plastic wallet, use large coloured dividers in your picture box, keep extra photocopies in cardboard trays, or wrap large folds of paper around connected items in an envelope folder. A few minutes spent thinking out a system that suits you will save you and your colleagues hours of scrabbling around desperately trying to find something just before a lesson.

Personal favourites

 Writers develop personal rituals and requirements that help them to work well. For example, apparently Kipling couldn't write anything worthwhile with a lead pencil, and Schiller filled his desk with rotting apples because the smell stimulated his creativity. In my experience we teachers are a bit the same when thinking about and teaching our lessons!

- Sort out in your own mind which items you absolutely cannot do without. For some people it's fresh chalk or good board pens, for others it's a decent tape recorder. Most teachers have some equipment or some configuration of furniture or space or sound that makes them feel ready to work with a class. Sometimes it's the lowly tools that make all the difference to a teacher. Whatever it is for you, make sure you can make it or buy it or organise it for use at all times! Put new pens in your bag or chalk in your pocket, for example. This keeps your blood pressure nice and low.

Part 2

5.9 A central tool: The coursebook

In Part 1 of this chapter, I looked at a range of tools available to us in the TESOL trade. Since the coursebook is totally different in scope and nature from any of the materials mentioned so far, I've given it a section all of its own. By the coursebook I mean not just the basic Student's and Teacher's Book designed to be used regularly in class as the basis of the syllabus, but also the accompanying recordings, workbooks, readers, etc. that we are offered in the package.

Many teachers choose to or have to use a coursebook much of the time. Some use it as their syllabus and test material, methodology, task guide and visual and auditory aid. It is their main resource. Others use it more as a supplement to their own syllabus and ideas, being very relaxed about omitting and adapting things. However we use coursebooks, we can learn a lot from them. We can learn language, things about language, ways of explaining things and exercise types. Let's look then, first of all, at the advantages and disadvantages of using a coursebook on a regular basis.

Advantages of using a coursebook

There is definitely a charm, from a student's point of view, no matter what you are learning, to working your way through a well written book and progressing to a new one. I personally felt a cheering sense of progress when I came to the end of my green, pre-beginner piano book and embarked on my new beginner's book with its optimistic red, shiny cover. A good coursebook can give a sense of clarity, direction and progress to a student. It can save a teacher wondering what to teach, how to teach it and with what materials. Written by experienced teachers, it can provide a balanced syllabus and ready-made materials in a reasonably cheap, portable form that teachers and students can use alone or in class. It contributes to learner independence as the learner can use it to review, look ahead and learn on their own.

If you and your students are really lucky, the coursebook you work with will be a perfect fit. By this I mean that the book covers all the things you and the students find important and does so in a way that fits the beginning, middle and end of your sort of lessons. With a perfect fit, the materials mentioned in the book are either provided, are available where you teach or are easily made and reusable by you and other teachers. The method suggested in the perfect coursebook for you will also be in line with your school, student and teacher ethos. This book will make planning easy and enjoyable.

Disadvantages of using a coursebook

Although coursebooks can be very useful, they do have their drawbacks. They can be filled with cardboard characters and situations that are not relevant or interesting to your learners. They have to suggest a lock-step syllabus rather than one tailored to your students' internal readiness. If the pattern in the units is too samey it can start to get very predictable and boring.

Often a coursebook is only a partial fit for the students or teacher. By this I mean that the book covers some of the things the teacher and students find important, but the conceptual chunks are mapped onto a different chronological structure from the one you have. In other words, the units are too long or too short for your lessons or the content is too dense, or steeply graded or too sparse for your students. Perhaps some of the materials mentioned are provided by the book but others have to be made or gathered by teachers. The methods suggested may not fit very easily with your class or your colleagues.

The worst case of course is a complete lack of fit between the book and you and your class. This coursebook would be different in level, density, unit length, layout and content from what you and your students like. The methodology and underlining principles are alien to you. You have to winnow each page carefully to glean anything useful. There are very few materials provided and the teacher has to really struggle to make the book work.

Below I'll describe ways of getting to know a coursebook better so that you can see if it's likely to be a good fit or not.

5.10 Using the whole coursebook: The stimulus-based approach

If you glance back at Chapter 2 you'll find *'Stimulus-based blocks'* (see page 56). I explained there how to apply five categories of teaching move to any learning stimulus. By way of review and extension of that work, I'd now like to apply those five categories to the coursebook since it is one of the main teaching materials used to stimulate learning. To refresh your memory, the categories were: meeting the stimulus, analysing it, personalising it, altering it and creating new work from it. We could apply these categories of work to any exercise, page or unit within a coursebook and/or to the whole book. The categories are not tightly defined nor meant to be scientific. They are mostly intended as a way of prompting and storing ideas. So if you find an idea in what seems to you the 'wrong' category, just relocate it to where you would be happier for it to be.

The main idea of applying the stimulus-based teaching model to the coursebook is to encourage you to do things with and to the coursebook rather than to follow it slavishly. After all, it's there for us to use as a tool in our work. It's not supposed to dominate our teaching!

Meeting the coursebook

Here are some ideas for when you or your students first hold a new coursebook in your hands.

A Me Teacher, You Book

Experienced teachers are able to pick up a new coursebook, flick through it looking at the contents page and the index, the blurb on the back cover and the introduction to the teacher's book, and gain a good idea of whether the book is possible for a particular group. If you're an inexperienced teacher, you may find this impossible to do fast. You may want to consider at least a couple of questions so that you can make the basic decision about whether to adopt it or not, always supposing this is your decision to make, of course! Let's look at these questions.

What does the book look like?   Have a look at the size, weight, colour, shape and general layout and style of the book. If you know that the book will immediately strike your students as, say, too frivolous or too dry, see if you can choose another one.

Who is the book aimed at?   Many coursebooks aim for as wide a market as possible. This often makes it bland for YOUR particular gang. I like to check the topics and activities to see if they hold relevance for my group. I also like a book that is challenging but not daunting for students.

What's the pace and timing like?   Check the pages and units to see if you can use them easily in the sort of time slots you have. As I like to use a combination of thread and block planning, I need a coursebook that does not have huge chunks of work that go on for pages.

Considering these three questions will help you on first meeting a coursebook. For a deeper analysis of the book see the next section.

A Sharing your reasoning

If you are going to use a coursebook for a while, student confidence in it needs to be built and maintained. Even if you know that the book has some serious gaps in its methodology, for example, it's important not to undermine the value of the work you do with the book by moaning about it. I'd suggest that you explain to students why you're going to use the book, what the book is good at, and where it needs supplementing.

If you skip something, share with the students why you are doing so. If you survey the book before using it or survey each unit as you get to it, invite the students to state their own priorities in the units too.

A Students survey the book in class

Most of the students' work in class with a coursebook will be of the purposeful study type. Survey reading is different in that it helps students to see what a book contains and how efficient use can be made of it. If the coursebook is going to be the students' companion for a while, it helps to get acquainted with it first. Although you might want to save a fully-fledged book survey for academic students (see Yorkey 1970), the steps in this activity will be useful for any teenage or adult learner meeting a book for the first time. If it's the first time the students have done a book survey, you could do it along with them.

1 You will need to pre-teach any new words such as 'blurb', or simplify the wording or do the whole thing in the mother tongue. Allow time for the students to handle the book to study the features.

2 Ask students to do the following tasks:
   * Look at the outside cover (front, back and spine) noting the title, author's name and anything useful in the blurb.
   * Check the place and date of publication to see how up to date the book is and which culture it's written from.
   * Check the contents page to see the names of the units and the types of things included in them.
   * Turn to the introduction to see what basic principles the book rests on.
   * Have a look at the text of a unit to see how the section headings, summaries, grammar or vocabulary review sections are indicated and what sort of symbols mark different types of activity.
   * Glance through several units to see what sort of pattern or rhythm is set up.
   * See if there are any glossaries, tapescripts, verb lists or other extra study aids.
   * Check the index to see how you can get back to work done or find new topics.

This activity combines nicely with the next one.

A Students write bibliography cards

1 Write on the board an example bibliographical entry for an imaginary book as below:

① ②③④⑤ ⑥⑦⑧   ⑨   ⑩   ⑪   ⑫

Smith, J. (2000). *The Nice Coursebook*, Cambridge: Cambridge University Press.
⑬   ⑭

EXAMPLE BIBLIOGRAPHICAL ENTRY

2 Write the numbers vertically down the blackboard and elicit the names in English of all these numbered parts:

1 Author's surname	6 Publication date	10 Comma
2 Comma	7 Close brackets	11 Place of publication
3 Author's initial	8 Full stop	12 Colon
4 Full stop	9 Title of the book	13 Publisher
5 Open brackets	in italics	14 Full stop

3 Ask students to write a bibliographical entry just like the one on the board but for an imaginary book which they have 'written'. The book can be about anything they like, from their favourite bicycle to a history of the universe in three volumes.
4 While students are musing and writing, go around and check that the entries are written correctly.
5 Ask students to dictate their entries to each other and check that their partner has written the entry down correctly.
6 For homework, ask the students to write an entry for their new coursebook in the same manner. If the students are academic, you can ask them to write the details for each of their set books on separate cards. This is a good habit to get into for when they are writing university papers with bibliographies, since the cards can be alphabetised and added to as they go along. This makes writing the bibliography a simple affair with no return trips to the library necessary.

A Looking ahead – Getting organised

Rather than have students sitting at home or in study centres for hours aimlessly staring at books and not really achieving anything, introduce them to a workable study system such as the organic study system in Buzan (1995a). Encourage students to decide before they start how much time they will spend on studying, decide on a study goal, mark the place they will stop at, and time themselves so that they stop at the previously decided time. You can help with the provision or negotiation of a suitable goal by giving them suggestions like these:

• Look at the section title or heading and guess what information or vocabulary will come up in the section.
• List all the vocabulary that you know associated with the topic.
• Write three questions to ask the teacher about the topic.
• Look up in the dictionary five new words in the section.
• Make a trailer for the section – just as in the cinema where trailers give a preview of films that are coming. The trailer can be in cartoon, mime or key word form.
• Start at the end of the section and read back to the start. This apparently illogical approach is excellent for cutting down students' anxiety, since they have in a sense already got to the end of their task when they start and so don't have to worry about not finishing.

Analysing the coursebook

The analysis stage of the stimulus-based teaching sequence aims to work with the stimulus more thoroughly, naming its parts, thinking about where it came from, considering its future. Here are some ideas for this more detailed meeting of the coursebook.

A Teacher guts the coursebook before use in class

We need to look at the book in more detail.

What does the book contain?   Let's consider all the possible things there are to put into a language lesson or course. This was the subject of Chapter 3 and in that chapter we moved a long way from just the inclusion of a few tenses, a few modal auxiliaries and some vocabulary. Below are the main headings from Chapter 3. Under each heading are a couple of things which I personally love to find in a coursebook. You will want to note mentally the things YOU would want to see on your shopping list and what seems to be present or missing in the book.

Classes and people   The sorts of things I would check a coursebook for in this area are the types of groupings mentioned. I mean, are the activities well divided between those that can be done in duos, trios, small and large groups? I like a mixture. What senses are appealed to? Visual, tactile? I like chances for students (and me) to move physically and to feast our eyes and ears.

Language patterns   Look at the coverage of lexical phrases and discourse patterns. I personally like to see work on isolated words, and sentences well supplemented with plenty of these. And what is the basis of the book? I quite like corpus-based books rather than those dependent solely on intuition or on traditionally included topics. See how the vocabulary is reviewed. I prefer to get extra information each time an item is reviewed, for example, on useful collocations or morphology.

Language skills   Have a look at the reading passages. I personally like to have some long, easy but interesting ones somewhere in the package as well as a variety of shorter ones, with differing layout and style and with interesting and/or realistic tasks to go with them.

You'll need to look at the listening available too. I prefer different lengths of monologue and dialogue and recordings that are as natural and interesting as possible for the level.

What about speaking work? I would look for the chance for students to take both longer and shorter turns so that they have a chance to practise fluency and discourse skills, such as turn-taking, as well as accuracy.

I'd suggest checking out the writing tasks too. I like to set optional writing tasks, often quite short ones and of different types, for homework after most classes. If there are some interesting ones already in the book, this saves me some time.

Combinations   You'll need to consider the situations, topics and human themes in the book to see if you and your students will find them interesting and relevant. I would check to see if they are likely to engage the students and allow them to do things that are genuinely worthwhile in class as well as learn English.

Culture and literature   See if there's any attempt to introduce interesting cultural differences. I would look to see if this gets beyond the level of, say, the difference between bus tickets and also to see if it is handled in an enlightened way!

Look to see if there's any literature in the broadest sense, including little rhymes, short stories, essays, and so on. I'd see if the students' own personal responses to the literature are allowed for in the tasks.

Study skills   I feel that work on study skills gives value to the work done with a coursebook so I'd suggest you look to see whether there's any help on that.

Now let's turn to our next question.

How does the coursebook suggest we work?   We need to think about how students learn and how we can teach, what the authors of the book think about this and so how they go about working with new and old material. I'd look to see if the organisation and methodology of the book allow students plenty of opportunity to meet new material, notice its features, remember it by review or depth of processing and use and refine their understanding. You might like to see too if there are chances for you, the teacher, to vary your approach; sometimes making things plain to the students, sometimes allowing them to find things out for themselves and sometimes learning peripherally. I get really bored with units that always deal with language in exactly the same way. And I always think that if I'm bored, it'll probably show and be transmitted to the students! Have a look at the exercises. You will need them to be motivating for your particular group.

You will think of other things to add to this checklist, things that are important to you in a coursebook, such as, perhaps, a good balance between work on accuracy and fluency or naturalness of language, different policies and methods for error correction, or lots of opportunities for personalisation.

This may seem an awful lot to consider, if you are an inexperienced teacher, but if you do it, you'll have a clear idea of which things you're going to have to leave out or put in.

A   The coursebook vocabulary thread for students in class

This activity involves identifying and naming in English the main parts of the coursebook and the main ways of working with it. You can start with just a few of the following words when the students start working with a book and then introduce a few more whenever you use the coursebook:

- Nouns: *front cover, blurb, index, glossary, workbook, tape, paragraph, line, caption, exercise, syllable, stress mark,* etc.
- Verbs: *pick up, turn over, look up, cover up, uncover, summarise, read,* etc.
- Adjectives: *interesting, thorough, incomplete, glossy, multi-coloured, dense,* etc.

Once the basic vocabulary has been covered, you can work later on with ideas that generate more vocabulary, for example, 'How does paper get made?' (*pulp, chemicals, bleach, dry, cut*) 'How does an author work?' (*key in, computer, proposal, draft, edit*) 'What happens to a book?' (*bookshop, shelf, home, tear, rip, dog-ear*).

Personalising the book

If we want the students to see their coursebook as a real resource, to enjoy using it and to want to spend time with it, we will need to help them to forge some kind of personal connection with it. Here are some ideas you might like to try.

A Covering the coursebook

Years ago when textbooks were hardback and expensive, my teachers required me to cover them with brown paper so that they would last longer. Although coursebooks are now paperback and a lot cheaper, asking students to cover them and decorate them any way they like is an exercise that generates plenty of useful vocabulary and thus their coursebook is personalised and distinguishable from any others.

A Coloured filters

Some students may experience mild to severe discomfort when reading or writing texts. Using coloured overlays can make reading easier for them by reducing blurring of words and letters, print movement and fading, and by stabilising text size in their vision. Even for students who have no real problems with text, choosing one or two coloured overlays they like and using them for reading the book is fun and can make them feel restful or cheerful. Testing packs and overlays are available from The Institute of Optometry (I.O.O. Marketing, 56–62 Newington Causeway, London SE1 6DS, England). (See also Rinvolucri 1998a.)

A Forging connections

In order to forge connections between the students and the books, take time every so often after looking at a page, picture or unit for students to state any of the following:

153

- Which character they feel they think, act or look most or least like, which character reminds them of someone they know, what they would do if they were in a situation such as the one in the text, which tasks they liked or disliked doing.

'Quantification' exercises are also fun. This is where students take any rather vague word or phrase in a text and decide what it means for them. Examples of vagueness could be: 'a short text', 'intermediate' or 'within walking distance'. Students can quantify, for example, 'a short text' as 'something I can read in five minutes', 'one paragraph' or 'something that's easy and interesting so that it feels short'.

A Inner voice

Inner voice work means encouraging students to talk in English but silently 'in their heads'. Most of us have inner monologues or dialogues quite naturally. Inner voice techniques merely recognise this and build on it. Students can talk to themselves using their inner voice in class or at home to enhance their connection with the coursebook. They can use their inner voice to 'talk' through:

- words they've just learnt in a unit
- snatches of English from recordings or stories in the coursebook
- structures that have appeared in the book. For example, the past simple tense can be personalised by students using their inner voice to think about what they did yesterday.
(I first learnt this idea from Chris Sion.)

A Teacher dissects the coursebook at home

If you have your own copy of the Teacher's Book and Student's Book you're going to work with for a while, I suggest you chop it up and put each unit in a different wallet or envelope. As you work with each unit, each wallet or envelope will contain not just the relevant pages from a particular unit but also any connected lesson notes you make, notes of any supplementary materials used, useful pictures and flashcards, and notes of any advantages or disadvantages of a particular section. (For an example of annotated pages from a Teacher's Book see page 200.) You might like to write comments by different exercises like 'Takes at least one hour with a slower group' or 'Too many forms in one exercise' or 'Very stimulating, use again.'

Altering the coursebook

Keeping a text pretty much intact and, for example, copying it and learning it by heart has the merit of helping us to commit it to memory. In some cultures this way of working shows respect for tradition and the wisdom of the author. Altering the text in some way which will be acceptable in other cultures has the merit of encouraging mental flexibility and personal relevance. Let's look first at how a teacher can alter a coursebook.

A Teacher selects, rejects and supplements parts of the coursebook before use in class

Having surveyed the coursebook, you may like to do this before you actually teach.

- What's good? Select the things you think are good. Perhaps the recordings are superbly natural, the periodic tests very well written and the pictures very useful.
- What's bad? Throw out what you feel is boring, irrelevant, confusing or wrong for your class. Perhaps you disagree with some of the grammar explanations or find the situations stiff and unnatural.
- What needs supplementing? Consider in what way you'll need to supplement some exercises and units. For example, you might find some of the tasks rather vague and in need of timing and focusing. You might find the book unhelpful when it comes to study skills or that it hasn't been written for multi-sensory teaching.

Whether you are experienced or inexperienced, it will be this kind of detailed consideration along with the time spent in class using the book with the students that will finally give you the feeling that you really know a book.

A Teacher and students alter texts that are too short

The traditional way of altering a text that's too short (especially if you haven't predicted its brevity and you're in class with ten minutes of the lesson left) is . . . to do it again. Here are some ways you and your students can do a text again.

- Read through the text and circle all the words in a particular set, e.g. adjectives, words connected with the topic, verbs in the same tense, or vague expressions.
- Dictate to students which parts of the text to underline. They underline those parts and then work on trying to form the question that would elicit the underlined 'answer' exactly. For example, 'The woman lived in a <u>small</u> wood.' The correct question to elicit 'small' would be 'What size wood did she live in?' or 'What was the wood like?'

- Dictate some sentences that could go in the text at certain points. The students have to decide where they should go.
- Take a sentence and ask students to expand it by putting one, two or three consecutive words into it wherever they can. The sentence must still make sense although it may make a different sense, e.g. 'Jake didn't want to go.' With one word added, 'Jake (really) didn't want to go.' With two, 'Jake really didn't want to go (home early).' With three, '(My elder brother) Jake ...'
- Add in to the text some senses, e.g. colour, sound, taste, smell, touch. For example, 'The van left with the goods' could become 'The noisy red van ...' or 'The van screeched off ...' or 'The dusty van lurched off down the road ...'
- Add in some speaker or writer distance by adding words and phrases such as: 'apparently', 'according to', 'I'm not sure if', 'it doesn't say'.
- Change the point in time of the text and thus the tenses. Or change the person ('he' to 'she' or 'they' to 'we'). Or change the style, e.g. from formal to informal. Or rewrite the text in another format or genre (as a list of events, table, poem, diagram, letter or news report) or rewrite it from a different point of view.
- Write the sentence or paragraph before and/or after the one you've been studying.

A Teacher and students alter texts that are too long

With upper-intermediate or advanced level books you may have the problem of a rather lengthy text on a subject that is not of particular interest to your group. Apart from simply skipping the text altogether, here are some further ideas.

- Ask students to read the title of the text and predict what it's about. Students then read the text through very swiftly to see if their predictions were basically right or not.
- Ask students to read either the first and last paragraphs or the first and last lines of all the paragraphs. They then tell each other or you what the text is about.
- Students read the first paragraph and write a one-sentence summary. Students then read the last paragraph and do the same thing. Are there any major differences between the two paragraphs? If so, what can your students speculate about the main body of the text from this?
- Read out a few words and challenge students to find them as quickly as they can.
- Read part of the text in class and ask the students to finish it at home.

Adding the students in

The coursebook can make the students feel as if English is an 'out there' subject fixed by others. It's essential for them to get beyond this feeling and really feel that English is a medium of self-expression. We thus need to involve the students and add them in as fast as possible. Ideas such as surveying a book (see above) can give a feeling of control and perspective at the outset. Here are some activities that increase this feeling.

A Read aloud and shadow

Read something out loud in class from the coursebook, leaving pauses after each sense group. Ask students to repeat what you say, in the way you say it, in the pauses you leave. Don't correct the students or take any notice of them while they do this, apart from just giving them time to shadow you as you read – sometimes swiftly, sometimes quietly, sometimes loudly. Each student can individually enjoy the feeling of speaking the target language at length and correctly without any interruption or stress.

A Different voices and gestures

When we're using language normally, we're not usually sitting behind a desk as students are in class. Instead, we're often moving, turning, glancing here or there, making gestures and moderating our volume depending on the circumstances. In order to allow students to integrate the target language from the coursebook naturally into their body memories, I believe it's important for them to be able to use the language while doing more than sitting at a desk. Ask students to speak English in the individual or pair exercises suggested in the coursebook while doing any of the following: using a sympathetic or surprised tone, speaking in a whisper, speaking slowly or very fast, shouting, walking around, searching for something in a bag, combing their hair, looking at a friend or poster, or looking out of the window.

A Reversals

I got the idea of reversing things from Keith Johnstone's book *Impro* (1981). Reversing things generates a power, and provides a range of possibilities. Some ideas follow for granting this power to the students:

- rewriting stories in the coursebook so that they convey the opposite message to their present one

- reversing pictures in the coursebook so that different people are on the left
- changing the order of the units in the coursebook so you do harder things first
- changing the biographical details of the characters so that young Sheila and John, who meet in a disco, are actually 80 years old when they meet and have to drink cocoa because coffee keeps them awake all night
- letting characters turn down invitations, storm out of job interviews and telephone to cancel or change arrangements

Creating things based on the coursebook

One of the categories in stimulus-based work is creation. Of course, within a coursebook there will be hundreds of chances for students to create things such as stories, dialogues, letters and so on. But what can you do based on the whole book?

A Using the pictures

There is a lot of mileage in the pictures in a coursebook. Here are just a few ideas.

- Encourage students to name everything they can see in a picture in English, including general and visible things such as the decor, the season, the geography, and also invisible things such as the degree of rapport between the characters. This will provide a challenge even at advanced level.
- Have a few students group themselves in a tableau, standing in the same relative positions as the people in the picture and copying the gestures and stance exactly. Ask them to say how they feel. This will often create laughter as well as a discussion of cultural points such as body language and eye contact in the target and home cultures. (I learnt this from Judy Baker.)
- Some planning is needed for this idea. Choose any picture (or dialogue) in the coursebook that depicts an interesting aspect of the target culture. Find a native speaker who's lived in the country under discussion and ask them to comment on the authenticity of the picture or dialogue according to their own experience. Record what they say on tape. You then have a comment on something in the coursebook, which is full of language to work on. (I learnt this from Peter Grundy.) For more ideas on how to exploit the recording you've made, see Lindstromberg (1997).

A Bringing out the coursebook characters

One option when working with the characters in a coursebook is to ignore them totally. The ideas in this section do the opposite and try to breathe some life into them.

- Use blackboard drawings or bring in real objects or glove puppets that speak the characters' lines and support the characters so that they come off the page a little.
- Spend time looking at the characters in the book with the students. Gradually build up the facts you are given about them, such as name, age, job, etc. and guess other facts, such as the kind of car they drive, the sort of person they would date, or other imaginary things depending on the age and interests of the students. Towards the end of a book you can compile character sound bites of the sort of thing character X is most likely to say.
- Rank the characters by preference. Which one would the students most like to go on holiday with, buy a used car from, or share a microphone with at a karaoke evening?
- Add thought and speech bubbles.

A Things you can do with the coursebook apart from studying it

This idea is taken from a party game. Groups brainstorm all the uses they can think of for a coursebook, apart from studying English. Students will note down things like 'swatting a fly', 'propping up a table with one short leg', 'a pillow', 'pressing flowers'. If you want, you can put some phrases on the board, e.g. 'You can use it to [verb] with', 'You can use it for [verb]-ing', 'You can use it as a [noun]', 'You can use it instead of a [noun]'. Ask students to read their ideas out. If you wish to make the activity competitive, you can score for unusualness of idea, number of ideas, speed of getting to ten ideas, or correct use of target phrases on the board.

A Finishing off

Once you've used the coursebook in any of the ways described above, you may want to offer students ways to round things off or review work done. Some ideas follow. You can ask students to:

- Finish off any work that was unfinished in class, e.g. read to the end of a text, write some more sentences, make a note of new vocabulary, etc.
- Read part of a unit again, stopping for a few minutes with the part masked and trying to remember the gist of it and any new words and phrases.

159

- Look up new words in the dictionary and practise saying them correctly and putting them into sentences.
- Make a list of words they like and want to remember and ones they dislike and feel they are sure to forget.
- Write test questions for other students for the next lesson. They can also write test questions for each unit and store these. Once a month they go back to old test questions to see if they can answer them.
- Make short, written summaries of work done, what they've learned and the difficulties they still have.
- Prepare to teach what they learnt in a lesson to a student who was absent.

5.11 Conclusion

I have to round off this chapter too. Whether you're experienced or inexperienced, I hope this chapter has been a reminder of how many tools of the trade we have and how important it is to use them as we want. After all, if you have a garden, the lawn mower may be a wonderful machine to have, but you only use it when you want the grass to look nicer. You don't use it every day just because you have it or because it cost a lot of money.

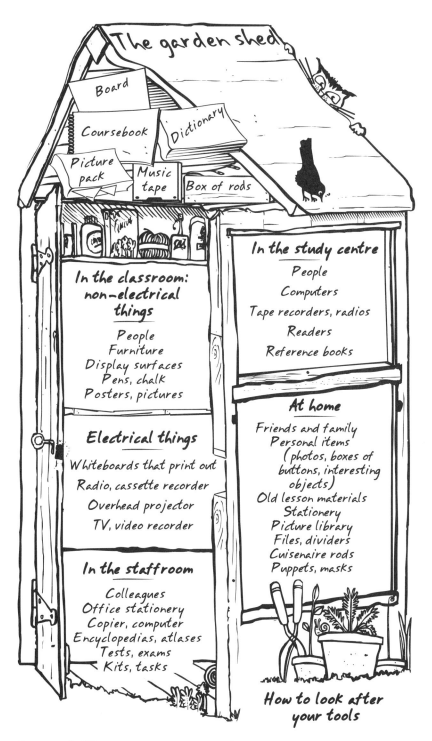

The garden shed

Board

Coursebook

Dictionary

Picture pack

Music tape

Box of rods

In the classroom: non-electrical things

People
Furniture
Display surfaces
Pens, chalk
Posters, pictures

Electrical things

Whiteboards that print out
Radio, cassette recorder
Overhead projector
TV, video recorder

In the staffroom

Colleagues
Office stationery
Copier, computer
Encyclopedias, atlases
Tests, exams
Kits, tasks

In the study centre

People
Computers
Tape recorders, radios
Readers
Reference books

At home

Friends and family
Personal items
(photos, boxes of
buttons, interesting
objects)
Old lesson materials
Stationery
Picture library
Files, dividers
Cuisenaire rods
Puppets, masks

How to look after your tools

CHAPTER 5: WHAT CAN WE TEACH WITH?

6   How can we vary the activities we do?

6.1 Introduction

Starter teachers need to build a bank of language learning activities to draw on in the classroom. More experienced teachers need to pick up new activities and vary old ones to keep themselves and their students motivated. In this chapter I'll start by describing and analysing an activity. I'll then show how the features of the activity can be changed to create many different variations to suit different circumstances. A bank of traditional activities follows, each one varied to suit radically different settings and teaching objectives. Some of the variations have been described in print elsewhere by teachers using a similarly creative approach to the use of conventional exercises.

6.2 Description of a learning activity

I'll now describe a useful activity for a language learning class.

A   The alphabet blackboard game

Basic type of activity
A fast-paced 'energiser'.

Goals, reasons and beliefs
This activity can be used to wake a class up, help them to enjoy themselves, learn spelling, encourage use of the board and the area by the teacher's desk, and improve general knowledge.

Content or topic
General knowledge and spelling.

Context
This game can be played quite peacefully with cooperative adults. Think carefully though before trying it out with teenagers coming from a competitive classroom ethos, as team members may get angry and upset if their team loses. If you use it with students from a different cultural background to yours, be prepared to learn about <u>their</u> composers and cities, etc. and don't expect them to know all about <u>yours</u>.

Materials and medium
You'll need a large, wide board and one pen or piece of chalk for each team for writing up single words.

Organisation of people and furniture
You need a space in front of the blackboard. Students stand in two or three teams. The first person is near the board, but behind a line. All the other team members stand behind the leader. Teams can be formed by mixing language levels, friendship pairs and genders, but need to be of roughly equal size.

Steps
Lay out the blackboard like this:

	Team A	Team B
City		
Country		
Composer		
Colour		
Object		
(with four or more letters)		

THE ALPHABET BLACKBOARD GAME

After an explanation of the game and a 'dry run', call out a letter, e.g. 'B!' The first student from each team runs to the board and writes one city name starting with B on the board, e.g. Bombay or Bangkok. The student then hands the chalk to the next team member and goes to the back of the line. The person with the chalk goes to the board and writes up a country name starting with B, e.g. Brazil, and so on, with different team members, through all the items in the list. When one team has finished, the teacher shouts, 'Stop!' Everyone checks the spelling of the words on the board. The team that has the most correctly spelled words is the winner of that round. To make sure everyone has a chance to write up an item on the board, you'll need to play two or three rounds of the game.

Timing
This activity works well at any point in a lesson when energy levels are flagging.
Preparation time   A minute to prepare the board.

Setting up time Three or four minutes to explain the game and to have a dry run.

Activity time If you play this game once, you'll use about three to five minutes of class time.

Clear up time A few seconds to wipe the board and for people to get back to their seats. Then a minute or two for them to make a note of any spelling mistakes they made in the game.

Follow up time You could set homework for students to think of three more countries beginning with B and be able to point out on a map where they are.

Language
There are many different aspects of language we can consider here.

Teacher set up language Minimal as you could use a lot of mime and demonstration to set up the game.

Student interaction language Students will need to know how to say, for example, 'Quick!' or 'Pass me the chalk!' in the target language or else they'll be forced to use the mother tongue.

Focus language of the activity The spelling of names of cities, countries, etc.

The skills used are reading, writing and listening (and whispering so the other teams can't hear!). If we consider the proportion of accuracy and fluency work in the activity, we're driving for written accuracy and spoken fluency. Plenty of meaningful language is likely to be generated if students get into the spirit of the game.

Teacher role
You need to explain the game clearly, watch carefully, inject a sense of fun, and arbitrate with good humour.

Student role
Students need to be good team players to enjoy the game, but not be over-competitive or to worry about details such as exactly how many people there are in each team.

Cognitive processes
Students have to understand the game, retrieve items from memory by category and by letter, think fast, evaluate team performance, skip what they are stuck on and concentrate on what they can do instead.

Level of difficulty
The activity can be done from elementary level to upper-intermediate but will constitute a challenge for those who can't work under time pressure

or aren't confident about spelling or writing in public, as well as those with very limited 'general' knowledge.

Correction policy
The correction happens within the teams while the game is being played and then between teams afterwards, with the teacher having the last say.

Other comments
Note the need to be prepared to add rules and penalties as you go along, as competitive groups will surely quibble over who's standing where and what happens if an item goes up in both teams' lists!

6.3 Definition of the features of an activity

I described the activity above under 15 headings. Since we can look at any activity from the perspective of these features, I'll say a little more about them.

Name and basic type of activity
Here we can include the standard names that every language teacher knows, such as 'Dictation', and also names that are personally coined for an activity, such as 'Ruth's hot seat idea'. As for the type of activity, you will have your own mental set of activity types, whether these are 'starters' and 'cool downs' or 'moral debates'.

Goals, reasons and beliefs
It's fundamental to consider what an activity is for, why you'd want to use it and what beliefs about people, learning, teaching and language it holds.

Content or topic
We need to know what an activity is about. Is its main theme 'cars' or 'joy' or 'the weather', for example?

Context
By context I mean the nation, culture, educational system, school and class ethos. This will make a huge difference to what you can do in class. If you work in a context, for example, where texts are expensive, considered extremely important, and where people like to learn them off by heart, then any activity involving altering or cutting up texts will go against everything students hold dear and will need to be introduced carefully and with a clear rationale.

Materials and medium
Here you consider what materials you will need for the activity, e.g. newspapers, graphs, flowcharts, tapes, and the main medium involved, e.g. pictures, numbers or texts.

Organisation of people and furniture
Another basic feature of an activity is the layout of the room and the way students are grouped for interaction, e.g. in plenary, milling around, in pairs or cooperative groups or working individually.

Steps
I mean here what actually happens in the classroom. How does the activity work? You may prefer to call this 'procedure'.

Timing
The time involved in an activity can be broken down into these stages:
Preparation time   How much time you need to arrange the room or make copies, for example.
Setting up time   How long it'll take you to explain to students what to do and get them started.
Activity time   How much class time the activity takes up.
Clear up time   The time it takes to get things back in order or to get ready to move onto the next phase of the lesson.
Follow up time   The work done in the activity may well lead to other profitable areas that you can ask students to do later on or for homework.
Under 'Timing', you might also like to think of which point in the lesson an activity would fit especially well into.

Language
There are many different aspects of language to consider when analysing an activity:
Teacher set up language   This is the language you need to get students settled profitably into their tasks.
Student interaction language   This is the language that students need before, during and after the activity. I would include language such as 'Shall I go first?', 'What do we do next?', or 'Have we finished do you think?' If you don't teach this language, students will naturally use their mother tongue.
Focus language of the activity   This is the target language that the activity is expressly designed to introduce or use.
   You'll want to note which skills (reading, writing, speaking, listening) are used in the activity.

Under 'language' we can also note the proportion of accuracy and fluency work, and the amounts of meaningful language likely to be generated by the activity.

Teacher role
You may need to behave differently in different activities. For example, sometimes you should be very central and at other times keep more in the background. It's good to note what teacher roles and personality types suit an activity best. How does the teacher work with the students, the materials and the content to mediate it best for students?

Student role
Roles and personality type need to be considered here too. We also need to think about student familiarity with the activity type, and any group rivalries or personal anxieties that might be in play. When considering teacher and student roles it's useful to think about what outcomes the two parties expect since these are often different and unpredictable.

Cognitive processes
An essential consideration when looking at an activity is the mental effort it encourages. I mean, for example, summarising, comparing, contrasting, ranking, and so on.

Level of difficulty
I mean more here than just thinking 'This idea would probably be OK for elementary up to advanced level students.' An activity can be challenging for many reasons such as the grammar involved, the length, information density, vocabulary, speed, number of people involved, visual support, degree of precision required, number of steps, level of abstractness and many other reasons (see Williams and Burden 1997 p. 171). And once these factors are considered, there remains the choice of which level of challenge to introduce to students. Most current thinking suggests setting tasks at a level just beyond that at which learners are currently capable of functioning, and also teaching principles so that students can make the next step unassisted.

Correction policy
This feature entails considering who (students, teacher, the dictionary?) corrects what (intonation, gesture, choice of word, hesitancy?), when (immediately, after a few seconds, after a few minutes?) and how (by interrupting, holding up a card, writing a note, pointing at a chart?). There is also the 'zero option' where no one deliberately corrects anything overtly.

Other comments
You may well find that there are lots of other things you find worth noting about an activity that don't fit very easily under the headings above, e.g. whether an activity is multi-sensory or not or which type of intelligence is challenged or rewarded.

6.4 Changing the features of an activity

While you've been reading through the activities in the book, I'm sure that, apart from liking some immediately, disliking others and remembering similar and related activities of your own, you've probably been thinking about how you could vary some of the activities to suit your setting and purposes. This is a very natural reaction and is part of the design process that every responsive teacher goes through. We shape and reshape our materials, activities, lesson and course shapes to fit the design problem set by a particular student group, syllabus or course goal.

 Continuing the gardening metaphor, we can alter our materials and activities a lot or a little to enhance our own style and setting, just as a gardener can add, take away or move single plants, rocks, paths or lawns to gain a better and better effect.

Let's look then at some of the changes we could make to the alphabet blackboard activity described above.

Content or topic
You can change the topics which are written down the left hand side of the board. You don't have to stick with 'City', 'Country', etc. If you've recently been working with students on, say, vocabulary connected with different rooms of the house, then you could write 'Kitchen', 'Lounge', etc. down the side of the board, thus encouraging students to remember and write up recently learned vocabulary.

Materials and medium
If you have a small, crowded classroom where it's difficult to have students moving around, you'll need to change the materials feature and let students do the game quietly and individually in their own notebooks. This will mean your neighbours don't complain about the noise but you'll need to think of a different way of checking that the spelling is correct as it won't be public any more.

Timing
If your students get stressed by fast games, you could allow longer for them to write their words down. This slower pace would work well especially if students work individually, and can no longer help each other in teams.

Steps
Perhaps you'd like to bring out some of your shyer, more imaginative students. If so, then instead of rewarding students for their speed in coming up with words, you could change the game to reward those who come up with an item that nobody else has thought of. Students could be encouraged to think for a while before recording their ideas.

Goals, reasons, beliefs
You could use a variation of the alphabet blackboard game for testing purposes rather than as an energiser. Warn the students in advance that they'll have a vocabulary test. Once students are settled in class, ask them to write their names at the top of a piece of paper and to hand in their lists for assessment at the end of the activity.

While playing with our activity, changing a feature here and there in order to address a particular design problem, other features will have changed apart from those deliberately tinkered with! Features such as the teacher set up language, the student interaction language, the correction policy and the degree of difficulty have all changed as we have adapted the materials or the goals, and so on.

As you can see then, an activity can be changed either slightly or greatly. Activities are plastic and malleable. This means that you can change most of the activities in this book to suit your group size, personality or curriculum. It also means that there's an infinite number of activities and variations on activities that could be mentioned in the activity bank which follows.

6.5 The activity bank

In this section I'll list some traditional activities used in language learning classrooms all over the world. Under each one I'll start with a description of the conventional way of running the activity. Next I'll consider ways of varying and improving the activity to achieve different ends. By changing some of the activity's features, you can make a new exercise with a radically different feel or purpose that works better in your classes.

A **Reading a text and then answering questions on it**

Conventional version
1 Elicit or teach a few words from the text.
2 Students read the text.

3 Students read comprehension questions and answer them individually.
4 Answers are checked in pairs or in plenary. You correct or explain as necessary.

Teaching objective 1
To encourage students to be more active and less dependent on you.

Variation
Change the teacher and student roles. So, instead of students being taught the pre-vocabulary, they go ahead and read the text. If they have any vocabulary problems, they consult dictionaries (thus changing the materials), ask each other or circle the words they don't know. They only ask the teacher for things they can't find out elsewhere.

Teaching objective 2
Perhaps your students hate comprehension questions but you still need to check that they *have* understood the text.

Variation 1
Change the steps and cognitive processes.

1 Ask students to read the text twice: once as themselves and then a second time through the eyes of someone in a relationship of some kind with the main character in the text, e.g. as if they were the parent, best friend, boss, lover, or even the dog of the main character.
2 When students read the text again from this new standpoint, they ask questions of and make comments to the main character, in role, as if in the stated relationship.

Variation 2
Change the materials and cognitive processes.

1 Prepare 20 or 30 questions on the text ranging from standard questions designed to retrieve basic information (on who did what, where, when and why) to questions designed to help students explore implications ('Why do you think X …?' 'What will happen if …?'), to questions that explore the mental images triggered by the text or recording ('In your mind's eye what colour was the …?'), to questions dealing with personal experience ('Have you ever …?') and the content itself ('What did you learn about …?').
2 Students read the text.
3 Students read the questions. Once they've understood them, ask them to cross out the ones they don't want to answer. You can, if you wish, give a maximum number that they are allowed to cross out.

4 Students pair up, swap papers and ask each other the questions they have decided to tolerate.

Teaching objective 3
To encourage the students to do more talking.

Variation
Change the organisation of the people and furniture by asking students to work together in pairs. Then change the language by asking them to compose their own questions for other pairs.

Most of the teaching objectives and variations above can be applied to conventional listening comprehension exercises as well as to reading comprehension.

A Dictation

Conventional version
1 Choose a text students haven't seen before.
2 Read the whole text out loud once.
3 Read the text out loud again in small chunks or 'sense groups'. Students write the text down as you dictate it.
4 Students swap texts and mark them against a perfect copy or give in their dictations for you to mark.

Teaching objective
To encourage students to ask more questions in class and to even up the power relationship a little.

Variation
Change teacher and student roles. You become a 'robot' and the students are your controllers! It works like this:

1 Choose a text that students may have seen before but which is funny or interesting.
2 Elicit or teach words for punctuation such as 'full stop', 'comma', etc., and phrases such as 'Hang on!', 'What was the word after ...?', 'How do you spell?', 'What does that mean?', etc. If this language is new for students, write it up on the board and leave it displayed during the next few phases of the activity. This changes the language focus of the activity.
3 Warn students that you'll be reading at high speed. They must use the phrases on the board to stop you and get what they need to write the

text down correctly. Thus the goal changes from testing knowledge of sound and symbol correspondence to oral communication.

4 Start reading aloud at high speed. Students stop you. You answer questions, etc. until the whole text has been written down by students.

5 Pairs of students check with each other and ask you about anything they need in order to write the text perfectly.

A Repeating after the teacher

Conventional version
1 New language is met and the meaning explained.
2 Students listen carefully.
3 Say the new language perhaps once or twice slowly and then at natural speed and then ask students to repeat it.
4 Students repeat chorally, or in pairs or groups or individually.
5 Correct where necessary and continue this cycle until student utterances are standardised.

Teaching objective
To give the students fun and choice.

Variation
Change the steps and cognitive processes by doing the activity as above except that students are encouraged to do one of the following:

- Shut their eyes as they listen to your voice.
- Practise saying the new language mentally or sotto voce once or twice.
- Practise saying only those parts they really like the sound of. This changes the students' role.
- Practise saying it with varying volume, pitch or emotions.
- Practise saying it like a jazz chant, snapping fingers and exaggerating the rhythm.
- Mime actions as you speak.

A Copying from the blackboard

Conventional version
After being taught some new language, students copy sample sentences from the board.

Teaching objective
To involve students in making language choices so that they'll be able to use new language for their own purposes sooner.

Variation

Change the steps and thus the level of difficulty and the cognitive processes involved.

1 After working with some new language, write up all its parts on the board but in random order, as shown:

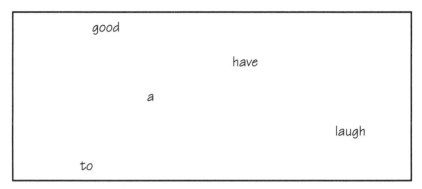

NEW LANGUAGE

Or write up all the parts met so far and also some spare parts, as here.

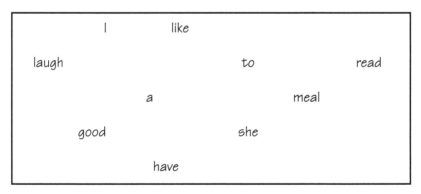

NEW LANGUAGE AND SPARE PARTS

2 Encourage students to read the words out loud to make either the original pattern or an acceptable variation such as 'She likes to have a good read.'
3 Allow time for fine-tuning and questions.
4 Students write down their preferred versions while you go around checking.

A **Reading a dialogue and then role playing it**

Conventional version
1 Students meet a dialogue, perhaps in a textbook, read it and discuss it in plenary.
2 Students are paired up. Each takes the part of one character.
3 Students read aloud in character.
4 Students then swap roles and read again while you walk around listening, correcting and helping.

Teaching objective
To increase the number of meaningful exchanges between the students.

Variation
Change the topic and the steps which, in turn, will change the level of challenge and other features of the activity. For example, you and/or the students could choose a human relations problem. Some examples could be: feelings when you're not chosen for a team, feelings when you're not asked on an outing by a friend, the temptation to shoplift, relationships between a class and an over-strict or over-lax teacher.

1 Work with the class to generate a story line and to identify and flesh out some characters.
2 Discuss and note possible dialogue exchanges.
3 Pairs or small groups role play the situation.
4 Discuss the language, content and the empathy gained by students with the character they role played.
5 Students change roles and have the chance to gain empathy with a different character.
6 Have a final discussion about what can be done in situations of the type chosen. In this discussion students need to be 'out of role' and thus in a genuine problem-solving rather than adversarial mood.

A **Checking homework around the class**

Conventional version
The teacher calls on students one by one, round the class, to read out their answers to exercises set for homework.

Teaching objective 1
To prevent students from mentally 'switching off' until it's their turn to answer.

Variation
Change the steps and the students' roles. Call on the first student, but then after they've answered, ask them to nominate the next student, and so on, so that students are nominating each other. This way they'll have less idea of when their turn is coming and so will stay more involved.

Teaching objective 2
To encourage autonomous thinking and self-checking.

Variation
Change the organisation of people and the steps by asking students to work in groups to decide what the right answers were. They only ask you if they have doubts or disagreements.

A   Filling in gaps in a cloze text

Conventional version
1 Choose a text and blank out one word in about every six so that the text is regularly gapped.
2 Students read the text all the way through once.
3 Students, alone or in pairs, try to fill in the gaps.
4 Students' answers are checked in plenary with discussion on why alternative choices are or aren't possible for reasons of collocation, word class, tense, etc.

Teaching objective
To give your students confidence in their ability to choose good collocations.

Variation
Change the materials, the goal of the exercise, the steps and the correction policy.

1 Choose a text and blank out words such as adjectives and adverbs which could be replaced by many other words of the same type. For example, in the phrase 'The .... woman looked around', the gap could be filled by: old, young, pleasant, peasant, rich, irritated, Spanish, laughing, etc.
2 Students read the whole text through.
3 Discuss the first gap so students can see that there are many possible alternatives for filling it.
4 Suggest that the students fill the gaps firstly to make the story as pleasant as possible and then a second time to make it as *un*pleasant as possible (or any other choices, e.g. formal/informal, vague/concrete).

5 Students try to fill the gaps accordingly, using dictionaries if they wish.
6 Students swap ideas in pairs.
7 Check students' attempts by discussing why some choices for filling the gaps are more or less appropriate than others, for reasons of collocation, word class, overall tone and register, etc.

A Student presentations

Conventional version
1 Each student is given time to prepare a topic and possibly write it down.
2 Each student talks for a pre-arranged amount of time to the rest of the class about their topic.

Teaching objective
To encourage students' concentration. Perhaps the quality of work that individual students have produced for this activity has been good, but you've noticed that while one student is presenting the others aren't really listening.

Variation
Change the steps and the students' and teacher's role so that students are more involved with the talks and are also graded on their participation throughout.

1 Each student writes their name at the top of a piece of paper and also the title of something they know about, e.g. 'Breeding rabbits' or 'Playing hockey' or 'How to win on the world stock market'.
2 Each sheet of paper is now passed to a different student who writes questions they'd like to know the answers to, e.g. 'Why do you breed rabbits? Do you kill them? Do you have names for them?'
3 The papers are passed around until students have had a chance to write questions on most of the sheets of paper.
4 Students then get their own sheet of paper back with lots of questions on.
5 Students have time to prepare a talk on their chosen topic, incorporating answers to as many questions as they wish and in any order they feel is logical.
6 Students give their talks.
7 Class members listen and then ask further questions. You listen too, offering comments and asking questions, and also grading the talks themselves and the participation of the rest of the class in writing interesting questions and asking further questions after the talks.

A Memorising

Conventional version

1 Give students some time in class or for homework to memorise some new language, for example, a list of new words.
2 Test students on the material and give them marks.

Teaching objective

To encourage cooperation. Perhaps it's been decided that cooperation should be encouraged in class more than competition.

Variation

The goals have been changed, so you can change the organisation of people and the steps.

1 After students have met some new language, put them into mixed ability groups of equal numbers.
2 Give students time in class to memorise the new material. Tell them that when they are tested, their individual marks will be totalled and they will be given an average group mark. This is gained by dividing the total by the number of students in the group. Here's an example for one group:

Student A gets 10 correct
Student B gets 8 correct
Student C gets 6 correct
Student D gets 7 correct
Student E gets 3 correct
———————————————
Group total = 34
Average score = 6.8

This average score is taken as the recorded score for each individual in the group. Thus Students A and E will both have the recorded score of 6.8. Once the students understand the scoring system, each group will work very hard to make sure that the scores of all group members are as high as possible.
3 The students are tested on the material and the scores are worked out as above.

6.6 Conclusion

If you've ever asked yourself 'What activities can I do in class?' I hope you'll feel, after reading this chapter, that you don't need to worry as there's plenty you can do. You can start from just a bank of a few very traditional activities that you have learned, perhaps from your own days as a student of a foreign language. Then, once you've thought about your students, setting and personal style, you can change a feature or two. You'll choose to change the features of a particular activity for different reasons. Perhaps the activity you know only works in a large classroom or with elementary or very motivated students or takes too much preparation time. You'll want to change those features so that you can use a variation of the activity in your own setting and circumstances. Every time you change some features of an activity, the goals, cognitive processes and other features usually change too in dynamic and organic ways.

CHAPTER 6: HOW CAN WE VARY THE ACTIVITIES WE DO?

7 Getting down to the preparation

7.1 Introduction

In the book so far I've looked at some important issues to consider before you teach. In this chapter I'll focus on getting down to course and lesson planning.

First of all, I'll look at a broad definition of planning because I don't believe it necessarily means the kind of detailed writing exercise that perhaps first springs to mind. Next, I'll consider the advantages and disadvantages of planning ahead for our teaching. I'll consider who you can plan with and when. Next, since many teachers are trained to feel that they should start from a consideration of aims when planning, I'll look at whether this is a wise or normal thing to do! I'll look at the 'starting from aims' view and at the 'starting from different angles' view and see how these two differ. The next section will be on types of plans, their general headings and styles. Planning doesn't just happen before classes, so there will be a section on things you can do during and after lessons too. To encompass all these planning options I'll introduce a model for lesson and course planning which I call the design model.

7.2 What is 'planning'?

By course and lesson 'planning', I don't necessarily mean writing pages of notes for scrutiny by someone else. That is a view of planning we can have if at some point in our teaching lives we have taken a course where such documentation was required and assessed by examiners. In this book I've taken a broader definition that represents the sort of mental image a working teacher might have. By 'planning' here then, I mean everything a teacher does when she SAYS she is planning! For example, listening to students, remembering, visualising, noting things down, flicking through magazines, rehearsing, or drinking tea while staring into space and deciding.

Why would we want to plan courses and lessons?

There are a number of reasons why we would want to plan our courses and lessons, including the following:

- Thinking things through before you teach helps to reduce feelings of uncertainty or panic and inspires you instead with a sense of confidence and clarity.
- It can inspire confidence in students who pick up a feeling of purpose, progression and coherence.
- It helps you to understand what research you need to do.
- It reminds you to marshal materials beforehand, and makes it easier for you to organise the time and activity flow in classes.
- If at least some of the planning is shared with students, they too will be able to gather their thoughts before class.
- Plans can be used in lessons to get things started, and prompt memory, and can help us to answer student questions.
- Working on planning *after* lessons, as well as before, ensures that the class you are teaching gets a balanced mixture of different kinds of materials, content and interaction types throughout the course.
- Course and lesson planning help you to develop a personal style since they involve sifting through all your information, resources and beliefs, and boiling them all down to a distillation for one particular group, time and place. This distillation, together with what happens in the classroom, represents a cross-section of the present state of your art!

Why would we not want to plan courses and lessons?

Despite its general usefulness, planning does have its drawbacks, including these:

- Thinking about your lessons and courses too far ahead and in too much detail can be a waste of time. This is because things change once you get settled into a course. Things you prepared earlier can turn out to be irrelevant or unsuitable.
- Planning in too much detail can also cause inflexibility in a programme, crippling the teacher's ability to respond to students. An 'I've prepared it now so I'm jolly well going to teach it' mood can set in!
- If the planning is written down for an observer or examiner who has set ideas about what should be covered and how, rather than an understanding of the language students or the teacher's development,

the result is a display lesson with attached documentation rather than a learning event prompted by a useful working document. Planning and writing lesson plans in this case is really being done for the wrong people, for outsiders and not for the learners.

Overall, however, when I think of all the hundreds of teachers I have known, if we take the broad definition of planning above, I can't think of a single teacher who doesn't plan at least a little, on the bus, in the bath, when walking the kids to school, during coffee breaks or in class. Most teachers take planning to be an integral part of the job and do it for individual lessons and for courses.

As for me, I do plan my lessons and courses. Before a course starts I write lists of things I could possibly include and sort them into sequences and groups. At the beginning of a course I want to make sure that the students get the message that it's OK to support each other. I'm keen to set up an interesting working atmosphere and I want to have my attention free to really listen to students. I thus plan in some detail. I gather all my materials the day before if I can, as I hate feeling rushed just before the lesson.

Once a course has started and people are working together well, with threads beginning to run from lesson to lesson and more content coming from the students themselves, I feel I can afford to sketch plans more lightly. I am happy to let students take me away from my plan. But it only takes one or two dull lessons or a couple of students looking bored and I'm back to detailed planning again! After every few lessons I think about how things are going. If I find I'm down a bit of a cul de sac, I start off in a new direction.

Who can you do your planning with?

On some pre-service courses, groups of teachers are encouraged to do their course and lesson planning together. It seems that, as with everything else in life, some people are loners and prefer to work on their own and others feel that two or more heads are better than one. The options, theoretically, are to plan alone, with the teacher you share the class with, with other colleagues including more experienced ones such as mentors, with students, or with friends and family members who have nothing much to do with your job. If you're sharing a class with a colleague, you need to plan at least a course outline together. Not to do so would be like playing a doubles tennis match with a blindfold on. Students would have to put up with the classroom equivalent of receiving two serves at a time or watching shots fall between you. If you're not sharing a class, it can still sometimes be a great help to talk a lesson through with someone else. They probably won't be terribly interested but can often restart you when you're stuck just by uttering a chance phrase or idea. If you're lucky enough to work in a friendly staffroom, you'll be used to people calling out things like 'Anybody know a study skills book that deals with book surveys?' There's usually a pause for a while but then some helpful soul will come up with a tip. It's all part of being a good colleague.

When can you plan your courses and lessons?

Most teachers will put some thought into a course before they teach it and once they have found out a little about the students, what they want or need and the time available for classes. Beverly Langsch-Brown, likes to make a course outline (see Langsch-Brown 1998). The course outline that makes sense in her situation usually covers 10–20 lessons and culminates at a holiday period or achievement of a learning goal. The goals can be externally set by, for example, the date of an exam or may coincide with the completion of a topic or a unit in the coursebook. A simple example follows. In real life this one was also supplemented by staff lists stating who was to teach when, materials files and lists of daily homework assignments.

COURSEWORK		
WEEK 1 Sept 4–8th	M T W T F	Group formation. Information re course. Library tour. Sample each of 4 exam papers. Set up systems. Working on the oral paper. Working on the reading paper. Tutorials. Reading laboratory.
WEEK 2 Sept 11–15th	M T W T F	Working on the writing paper. Working on the listening paper. Studio day. Discuss/write up the Studio day. Library. Tutorials. Group presentations.
WEEK 3 Sept 18–22nd	M T W T F	Reading and writing prep. Oral and listening prep. Mock exam. Studio day. Tutorials. Write up Studio day. Library.
WEEK 4 Sept 25–29th	M T W T F	Working on subject specific dictionaries. Optional guided study. THE EXAM ! Producing learning portfolios in studio space. Present portfolios. Party !

(See staff list, materials list, homework task lists.)

A FOUR-WEEK PRE-COLLEGE EXAM PREPARATION COURSE OUTLINE

A distinction is made by Julia Vogel, between 'instant' and 'constant' planning and preparation (see Vogel 1998). Instant preparation is the type you do in a lesson while you are teaching. An idea comes to you and you note it down quickly for later. Constant preparation is the kind that happens all the time in life, while you are reading the paper or washing up, without your necessarily being aware of it. Then of course there's the kind we do when we think, 'OK, I'd better think about that class now!' This is 'advance planning'. I won't deal much with instant or constant preparation, the more intuitive types of planning. Where I can be of more use is, I think, with the advance planning.

7.3 Specifying objectives

Perhaps you have been trained to think you must start your planning from a specified aim or objective such as 'By the end of the lesson the students will be able to make a phone call to a travel agent asking for dates and times of flights and be able to understand and write down the replies.' You may have been taught that only after this should you think about the material, activities, grouping possibilities and so on. Perhaps you've been taught to write 'Aim' at the top of your lesson notes and headings such as 'Steps' or 'Materials' below. Perhaps your teaching, in the past, has been assessed on this type of thing. If so, then we need to consider the matter of specifying objectives right away. Let's look at terms first.

There are a lot of possible terms we can use here, e.g. 'goal', 'aim' and 'objective'. Different people use these terms in different ways. Roughly speaking, most people think 'goals' tend to be broader, then come 'aims' and finally, the narrowest in focus, 'objectives'. People do, however, talk about broad, specific and detailed goals, aims and objectives. Let's look at a couple of examples. A very broad goal would be 'to improve their English'. Another broad goal might be the name of a course, 'Improve your conversation skills'. Try substituting 'aims' or 'objectives' in those last two sentences, however, and you will see that they sound just fine too! Rather than worrying about this, I'll take the word 'goal' from now on.

It is of course possible to set goals before you teach. Some people I've talked to who set goals at some point in the planning and teaching process are happy with a formula that goes something like 'By a particular time, I hope the students will be able to do X, in setting Y, and to Z degree of competence.' Most teachers would like to add, 'I'll divide the time thus and use this or that material and activity.'

Many teachers, however, first concentrate on materials and activities, crafting useful, interesting lessons without thinking too much about goals first. After teaching they may reflect on what happened in the lesson and thus draw conclusions about what goals the students have achieved. The many teachers who start from materials, topics or tasks, would probably say something like 'This week I'm going to use material M, topics T and activities A' and then, when asked why, would be able to say 'Because I want the students to be able to ...' in reply. If you ask a teacher why they chose to use a particular activity or piece of material, detailed linguistic and other objectives will be uncovered. But, at a certain point, the conversation will tend to flip into a discussion of beliefs and assumptions. Because of the way we are and the values, attitudes and knowledge we have, we see certain things as valuable to work towards and have our preferred ways and means of getting there.

The traditional view

In this view a teacher may feel that language is an 'out there' subject, like historical dates or mathematical equations, that has to be learnt about or memorised by students, or that language is a set of trainable skills that need lots of mechanical practice. If you feel that language learning and teaching are like this, then when you plan you may well tend to ask the following questions: 'Where do I want my students to go? How will I get them there? Will my route map coincide with reality? How will I know if we've arrived?' Put another way, you will want to find out what your students can do, specify broad and detailed goals, break these down into a 'logical' order, select learning activities and materials which are designed to bring about change, put these in place, and then test to make sure that the changes have occurred. This is the view of language and learning presented on many assessed training courses, which is understandable since working with teachers this way makes assessment of their work easier! The problems with this view are that students may have objectives of their own, language may not be this kind of subject matter, the value of unintended outcomes may be discounted, and the planning may lead to inflexibility. However, if students and other stakeholders are also allowed to initiate and contribute to the plans and if the plans are treated as 'roads to travel rather than terminal points' (Taba, p. 62 in Cohen and Manion 1989), then this kind of planning is perfectly viable. At the level of the individual lesson, this is what this kind of planning looks like.

LESSON PLAN EXTRACT
Students at present write their ideas about one topic in single sentences using a new line for each sentence. They also include sentences that are irrelevant to the topic.

Broad goal
To have students write a paragraph that looks and reads as a paragraph should.

Detailed goals
- Students to indent the first line of a paragraph.
- Students to start new sentences just after the previous sentence ends.
- Students to put all sentences on a similar topic together and recognise as irrelevant sentences on different topics.

Activities
1 Guessing game: Look at figs below. Guess and discuss differences.

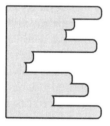 

BAD AND GOOD PARAGRAPHS

2 Students, in pairs, receive sentences on slips of paper. The sentences relate to two different but closely related topics. Students sort the sentences, first into two groups according to topic, and then into a logical order. Student A writes a paragraph using one group of sentences. Student B does the same with the other group. Students swap and compare each other's work with the figures above.
3 Individual students look back through old homework and rewrite any 'paragraphs' I've marked with an asterisk because they're incorrectly laid out or contain irrelevant sentences.

The 'starting from different angles' view

Specifying testable, short-term goals and then creating step-by-step procedures for moving students towards these objectives is NOT the way many teachers instinctively work. Many teachers use a different component of the teaching–learning encounter first, whether materials or activities or something else, to get them started and as a trigger for ideas. This may be because they view language and learning more organically. You too may feel language learning is a slow process that happens gradually as perception shifts, as knowledge and skill slowly improve and are refined. You may accept that students often plateau for long periods and seem to have an internal, natural syllabus that moves things at a different pace from your own. You may feel that the most important thing is to get students motivated, keep them interested and do something worthwhile in class. You may well feel that, if this is achieved, learning will inevitably happen. If so, you may make 'plans looking for a goal' (Woods 1996, p. 173). Many teachers work this way. When asked about their goals and aims, they can give reasonable and full answers in retrospect, after a class or course has finished, but would not choose to do this beforehand. Some of the many experienced and competent teachers who work this way feel a little guilty about it since it is often not what they were trained to think was the right way of working. It is not the traditional model. There is, however, absolutely no reason to feel guilty about working in this more natural way, as long as this kind of ongoing planning, with aims and rationale considered during or after lessons, is not used as an excuse for not thinking things through or not involving students. If you work this way, you'll come at your planning from different angles on different days. In the book so far, we've looked at different angles: the students, the timing, generative frameworks, different sorts of content, how people learn and teach, and teaching materials and activities. We have built lessons and sets of lessons from a different starting point in each chapter. Let's have another look at these different triggers. The following sections relate to lesson planning. This will give us a shared vocabulary with which to discuss course planning later in the chapter.

The students

In Chapter 1 we took the students as the starting point for planning parts of first and later lessons, finding sequences of activities that enabled us to find out more about our participants. If you're the sort of teacher who asks 'Who are they and what are they like?' when taking on a new group, you'll find Chapter 1 and this starting point useful. The students are a logical place to start since the more we can use students' own ideas and requests as our starting point the more relevant and motivating classes can be for them.

EXTRACT FROM A STUDENT-CENTRED LESSON PLAN

Students will have just come from a swimming lesson and will straggle in so ...

1 Early birds finish their dialogue journals.
2 When everybody's in and settled, Carmela's group asks the others their review questions on the last lesson.
3 Pairs brainstorm all the words associated with the topic they've chosen for this lesson.
4 Student on poster duty writes them up asking for help with spelling, stress marking, collocation and meaning, if unsure.
5 Give student on cassette recorder duty the cassette of two people discussing the topic. The class says when the student should stop, rewind, play the tape, etc.

Time

In Chapter 2 we took time as our starting point for planning lessons and looked at the basic chronological unit of a beginning, a middle and an end, plus generative ways of filling in the spaces in between. If you're conscious of time and often ask 'How long are the classes and how many weeks have we got?' then this will be a major way of structuring your thoughts. You may jot down the start time, finish time, rough timings for activities and so on, as in the lesson notes below.

EXTRACT FROM TIME-CONSCIOUS LESSON NOTES

Thursday, 2–3 pm

1 What can they remember re political correctness (PC) language from last time? (5mins)
2 I dictate ten PC terms. They write down the blunt versions, e.g. Me: *vertically challenged*; SS: *short* (5mins)
3 Allow time for questions, productive examples and reteaching if necessary. (10mins)
4 Check what they wrote in cartoon bubbles for homework and finish last picture strip in pairs. (15mins 2.40 pm?)

Start coursebook pp. 43–5 in class. If no time, set p. 43 for homework.

Generative activity frameworks

In Chapter 2 we took generative frameworks such as threads, stimulus-based lessons and Maley's short and sweet ideas, and saw how they could be applied to any content area or piece of material, providing you with an endless supply of lesson ideas. As you can use that chapter as a starting point once you know what material you are going to use, I haven't supplied an example here. You can also use Chapter 6 to help you adapt traditional activities for your lessons.

Content

In Chapter 3 we took perceptions of what there is to put into a language lesson as the starting point for planning. The trigger here is not just thinking 'What have they done already?', 'What do I normally teach?' or 'What is in the textbook?', but also considering the students' perceptions of what there is to learn and what you or the coursebook usually leave out!

EXTRACT FROM A CONTENT-BASED LESSON PLAN

Language area: hesitation and stalling devices

- Ask a couple of students some hard, fast questions in target language. Wait for slight embarrassment and pauses.
- Be reassuring! Switch to mother tongue and do same again, then asking what sorts of noises, phrases, etc. students would use in mother tongue if put in the spotlight in this way.
- Explain that today's lesson will be about what to say and do in the target language when you don't know what to say and do.
- Ask students to prepare some questions for me that they think I won't know how to/want to answer.
- Students shoot questions at me. I field them. This activity is called the 'Hot seat game'.
- Students repeat back to me as many of my phrases as poss.
- Oral practice and written phase.
- Hot seat game played twice more, with a student in the hot seat instead of the teacher.
- Explain hot seat will be a 5 min thread in future classes.

How people learn

In Chapter 3 we looked at the sorts of things people need to do in order to be able to learn. If this interests you, you'll want to make sure your lessons contain chances for students to meet new language, notice things about it, remember it and use and refine it. These four could form headings for lesson notes as below.

EXTRACT FROM LESSON NOTES FOR A SATURDAY MORNING BUSINESS CLASS

<u>New language</u> useful for a SWOT analysis. A SWOT analysis is when you think about your company (or department or product) in terms of its Strengths, Weaknesses, Opportunities and Threats from, say, its competitors outside the company. You can then give a presentation about your product to a group, based on the SWOT analysis.

<u>Meet</u> the new language:
- Students pool what they know
- I start a SWOT of my school

<u>Notice</u> things about the language:
- Draw students' attention to similar forms and stress
- Formal and informal alternatives
- Importance of varying the phrases and of eye contact, voice volume, presence, etc.

<u>Remember</u> it:
- Standardising by shadowing me in different voices
- Write down with stress marks, etc.
- One minute silent memorisation time
- Pair practice saying alternate phrases

<u>Use and refine</u> it:
- I give them an object each; they prepare a SWOT analysis
- Each student performs in front of the others
- Group assessment. Points for improvement?

How teaching can be handled

In Chapter 4 we looked at some of the ways of working in the classroom. We saw how you can set up activities so that students can find out

190

for themselves, have things made plain to them or absorb them via periphery learning. You can use Chapter 4 in conjunction with Chapter 3 as a starting point for planning lessons since it contains common instructional sequences applicable to any content you or your students choose.

Materials

Materials have been implied in every chapter so far, for example, letters and questionnaires in Chapter 1, texts and interactive dialogue journals in Chapter 2. But materials can be the starting point for planning as well. Many teachers will find a poem, a page or even a seashell and this will spark off ideas for whole units and projects as well as individual lessons. This was the approach we saw in the stimulus-based lesson in Chapter 2. In Chapter 5 we looked at an important teacher resource, the coursebook. Coursebooks are used by many teachers as jumping off points in planning courses and lessons too.

EXTRACT FROM LESSON NOTES BASED ON MATERIALS

NB Take in magnets!!

1 Write poem up on board in 'dash' form, e.g.

— — — — —
— — — — —
— — —
— — — — —
— — — — —
— — — —

> **London Airport**
>
> Last night in London Airport
> I saw a wooden bin
> labelled UNWANTED LITERATURE
> IS TO BE PLACED HEREIN.
> So I wrote a poem
> and popped it in.
>
> Christopher Logue

2 Elicit words from students using mime, pictures, sound, etc. and write up until poem complete. Provide simple grammatical items like 'a', 'the', etc. quickly if students don't get them right away.
3 Discuss any problem words.
4 Discuss possible meanings.
5 Students in pairs say alternate lines to each other two or three times while I rub out occasional words from board until all words have gone but dashes remain.
6 Students write the poem from memory and we check.

7.4 What happens once you get some starting points

The starting points for lesson planning described above are the practical, everyday, realistic starting points for most working teachers. It's not usually a discussion of the theory of planning or a detailed consideration of goals, aims and objectives that enables people to start thinking about their next course or class. It's more often looking in the coursebook, coming across a nice piece of material or listening to a student request. Above I've written up the different bases or triggers for lesson plans separately. In real life, of course, our lesson plans often come from an amalgam of starting points, though our own personality may well determine which bases tend to be more dominant and which less. Before starting a course or around the time you first meet the students you might like to brainstorm ideas you can use with them, whether these are materials, activities, different types of content or different skills. Don't worry about what kind of idea it is. Don't think you MUST start with aims or content or timings. Just get some ideas down on paper to start you off.

After that, try deliberately using different starting points at different times before individual sections of work. I'd also recommend that you don't feel guilty about it! You will still know why you are doing things and will still have goals. You may well have a map in your head of all the components of the language learning and teaching classroom and tend to plan as you go along, with different starting points on different days, rather than setting out with extremely clear ideas about where you want to get to in a course. You start the teaching and learning first and you worry about the phases you've been through and the balancing up later on. Only in retrospect can you really understand a course and why you made the decisions you did. As Devon Woods says, 'The course is the trail made by the decisions that were taken' (Woods 1996).

We've seen that different elements of learning and teaching are likely to spark you off in your lesson planning. I'd like to consider now what you do once you've got some starting points. If you think of these starting points as making up a pack of 'cards', how are you going to play them in the game of course planning? You have things you want to do with students, things like listening to a story, writing an e-mail message, practising some vocabulary, exploring ways of talking about the past. These are your 'cards'. Are you going to play each card once and consider it done? Play it several times during a course? These are the sorts of decisions I'll look at next.

Building courses, playing your course cards

Laying down one card, or the one card trick

Here you plan one lesson at a time as a one-off block. In some circumstances there is little continuity possible between different lessons in a course, for example, in shared classes when you cannot liaise with the other teacher, in classes where different people come each time, in 'courses' where classes are held at extremely long intervals, or when you are substituting for a teacher who is ill and has left you no notes. In these cases it is probably easiest to plan one-off classes that can stand on their own. If you are a novice teacher, spending an enormous amount of time planning exactly what you will do and say in a class, you'll often find that lesson by lesson planning is all that you can manage at first.

In these cases, any starting point or combination of starting points could be used for individual, discrete classes and almost no attempt made to connect the classes. If you share a class with someone you rarely see, you can divide up components and topics between you at an early meeting and then work on them bit by bit in discrete blocks. This way of playing the cards means they are simply laid down one after the other on the table. The disadvantage is that students who manage to attend regularly may feel a lack of continuity. Of course it is extremely hard in reality to keep everything discrete. Long stories tend to need finishing in the next lesson, words need reviewing, and so on. But one-offs are a useful option for the circumstances mentioned above. All the lessons described earlier, except for the ones using the threads framework, could be used as 'one-offs'.

Playing similar sorts of cards

Here you teach similar sorts of lessons each time you meet a class. In most settings there *is* a connection between different lessons. Lessons are not seen as one-off blocks but as exchanges in a conversation between learners and teachers. There is time to get into a rhythm and routine. You have a choice here of what exactly you are repeating. You can repeat student groupings, for example, doing a lot of trio work, or repeat channels, always including plenty of visuals, or repeat activity types, always having, for example, a dictation at some point in the lesson. You can repeat the same method over and over again, always having the same chronological structure, say a warm-up and filler in every class. Most teachers have elements of repetition in their teaching. I personally like some elements of routine in my work. I like to start language classes with background music and review questions (see page 51). Routines free you up from worrying about classroom mechanics and allow you time to consider higher order concerns such as how much people are learning. To return to our card metaphor, in this way of playing the cards laid down on the table are, say, always clubs.

Heart, club, diamond, heart, club, diamond

This way of working involves rotating your starting points and so avoiding the rhythm and routine described above. If you are the only teacher of the class and you have them often or for long periods, you will need to vary things. You can rotate content types, sometimes working on discourse, sometimes lexical phrases, sometimes situations. You can rotate ways of working, sometimes using an experiential encounter, sometimes telling students directly what you want them to focus on or sometimes using a 'test, teach, test' lesson model and sometimes a task-based model. You can have a series of things you and the students like to do and work through them from beginning to end before starting again at the beginning. If you share the class, once you know your colleague's normal routine, you can make sure you don't duplicate and also make sure that your rotations are complementary from the students' point of view. In this way of playing the course cards, you lay down on the table a club one day, a heart the next, then a diamond and then a spade. You then go back to clubs again. You may like to work with a large number of cards and keep rotating them. I have a colleague who likes to work with two or three main cards. His rotation goes like this:

> Day 1: Presentation and practice of a language item. Break. Pre-, in-, post-receptive skills slot.
> Day 2: Review, practice and production of the language item from Day 1. Break. Short productive skills slot.
> Day 3: As Day 1.
> Day 4: As Day 2.
> Day 5: Weekly review. Discussion of weekend task. Song or story.

The presentation is of a different type of language item each time, that is, some vocabulary one day, an exponent or two in a functional area two days later. To ensure variety, the skills slot is devoted to a different skill each day.

One of spades, one of hearts, one of clubs

Here we make connections across several lessons rather than within one lesson. In Chapter 2 we discussed this idea of threads, that is, the gradual introduction, revision and extension of ideas over a series of lessons (see page 55). Threads are an excellent way of working with groups composed of some students who get bored easily and some who like review. A threads approach to a series of lessons would mean having, at any one time, perhaps four or five different types of content running side by side in a lesson. See the notes below for a week of 'three thread' lessons.

LESSON NOTES

Threads	MONDAY	TUESDAY	WEDNESDAY	THURSDAY	FRIDAY
Animals vocabulary thread (10 mins each time)	Parts of cat's body	Review + cat verbs	Review + cat metaphors	Review and start fish vocab	Review and start fish verbs
Tenses thread (30 mins each time)	Regular past simple first person	Review + all persons	Review + negatives	Review + some irregulars	Review and start 'Did you ...?' questions
Reading thread (20 mins each time)	Introduction of graded reader	First two pages + comp. questions	Review and Chap. 1	Study of past forms in Chap. 1	Oral summary of Chap. 1 + vocab in notebooks

This way of playing is like laying down spades first in a lesson, and, over a series of lessons playing the one, two and three of spades. The hearts represent the second thread in a lesson and again will be played one, two, three over a series of lessons. Of course you've no obligation to proceed at exactly the same pace with each thread or to start all the threads in the same lesson. You'll start one or two threads, then later on start one or two more. If people get bored with a particular thread you drop it and replace it with another. So any lesson could contain, say, the one of spades followed by the six of clubs, followed by the eight of diamonds.

Building a pack of cards

Here you break the content into little bits and build up very carefully over time. You never teach something new unless the ground has been prepared beforehand. The last thing has to be firm in your students' minds before the next thing is started.

The building a house metaphor has been the mainstay of general education syllabuses for years. Progression through a course is equated with stacking identically sized units on top of each other in a certain order. The order is determined in advance by the relative ease with which items can be learned, their formal complexity and relative usefulness. Although the building block metaphor seems neat and logical, it has proved difficult to break a whole language into tiny bits. Teachers and students who use this approach regularly can also become fearful when asked to skip stages and work with long stretches of language or roughly tuned input. In my own work I prefer to think of the 'building' you end up with as referring to a class newspaper, a school play, or other educational project that involves talking and planning, recording and editing and an intense flurry of activity towards the end when there is a finished product.

Face down concentration

This review technique can be used as a component of any lesson or course. In a series of lessons, make sure that material covered is brought back for students to consider and use again in different settings, skills, registers and role relationships. Revisiting material means that you and students have to keep records of what has come up and have to be organised about allowing time to review. Constant cyclical review is very popular with students who have a fear of forgetting and who like to get one thing straight before going on with another. Some students, however, find it tedious to go over old ground again and again. They need the stimulus of lots of new material. These are students who can cope with the feeling that they don't know everything perfectly.

Review is like playing some cards this lesson and then in the next lesson laying those same cards face down and asking people if they can remember what's on the cards and which card is where. If they can, you play some new cards face up.

So, to recap, we've mentally put all our teaching points on cards and we have considered the different ways we can play them – one by one or in repetitive combinations, etc. It's unlikely in reality that you will choose one type of playing style. Depending on the situations I've mentioned above, for example, substituting at short notice for a colleague who leaves no notes or working on a school play, you will use different ways of working. Most teachers have their favourite combinations though. (See also Woodward 1991.)

Once you've decided on one or more playing patterns, you may want to record your decisions somehow. Every teacher seems to need to write out their syllabus or timetable in a different way and very few teachers can make head or tail of each other's! Some people prefer grids with vertical columns (see page 183), others prefer horizontal lines, circles, lists, mind maps or flowcharts. (See Graves 2000 for examples of mind maps pp. 61, 62, 64, and flowcharts pp. 67–9. See also Buzan 1995a.) The important thing is to have a system that works for you. I'll say more about this below.

7.5 Before individual lessons

We looked earlier at what starting points can be used to generate course ideas and some different ways of working with those course ideas. I'd now like to look at the sorts of things we can do before individual lessons. I'll look at the zero option, writing different types of lesson notes and visualisation.

The zero option

This is when you walk into class with some ideas in your head but having written nothing down at all. You may have to do this at some time if there's been a disaster in the school. You may even choose to do it when you're really experienced just to see how you manage when forced to work totally from memory. There are also times with small, high level, highly motivated classes when you never have the chance to use your written notes or plans because the students have so much they want to work on. They bombard you with questions or comments from the moment you get in the door. Groups I've had like this have been composed of, for example, Swedish politicians, Berlin policemen and international groups of teacher trainers. I have to say though that I still had some written notes when I went in, even if they were just the unused ones from the day before! I would strongly recommend writing lesson notes, however brief, for the reasons below.

Writing lesson notes

Although you can make your lesson notes mentally, many teachers, whether novice or experienced do write them down. The act of writing or typing helps many to organise their thinking. The physical act and the sight of the page mean that you've usually partly memorised your lesson steps by the time you've finished writing. If you're a novice teacher, doing this a few times with the same instructional sequences will help you to remember them. Clarifying your thoughts by writing them down means students are less likely to get confusing or incoherent messages!

One important thing to remember is that no teacher writes absolutely everything down. We also all differ in how much we actually refer to our lesson notes while teaching. Writing a complete 'movie script' would not only be very time consuming, it would also lead to you clutching your 'lines', reading them out loud in class and being unable to respond to real events. It's better to have a working document visible from a couple of feet away that can act as a prompt which you can refer to while working. Let's look at the different types of notes about lessons and courses you can make.

Different sorts of notes

Preliminary background notes
If you want to get straight in your own mind what you know about the context of the course or lesson you're going to teach, you might like to use preliminary background notes. Some possible headings for these are:

What do I know about the students?

Goals and expectations (from the course name/adverts, students, other stakeholders, syllabus, exam, etc.)

Timing (length of course, frequency of classes, time of day, length, built in gaps or holidays)

Work context (rules, room size, acoustics, heat, light, etc.)

Materials I can draw on

After you've taught the class for a while, you will internalise these background points and take them for granted. When starting out, however, it doesn't hurt to write them down.

Starter notes
You wouldn't expect your language students to be perfect first time if they write something for you, so give yourself too an understanding start

with your lesson plans. Start with a few headings that make sense to you and build up gradually to fuller 'better' plans. I mean better in respect of degree of detail and usefulness. The headings you choose for starter notes will echo your views on language and learning. Here's a skeleton plan as an offering but it can be changed to suit your own beliefs.

<u>S/S</u> (level, no., room   <u>Time</u>

    <u>Materials</u>

    <u>Steps</u>
    1
    2
    3

    <u>Homework</u>

    Main aims of classwork:
    Main aims of homework:

SKELETON STARTER NOTES

The Teacher's Book notes
You may plan to use a unit of the coursebook in a lesson and wish to follow the notes for it in the accompanying Teacher's Book. You may want to alter some activities to suit your class, and so your notes may look like this:

7 Getting down to the preparation

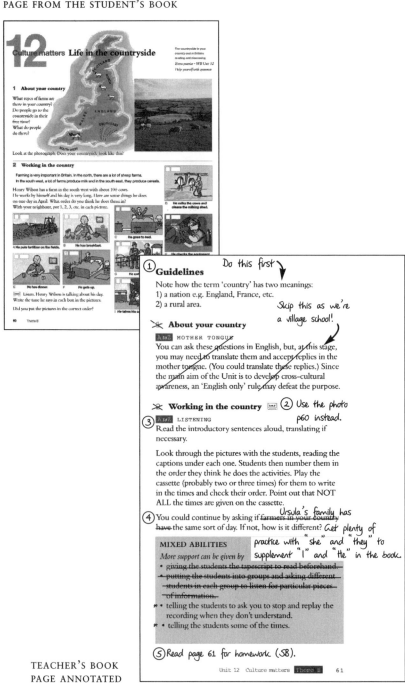

Who and what go where notes
If you're experimenting with different student groupings or with moving around more yourself, or are trying to get your boardwork more organised, you might want to make notes like these:

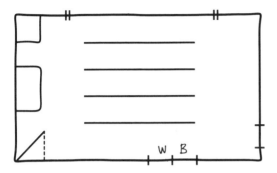

THE CLASSROOM

Ask S/S to brainstorm in pairs...   In fours to...

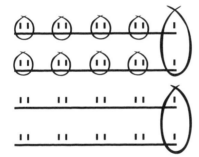 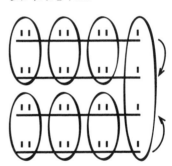

STUDENT GROUPINGS

Menu		Vocabulary
Homework		

BOARD LAYOUT

201

Building better lesson notes

By the time you've worked with a class a couple of times, you'll notice more about the students, the activities you plan and so on. If you're an inexperienced teacher, this may well lead you to use more headings and fuller lesson notes the next time you plan. If you're experienced, it'll probably mean you write shorter notes since there's much more you can take for granted.

Whether you write a lot or a little, the layout of your notes can do a lot to enhance their usefulness. Some people find that if they write things down in a linear way (that is in straight lines with one point under the other), before class, it makes it more difficult for them to adapt their ideas once in class. If you feel this way, then you may find that non-linear notes have more potential flexibility built in. Here's an example.

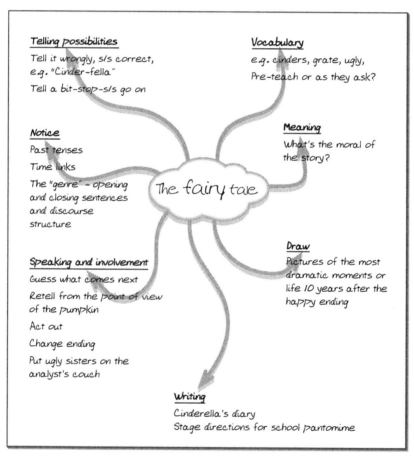

Telling possibilities
Tell it wrongly, s/s correct,
e.g. "Cinder-fella"
Tell a bit-stop-s/s go on

Vocabulary
e.g. cinders, grate, ugly,
Pre-teach or as they ask?

Notice
Past tenses
Time links
The "genre" - opening
and closing sentences
and discourse
structure

The fairy tale

Meaning
What's the moral of
the story?

Speaking and involvement
Guess what comes next
Retell from the point of view
of the pumpkin
Act out
Change ending
Put ugly sisters on the
analyst's couch

Draw
Pictures of the most
dramatic moments or
life 10 years after the
happy ending

Writing
Cinderella's diary
Stage directions for school pantomime

FLEXIBLE LESSON NOTES

In the central box you write the name of the main stimulus or starting point, e.g. 'page 13' or 'The fairy tale'. From the central box you draw rays or arrows pointing out in different directions. The arrows represent the various ways you could exploit the material. If you like the generative frameworks used in Chapter 2 then each arrow might say, for example, Meeting the stimulus, Analysis, Personalisation, etc. (see page 56). Each arrow is a possible path for you to take in the lesson. This type of notation means you are left free to decide which order to do things in. This may depend on how tired students are when you meet them or how you feel on the day.

Many other flexible planning systems exist. If you are lucky enough to teach near a stock of materials, all well-known and annotated by you and ready to go, you could select literally by finger tip as the lesson progressed. Your flexible lesson notes would be accompanied by a box of filed materials.

Teacher development notes
You may want to have a section that reminds you to think about your own personal and professional development. If so, you might like to use some of these headings:

> What am I going to try out this lesson? (perhaps new activities, materials or matters of personal style, e.g. sitting down more)

And headings after you've taught the lesson (see page 205):

> What problems did I hit?
> What can I try out next time?

If you have a specific problem with, say, clarity of instructional language or giving clear explanations you could plan your language carefully and write the sentences onto your lesson notes.

If you want to make your own notes into a useful working document for class, you can add diagrams, circles, colour, capitals, arrows, highlighting, key words and mind maps or write them on coloured paper or hand held cards. For a thorough explanation and examples of the kind of lesson notes you might write if working with a colleague on a new area of learning or teaching, see Joyce et al (1997, Chapter 12 and Appendix Two).

Lesson notes for when you are being observed
If you are being observed within a controlled programme, then you may well have to produce a lesson plan or notes according to a particular

format. It may be possible to have a section 'For the observer' where you write a request such as 'Please could you watch X and let me know afterwards what you think?' This way you can use the opportunity of having a new pair of eyes and ears in the classroom and may also feel slightly more involved in the observation from the control point of view than you otherwise might!

Visualising the class

Whatever kind of lesson notes you write, once you've written them and prepared the materials you'll need in class, here's an option for just before you teach. It's a mental rehearsal of your lesson. Many teachers do this naturally while planning anyway, but sports training has built on this uncontrived process and proposes it as a confidence booster, a way of training for flexibility and find that it actually improves performance. Here's how you can go about it. I'll give the short version first.

- Simply talk yourself (maybe not out loud if you're in company!) through your plan, visualising it actually happening in class. This will help you 'learn' it and spot any wildly over-ambitious steps.

Now for the slightly more detailed version.

1 Cover your notes or close your eyes and think your way through your lesson, mentally seeing the students react as you would like them to at various stages of the lesson.
2 Visualise the students again but this time try to see them doing different things either because they don't understand or are bored.
3 Spend some time thinking through what you will do if things don't go the way you want them to. This way you are less likely to be completely thrown when it happens in reality.

The advice here is for decision making to become part of your planning process. You will sometimes need to make decisions fast because they are actually planned into the lessons, e.g. with the menu style lesson start in Chapter 2. If you're a novice teacher or have a difficult class, I'd also suggest you think to yourself 'What will I be happy with?' By this, I mean you should ask yourself what as a minimum would make you feel you had achieved something by the end. For example, if you could just hold the students' attention for the instructions and have them complete tasks A and B, would you be reasonably satisfied with that? Keep your expectations low and set yourself the lowest target you'd feel happy with.

In-class ideas

If you allow students time to complete tasks or perhaps to do some reading and writing, then there is something useful you can do to stop yourself interrupting students unnecessarily. Have a quick look through your plan and note down:

> Anything ...
> which has turned out radically different in timing or effect
> which is left unfinished or has not been satisfactorily dealt with
> which you need to bring with you next time
> which students have asked questions about
> for another lesson that has been sparked by something in this one!

This kind of in-class work, plus the feelings you get as you watch students interacting with you, each other, the materials and activities, signals the beginning of your own evaluation of the lesson.

Immediately after class

Once you've come out of class, put your books down, and decided whether to have tea or coffee, you might want to do some of the following:

- Make some sort of record on your lesson notes of what actually happened, even if this just involves crossing off things that didn't happen, adding the extra things that came up and noting what went well or badly.
- Research the questions students asked in class and that you noted down.
- Write notes about any teacher development points you were working on.
- Decide what to do with your lesson notes and personal materials.

Your options for storage are to:

- Save everything for years, including extra copies of handouts, until your house is completely full and you have to have a bonfire.
- Annotate your lesson notes with little remarks such as 'Takes too long' or 'Very stimulating' and keep the best ideas and materials for when you reteach the course.
- Keep everything for a while and then periodically copy out and file good ideas and materials and discard the rest.
- Throw everything away immediately.

Personally, I recommend keeping records at least until the end of the course, and longer if you're going to do a similar course again soon. If you do this, you'll be able to do the balancing up (see below), which can also include checking what you've covered against expectations raised in '*Bartering*' at the start of the course (see page 30).

More ambitious ideas for later on

Keeping track

I like to keep a little exercise book for each class I teach. I put the name of the class on the front of it. I note down, while I'm in class or just after I leave, what I didn't have time to finish, what needs more work, things the students expressed interest in, any questions they asked that I didn't have time to answer or feelings I have about how the class went and why. I have the book by me when I'm reading their homework too so that general problem areas or information on students can be noted. This little notebook helps me with ideas for the next lesson and I find the system especially useful because I teach a lot of different classes in different places. It also means that by noting down what actually happened I have an informal, retrospective syllabus recorded.

Analysis of tapes

If you've made tapes of parts of your lessons, put them in a drawer for a while and then, when you've forgotten which one relates to which lesson, pull one out and listen to it. You can just listen and see what strikes you about your classroom encounter or you can set out deliberately to check some aspect of the lesson, for example, how long you waited after asking students questions and after receiving a student response. (See Woodward and Lindstromberg 1995 pp. 105–109 for more ideas on what to listen for.)

Ideas for balancing up

Whether or not you use a coursebook, once you've taught your class(es) for a while, you'll want to consider what you've been doing. However balanced a programme you've tried to plan, there's always a possibility that you've missed something out, over-stressed something, have changed your mind or have had it changed by student feedback. I suggest then, as a way of monitoring the balance of ingredients in your lessons, that you keep all your lesson notes, however tatty they look, for a while and periodically go through them. Think about the balance of activities and types of lessons from your point of view and from your students'. You can mark where individual lessons or phases of lessons fall along balancing scales such as the ones that follow.

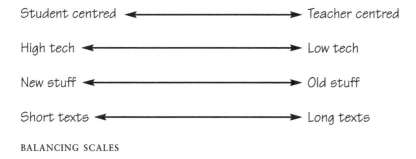

BALANCING SCALES

Of course, what you put at either end of a scale, will depend on you and your students' priorities and what you want to evaluate. Some things don't fit on scales and sit better in a list which you can tick items on, as follows.

Culture
Discourse
Topics
Vocabulary
Lexical phrases
Work on noun phrases
Work on verb phrases
Etc.

WHAT HAVE WE WORKED ON?

Again, you and your students will want to add your own items to the list.

Once you see where your marks are clustered on your balancing scales or which items in your checklist have been ticked most often, you will know what your main patterns are.

Variety stars

Once I've had a think about a sequence of lessons I've just taught and have considered any mid-course evaluation done or feedback collected, I like to get myself a brightly coloured sheet of paper and write on it things I want to remember to include from now on. My notes might look like this:

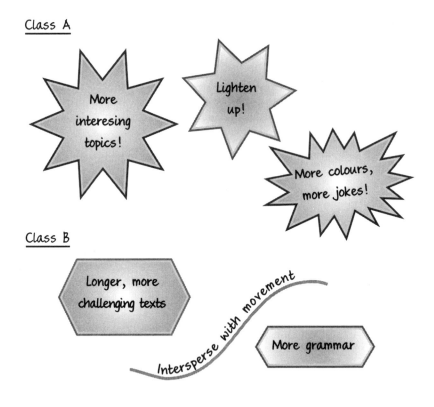

Class A

More interesing topics!

Lighten up!

More colours, more jokes!

Class B

Longer, more challenging texts

Intersperse with movement

More grammar

VARIETY STARS

The ideas above illustrate the way many teachers work. As well as running large-scale tests or evaluations on our planning and teaching, we often gather information and impressions as we go along and adjust accordingly. I'll say more about this below.

7.6 The design model for planning

This chapter has been about some of the starting points for concrete advance planning. Most teachers probably, at heart, consider that language is partly a skill that can be trained, partly a subject matter that you can know about, partly an instinct, and partly a natural organic system that grows slowly over a number of years. To be able to encompass this mixed view, we need to use different starting points for our planning on different days. Sometimes we'll identify language items as our goals and expect the items to be learnt to a certain degree of accuracy within a certain time period. Sometimes we'll encourage students to do tasks and to notice what they've done, and we hope they get better at the language in the process. We'll need to do different things at different times.

Whatever your starting point, you may want to write some notes, do some mental rehearsal and then, after teaching, have a ponder to make sure your classes are getting a varied and balanced diet. Since starting points, lesson notes and planning behaviour all depend on your personality and what you think language, learning, teaching and people are all about, we need a course and lesson planning model that can encompass differences. The one I'd like to propose is the 'design model'. The design model of lesson and course planning provides a clear framework for all the options I've mentioned in this chapter and before. The design model looks at a lesson or a course as a creation, a structuring of time and experience for our learners using a set of resources (time, people, materials) in order to achieve learning.

In all jobs there are times when you have to consider the future, think about what needs to be achieved, assess your resources and work context, define the problems or issues, consult references, mull things over to see what's possible, construct things, and adjust them when their inherent problems become clear.

 I've seen furniture makers come back from listening to clients and then work for hours placing pieces of wood on the floor, arranging them this way and that, turning them over, matching them, swapping them and then going for a walk to have a think. I've watched a quilter choose and cut out pieces of material, placing them here and there on a table until an agreeable solution to a design problem is found. And I've seen people planning large and small gardens by talking things over with the owners, sketching things out, transferring workable ideas to graph paper, filling in planting programmes, standing back, seeing how things take, moving the mistakes, transplanting the successes, watching and waiting for the weather. They are all working hard, but also enjoying the work and the results.

We could liken course and lesson planning to setting and solving design problems in a principled way. We too can try out, discard, combine and redesign without a feeling of guilt if things don't go right first time. We also need times when we just watch and wait and times when we're more active.

209

During the lesson or course
Watch and listen to the students.
How's the time going?
Note down questions and reactions.

Before the lesson or course
What do students know?
What resources do I have?
What shall I do?

THE DESIGN MODEL

After the lesson or course
What's left over?
Hmm, I need to change that.
How has what we did shifted
student perception and skill?
I need to calm down and think!

THE DESIGN MODEL

7.7 Conclusion

We play a part in the business of teaching and learning, but like gardeners, we know that the other forces at work, the weather, the students, the germination times, are just as important as we are. There is room in this design model for both large-scale, broad sweep planning and detailed adjustment. There is room for goals of many different types before, during and after teaching. It is a cyclical rather than a linear model and there's time in it for planning and evaluating before, during and after teaching.

8 What are our freedoms and constraints?

8.1 Introduction

In this chapter, I'll look at some factors that we all have to bear in mind when we plan lessons and courses, factors which will differ from setting to setting. I'll look at external variables such as the type of organisation and the type of class, whether it's heterogeneous, very large, very small, exam or a substitute class. I'll also mention the sheer unpredictability of work that includes people (including ourselves!) as its main ingredient. In that section I'll work from the give and take of a normal class to classes whose students don't like each other, through classes that are a bit undisciplined, and on to the sort of pleasant and unpleasant surprises that can constitute a complete hijack! In each case I'll suggest that the feature can constitute a freedom or a constraint and I'll also suggest some practical principles for working with it.

External variables

8.2 Type of organisation

Your teaching life will be affected by the type of institution you work in, whether it's a primary or secondary school, an after-school language club, a private language school or university, a secondary or vocational school. More important than the type of institution though will be its 'organisational culture', that is, its normal practices and attitudes. For example, is there clear communication in your organisation? Is there an ethos of community service or is the whole place deserted when the bell goes and the offices locked up tight as a drum when you need to get into them? Are things organised for the marketing department's convenience or just for the students or as a good compromise between everyone?

The restaurant class
A friend of mine did some in-company language teaching for a business in Switzerland. As all the rooms in the company building were too small, a large room in a local restaurant was hired for the English classes. As an idea it sounded fine but my friend found out on arrival that he was expected to teach *through* *lunch*, i.e. through the business of discussing menus, ordering food, eating, socialising in the mother tongue with late arrivals who had missed the food information, calls for more mineral water, and so on. It was impossible, with or without planning, to sustain an English class through all the interruptions.

Of course, an organisation's practices and attitudes can work very much in your favour if, for example, professional development is taken seriously, or you get loads of free stationery, or if you drop your standards and join in the eating in the situation above, free lunches!

The best advice I can give on organisational and community culture is to learn as much as you can about the attitude or culture of the system you work in and to struggle to find your own particular peace with it. This may involve deciding which battles are not worth fighting and saving your energy for the ones you feel are crucial.

8.3 Type of class

Another very important factor in a teacher's work is the type of class, whether it's heterogeneous, large, small, an exam class, a substitute class or a class with very few resources. I'll deal with each of these types of class in turn now. Then in the next section I'll deal with classes with a challenging atmosphere.

Heterogeneous classes

If we think of a mixed class as being mixed in language skills and levels, age, academic background, mother tongue, sex, personality, language aptitude, learning style and other factors, then really every class we teach is mixed. It's strange that we tend to regard heterogeneous classes as a special category when they are our everyday reality.

There are in fact many attractions to teaching heterogeneous classes. They are interesting because of the sheer richness of their human resources. They are often bursting with energy precisely because of all the differences they contain. They give scope for peer teaching too and are challenging to teach.

They do however have some drawbacks. It's difficult to meet all the widely differing expectations held by individual students and difficult too to make sure that everyone learns. It's tricky to find materials, activities, topics and a pace to suit most participants, and those who are not catered for can soon become disaffected or bored. So until you have some satisfactory ploys to use while thinking on your feet, planning for heterogeneous classes will be very important. There are a number of very good sources to help and I recommend Ur (1987 and 1996), Prodroumou (1992) and Bell (1994). The practical principles below come from these and other sources.

Practical principles for working with heterogeneous classes

Syllabus and content

- Rather than having one syllabus for everyone in the class, try having two. One is the minimum compulsory syllabus you expect all students to follow, the other is an optional extended syllabus. Imagine you're tackling a reading text and vocabulary from it. In your preparation you note down what words and expressions from the text you consider essential, and make sure all the students write them down, learn them, review them and are tested on them. But you also give another set of 'optional' items, which will later appear in 'optional' sections in tests for the more advanced students to learn (Ur 1987, p. 11). Students can choose which syllabus they follow according to how much challenge they want or their perception of their own level. This work does presuppose that you know plenty about the things you plan to teach. A prerequisite is thus a willingness to research the content. Keep a notebook for each class too. If you're working with minimum and optional syllabuses (and also the self-access or other individualised work mentioned below), you'll need, more than ever, to keep track of who's doing what in which class and what goals students have set themselves.
- Jill Bell suggests altering the type of syllabus used too, from a 'hierarchical' one where 'material presented in any given lesson assumes that the student has worked with and understood previous units' to a student skills syllabus (Bell 1994 p. 29). This type of syllabus identifies skills that students need to practise, e.g. listening for the main idea or expressing information concisely, and it identifies areas that all students can work on and improve. Bell also suggests using a theme-based syllabus dealing with topics such as

'food', thus linking activities at all levels as well as bringing in the interesting content so vital in heterogeneous classes.

- If lessons are based on interesting and varied content, even native speakers will be engaged and can contribute to the proceedings. Less advanced students still have plenty of opportunity for profitable language practice and use.
- As Luke Prodromou points out, students who seem to be lacking in linguistic aptitude are often voluble and witty in their own language and culture. We thus need to build on what students know rather than incessantly reminding them of what they don't, so that all members of a mixed aptitude group are seen to be as bright as each other, only in different ways. This involves not only working on topics students themselves are interested in, but also on general knowledge, questionnaires about travel, culture and social behaviour, and using cognates, translation and paraphrase (Prodromou 1992, p. 49).

Materials and tasks

- The option of having the same materials and tasks for each student is not a workable one in a heterogeneous class. You can give differently graded materials to different people and expect them all to do roughly the same task. I'll give an example here in the form of a mixed ability dictation.

A Mixed ability dictation

Dictate a text. Advanced students have a blank sheet of paper each and write everything down, intermediate students are given a handout with the text gapped on it (they fill in the gaps), elementary students have a handout with the full text on it including, at some points, a choice between different words (they simply circle the word they think they heard). Once the dictation is finished, students are placed in threes across levels to check their answers. The only ground rule is that there should be no switching of papers. With this configuration, unusually, the advanced student in each trio will really need the intermediate and elementary students in order to check that their own writing is totally accurate.

- It's possible to have self-access phases in lessons where students can use colour coded materials banks to complete different tasks, thus fulfilling separate learning contracts (see page 40). The individualisation implied here can be based on quantity, difficulty, content, skill or activity type and it's important for students to judge for themselves if a task is right for them.

- Although very helpful to students, any approach which involves giving different materials to different students dramatically increases your preparation time. It's more time and energy efficient to use the same material for all students and then to vary the demands on different students by leaving tasks open-ended (see below).

Success orientation

All members of the class should be able to do the tasks set to an acceptable level so that the teacher doesn't have to make negative assessments of the weaker students. On the other hand, different levels of success can be set for different students. This works by asking all the students to find, say, three facts or do at least five questions or read at least the first paragraph, while the advanced students have to do more than this. Thus the 'compulsory plus optional' idea mentioned under 'Syllabus and content' above is carried through into the materials and tasks. Later on it's carried through too into tests. The main part of the test can be compulsory and a final section or sections made optional.

Teacher assistance

Preparation in class before all task work should be thorough so that everybody, including the weaker students, knows what to do. Your attitude should be to help students to produce successful work rather than wait until students make mistakes and then correct them. While this is obviously a good idea for all classes, it's especially true of heterogeneous classes where there is greater potential for embarrassment and loss of face of less advanced students in front of the more advanced students.

Open-endedness

Open-endedness means that each student can respond to their own level and to their own taste. Penny Ur (1987 p. 11) gives an example of a brainstorming exercise where students are asked to tell her all the things they can think of that are going on at the moment in the school. Thus the simplest response ('I am sitting') is as successful as the most sophisticated ('The caretaker's probably sitting down to a nice cuppa about now') and there is no clear limit to the number of responses possible. Students can express personal, original or humorous contributions.

The pleasure principle

Heterogeneous classes are riddled with differences of talent, personality, level and opinion. Yet virtually all learners fortunately agree on the importance of pleasure, whether this takes the form of humour, performance, games, mysteries or 'just' a sense of well-being. We need, thus, to remember when planning that lessons are best when they are purposeful and pleasurable. This means planning to include games, quizzes and stories as well as seemingly more important matters (see Prodromou 1992). This is important in any class but will particularly help to allay any of the divisiveness possible in very mixed groups.

Working together

- It's important to plan in some whole group time, for example, at the start of class, to bond the whole class together despite their differences. This can be a good time for non-language focus tasks such as moving furniture, showing photos or listening to music.
- In large heterogeneous classes you'll want to plan in plenty of peer teaching. In any group activity a certain amount of peer teaching and learning will be happening informally as people listen to and read each other's work, but I mean more than this. It's not just a question of asking advanced students to teach things to less advanced students since, if this is done too often, the advanced students will feel they're not learning anything and the less advanced will feel small and a nuisance. I mean that tasks can be given that build in collaboration (see the scoring system in '*Memorising*' on page 177). In tasks like this, less advanced students will gain the benefit, almost without noticing it, of working with students whose target language is better developed than theirs. More advanced students will get ideas, organisational help or social tips from the students who are not as able as they are in the target language. Thus the advanced students won't feel they're wasting their time. This kind of interdependence is deliberately planned into tasks for classes in cooperative language learning (see Johnson et al 1993).
- Employ different criteria at different times for grouping and for assessing group performance. Thus, while sometimes you will want to put all the strong students together and all the weaker students together, there must be times when groups are mixed as to level. The same goes for any other criterion, for example, sometimes all women together, sometimes women and men mixed. Mixing groups in this way will help stop cliques from forming and can encourage students to value each other's contributions, especially if the criteria by which work is evaluated are also varied. For example, sometimes speed will get an 'A' grade, and sometimes imagination. You can note down a reminder as to which grouping and grading criteria you'll use for any particular activity.

- In class ensure that students listen to each other, despite any cliques or differences, by periodically asking them to report back on each other's utterances. You can prompt this by asking, for example, 'X, what did Y just say?' or 'Z, do you agree with what A has just said?'

Very large classes

 I remember once, in an international teachers' group, a Swiss teacher talking about a 'large' class of 25 students. Some of the other participants laughed. 'That's not large', said a Japanese teacher, 'I regularly teach classes of 55.' Some participants gasped. There was a chuckle from a teacher from India, 'My largest class has about 120 pupils in it.' So I suppose a definition of a large class is one that *feels* large to you.

With a definition like this, we are then mostly thinking of the problem associated with classes that feel too large. These problems include noise, too many people and fixed objects in a restricted space, not enough materials for everyone, not being able to respond to differing needs, the difficulty of organising anything more than lockstep teaching and the lack of target language use if students speak common languages.

Practical principles for working with large classes

Crowd control

- Plan to invest plenty of time in learning students' names so that you can nominate individuals, so breaking up the group and having fleeting one-to-one encounters with lots of different students.
- Use clear eye contact with individuals.
- Don't bank on achieving group control by simply speaking more loudly, as you'll be hoarse within an hour. Use other systems for attracting students' attention such as hands up, tapping on the board, ringing a little bell or shaking a tambourine. Remember to explain whichever system you plan to use beforehand. Also work out how you would like students to attract *your* attention.
- Plan to establish a certain amount of routine. Don't make the routines too fixed, though, or the class will go into automatic pilot and it'll be very difficult to turn them once they've started.
- Keep students involved from the start of the lesson so that a working atmosphere is achieved while social energy is high.

- Use plenary phases and large display surfaces, such as the board, as a way of returning the whole class to cohesion after group work.

(See the section on page 232 on undisciplined classes for more practical tips.)

Basic chores

- Number or colour code materials so you can check quickly who's got what and get back any returns.
- Allot roles to students so that basic chores like checking the register, handing out materials and cleaning the classroom up are done with a team of helpers.

Group work

Contrary to what teachers of smaller groups sometimes think, teachers of large classes need to use pair and group work a lot in order to give students natural oral/aural target language practice and use. When doing group work with large classes, you need to plan it well otherwise there will be chaos. Plan to attend to all the following points:

- Make sure that the whole class works together quite well before you consider breaking down into smaller units.
- Give the smaller units a chance to bond and form an identity.
- Make sure the tasks you plan are clear. Go through them beforehand to make sure that the instructions are unambiguous, the time given realistic and the outcome achievable by your group.
- Make sure the tasks are interesting and explain to the students why they are useful. Students need to perceive the value of a task before they feel like putting in time, energy and commitment as well as, nearly always, suspending disbelief.
- Make sure that pair and group tasks involve student interdependence. This means that no one student can complete the task on their own. They need others to organise, complete or be graded on the task.(See Johnson et al 1993 for help on how to do this.)
- Work out who is going to work with whom and how you are going to explain this.
- Plan clear step-by-step instructions with demonstrations and checks where necessary.
- Work out clear timings and how you are going to communicate these.
- Work out who in the group is going to have what role. For example, one person can act as chair, another as scribe for the task, another as

the ideas person. Ask one person to be responsible for writing down verbatim the main things that were said during the task work in the mother tongue.
- Plan what you will do yourself during the task work, for example, listen and write correction slips.
- Remember to give timing warnings towards the end of the group work. If you have checked the task beforehand and planned the timing realistically, you should avoid the desperate cry so annoying to students, 'Stop now! It doesn't matter if you haven't finished!' ('Doesn't matter to whom?' I always want to rejoin!)
- Plan how you will check the work and make students accountable for it.
- Plan your evaluation stage, which in my view should include not simply an evaluation of language used, but also of task content, how well groups worked together, and which mother tongue utterances need translating into target language for next time, etc.

This may seem an encyclopedic list but the sort of gentle, unstructured task work that seems charming to a small group of adult learners can get you slaughtered in a large class of energetic teenagers. Because large classes are always heterogeneous ones too, you may like to look back to the practical principles for heterogeneous classes on page 214 as they may well be relevant to your class too (see also Cross 1995).

One-to-one (or very small group) teaching

When you start (or switch to) one-to-one work, several things may strike you – that it feels personal and intense, that instructions that include 'everyone', 'all of you' or 'get into pairs', which may come out of your mouth naturally, are no longer appropriate! Yet, if you've found it difficult to cater for everyone in a large mixed class, in one-to-one work you can now adjust to student pace and interests and have authentic conversations to your heart's content. These classes are a real luxury. You just have to learn how to keep things interesting without you or the student feeling that the heat is on you perpetually. There are some very useful books on teaching one-to-one. My advice is to look at Murphey (1991) and Wilberg (1987), in that order. The sort of practical guidelines they and I would give for planning follow.

Practical principles for teaching one-to-one or very small groups

- Plan plenty of time at the first meeting for getting to know each other, letting the student take as much responsibility as they wish, and completing personal profile forms on the student's background wants.

- Make the encounters as equal as possible by, for example, doing the work you ask the student to do yourself, either before or after the student does it, sitting near rather than opposite the student, letting the student handle any equipment, and so on.
- Make the occasions you meet a real exchange of information and underline this metaphorically by exchanging things such as poems, books, CDs or cassettes with the student.
- Use the student as a resource by, for example, asking them to demonstrate their job to you, draw a diagram of their home, tell you what they've been doing and plan to do, and ask them to teach you things.
- Bring other people in (by photo, letter, phone call, anecdote, etc.) so that neither of you feels lonely or bored.
- Use the local environment, e.g. corridor, coffee area, street, park, so that neither of you feels cooped up.
- Bring in more materials and activities than you would normally so that you can be very flexible as to level and interests.
- Bring in plenty of variety in the way of movement, music, colour, objects, pictures, jokes.
- Adjust to appropriate forms of error correction such as 'reformulation', where whole texts and utterances are rephrased so that they are natural. Reformulation can also include reformatting, which is typing out or transferring work to text, tape or graph (see Wilberg 1987, p. 5).
- Make plans, recaps and summaries even more clearly and jointly than usual.
- Try to extend your contact time with the student (unless, of course, you're meeting very intensively), by exchanging postcards or phone calls between classes.

Exam classes

If students are working towards an exam, the advantages are that the syllabus is external and thus clear and already written for you. The learners' aims are clear too since most of them will want to cover the syllabus and pass the exam. This gives a certain amount of motivation. There are usually lots of practice materials available commercially so you probably won't have to make your own.

There are disadvantages to exam classes though. Students may be nowhere near the level necessary to pass the exam. An over-concentration on exam technique can lead to too little actual language learning and an unbalanced diet of exam type tasks. Two useful sources to help you work on studying language as well as studying the exam and on teaching as well as testing are May (1996) and Prodromou (1995). Here are some practical principles from this and other sources to bear in mind when planning work with exam classes.

Practical principles for working with exam classes

Transparency

- Give students the syllabus and sets of real exams so that there is no misconception about what they will face. Show them all the question and task types. Make sure students know the names of all the main types of exercise, such as 'Cloze', etc. and the vocabulary in all the rubrics, e.g. 'cross out', 'fill in', 'underline'.
- When looking at tests and discussing answers, always try to help students understand why a particular answer was wrong and not simply that it was wrong.

Similarity

- Whatever the exam your students are working towards is based on, make sure that you plan plenty of work in class that is similar. For example, if the exam is based, as many are today, on authentic material (e.g. reading comprehension questions based on newspaper articles or public notices, orals with native speakers, listening tests devised from radio programmes, etc.), provide plenty of authentic material, a wide range of text types, practice in all four skills and a wide range of vocabulary and structures. Do plenty of pairwork if there is an interview component to the exam.

Get students in the study mood

- Give homework and encourage students to keep their old work. This is so they can periodically go through the corrected papers, see how they are improving and make lists of their 'favourite mistakes'. Keep a note yourself of the homework you've set so that you remember to collect it in.
- Encourage students to keep learning diaries so they can see how useful the class is even if they don't end up passing the exam.
- Encourage them to become more independent in their use of dictionaries and grammar reference books and also encourage student-to-student and student self-correction.

- Help them to understand the examiner's point of view by, for example, letting them make up their own comprehension questions and write test items to reflect their own interests and gender.

Balance

- When you're doing exam exercises point out how useful the work is for other things apart from the exam. Do plenty of work which is NOT aimed at a particular section of the exam. Point out how essential it is for real life and the exam to keep learning, for example, vocabulary, and to gain cultural and general knowledge from extensive listening and reading. Thus students will see that exam preparation can be good general learning and general learning can be useful for the exam.

Exam tips

- Plan in time to develop good exam strategy. Show students how to time their work, plan it, proofread it and check it for their own favourite mistakes.

Sort yourself out!

- With the help of other teachers when possible, make information banks containing past papers, examples of past student work graded at different levels, and lists of the usual topics, text types, situations, etc. that tend to come up in the exam. Gather folders of interesting texts and topics, pictures and photos, etc. as you will get through an immense amount of material in the life of an exam course.
- Make sure that while keeping a steady pace you still allow thinking and learning time, the right to make mistakes, experiment and discuss. Build student confidence by graduating the degree of accuracy you expect according to the student and their distance in time and level from the exam.

Substitution classes

Some teachers asked to stand in for a colleague who is absent for some reason, will groan inwardly (or even outwardly!). The reasons for their disgruntlement are not just that they'll miss a potentially free period but that they are usually told at short notice and thus don't have much time to prepare, and that classes would often rather have their own teacher. Other problems with being asked to substitute can be that you don't know the students or what they've done, especially if the colleague who's away is a poor record keeper. Also, you may not know how many times you'll see them and so you may have to teach one-off block lessons for a while.

On the other hand, the pleasures of substituting are that you get plenty of variety, can find out what other teachers have been doing with their classes and are relatively free from homework drudgery and long-term responsibility.

Practical principles for working with substitution classes

• When you meet the class in which you are the substitute teacher, explain the reason why you're there and sort out a quick routine for names, such as asking students to write their names on cards and to prop these up on their desks.

One approach is to have some activities in reserve that will work at different levels. Some ideas follow.

A Using pictures

Precisely because pictures are free from words and thus don't tie you to any specific language, they're ideal for using with classes you haven't taught much and so don't know the level of. I particularly like working with sequences of pictures or picture stories. The rather old-fashioned ELT picture composition books can be useful here, but the cartoon strips without words that appear in magazines and newspapers tend to appeal to students more. They often have amusing or unexpected last pictures that make a good 'punchline'. I clip these out whenever I find them and keep them on hand for when I have time to do Step 1 below.

1 When you have a spare ten minutes, number each picture in the story, and write out a skeleton text for it at elementary level. Then write down extra things you could elicit or teach at higher levels. This will save you thinking on your feet when you're teaching.
2 In class, hand out a part of the picture story and then start work on picture 1. Elicit ideas for the name of the main character and the setting. Write up the numbers of the pictures on the board and store elicited ideas under the appropriate number. Ask students not to write yet. Promise them there'll be plenty of time to write later. Then work on each picture in much the same way. Elicit ideas and language, refine the language if necessary, striking a balance between accepting as much of the less advanced student's offering as possible and stretching the more advanced student as much as possible with challenging paraphrases.

3 Let students practise orally in pairs or plenary. After every couple of pictures, loop back and ask a student to tell the story from two or three pictures back. Continue looping back with some pair practice until most of the picture story is told. Keep the last one or two 'punchline' pictures to the very end so that interest is rekindled.
4 Finally, give the students the promised writing time. Then check their stories to make sure they are correctly written up.

A Using an unusual methodology

Some slightly unusual methodologies (which are hard to use with enormous mainstream classes) are perfect to use with small classes into which you come as a substitute teacher. Here is a good example.

Counselling Learning
Counselling Learning is an entire method created by Rev. Charles Curran (Stevick 1980). Teachers all over the world now use part of the method, the 'circle around the tape recorder idea', without necessarily knowing a lot about the original method or its philosophy.

For the idea to work well you need a small group of about ten lower-intermediate students or above or you need to share the students' mother tongue. Draw the chairs together into a circle and use either a cassette recorder which is passed around the circle or a tape recorder with a built-in or hand-held microphone. Students first decide what they will talk about. It's important that they decide this for themselves even if it does take a while for them to gain a consensus. They start their discussion in the target language. Every time they feel they need you to help with a word or expression they call you over. You quietly give them the best word or phrase you can think of for what they wish to express. They may want to practise saying it a few times. Then, when they feel sure they can say it, they record it using the microphone. When someone else feels they want to say something, they either record it straight away if it sounds natural and correct or call you over if they need help. Keep going until you have at least a few minutes' worth of discussion recorded.

What happens next depends on the structure of your lesson. If there's a break or that's the end of the class, you can transcribe the tape at home. If the class is a long one without a break, you can do the transcription in class with the students. Write the transcription up on an overhead projector or write it out by hand and make a photocopy for everyone. If you share the students' mother tongue, you can write in English on the left of the paper and a mother tongue translation on the right. Next, students read the transcription while listening to the recording. They then ask you any questions they want about patterns they spot or anything they don't understand. (See Thornbury 1997 for the usefulness of this method for working on noticing language.)

That's the basic idea. All you need is a small class, a circle of chairs, a blank cassette and a tape recorder. You don't need to prepare any topics or materials. That's what makes this a useful activity for when you're substituting.

Using teacher resource books

Another way of coping if you are called on to substitute for a teacher who is away is by using 'recipe books' or ideas books. There are so many good ones that it's hard to know which to list. I solved this problem by asking colleagues to nominate their favourites and by going into busy staffrooms to look at the shelves of resource books. The list that follows includes my own and other people's recommendations: Campbell and Kryszewska (1992), Frank and Rinvolucri (1983), Grange (1993), Hadfield (1984 and 1995), Hancock (1995), Kay (1994, 1995 and 1996), Lindstromberg (1990 and 1997), Porter Ladousse (1983), Watcyn-Jones (1993 and 1995).

Whenever you have a moment, flick through one of these ideas books. Mark the ideas that look promising and which say 'Any level' or 'No materials preparation necessary'. Then, when you are next asked to substitute, you can try one out. You can tell the class that you haven't tried the activity before but that it looks interesting. Give it a fair trial and then ask the students what they thought of it. Many students, having a change from their normal teacher, will enter into the spirit of doing something outside their normal routine. The joint exploration can get students on your side. Even if the activity isn't a raging success, at least you've started to get to know a new book.

Using a topic-based lesson

Provided the class you're going into as a substitute teacher is 'intermediate' or above, the topic-based lesson can be a useful one to use. You will need to do a little preparation beforehand but this could be done whenever you have some free time. First you find a couple of topics. They need to be ones that are unlikely to be found in the normal range of coursebooks and thus not already 'done' by the class. They also need to be ones that are right for the kind of classes you're going into. Thinking of groups that I could presently be asked to cover for, I could take any of the following topics: 'Breaking bad habits', 'TV chat shows', 'Headaches', 'Relationships' or 'The influence of US culture on our country'. Once you have some possible topics, jot down on paper some things that could come up under each one, as here:

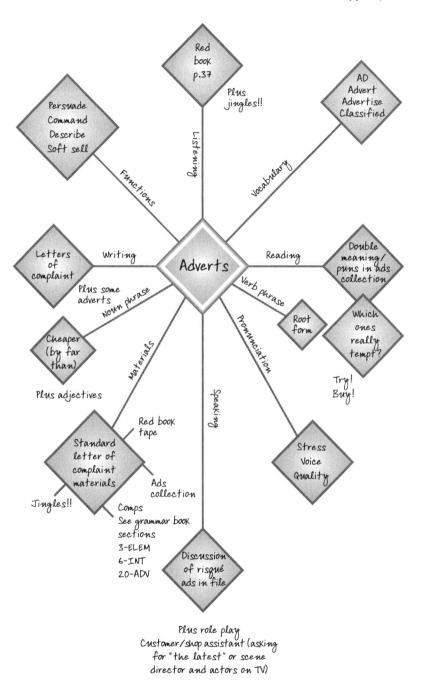

Red
book
p.37

Plus
jingles!!

AD
Advert
Advertise
Classified

Persuade
Command
Describe
Soft sell

Listening

Functions

Vocabulary

Letters
of
complaint

Writing

Adverts

Reading

Double
meaning/
puns in ads
collection

Verb phrase

Plus some
adverts

Noun phrase

Root
form

Which
ones
really
tempt?

Cheaper
(by far
than)

Materials

Pronunciation

Try!
Buy!

Plus adjectives

Speaking

Red book
tape

Standard
letter of
complaint
materials

Ads
collection

Stress
Voice
Quality

Jingles!!

Comps
See grammar book
sections
3-ELEM
6-INT
20-ADV

Discussion
of risqué
ads in file

Plus role play
Customer/shop assistant (asking
for "the latest" or scene
director and actors on TV)

TOPIC-BASED LESSON NOTES

You'll notice I've jotted down my ideas in a sort of snowflake pattern rather than in lines. This is so that once I get in class, I can start off with an idea from any section. I won't feel I have to follow any particular order of steps but can think on my feet in response to the class.

Once you've jotted down some ideas and found any texts, pictures or activities that fit the topic and popped them into an envelope with the notes, you'll have a head start when suddenly called on to go into a class as a substitute teacher.

If you'd like to do a topic-based lesson but have literally two minutes' warning that you'll have to substitute, have a look at the *Cambridge International Dictionary of English*. It has 'Language portrait' pages which, at a stretch, could get you through a class. Some pages show pictures of vocabulary linked by place (e.g. the bedroom), other pages show a semantic link, such as all the words for different kinds of coverings (e.g. lids, tops, etc.). Yet other pages illustrate all the meanings for one word (e.g. crop) or take, say, a topic like 'Relationships' and show pictures and phrases (e.g. 'to get engaged'). These pages would certainly get you started and meanwhile you can be planning what to do in the rest of the lesson!

Classes with few resources or facilities

Just as I defined a large class as one that *feels* large to the teacher, I'd like to define meagrely resourced classes as ones that don't contain some of the resources that the teacher and students are used to.

I've seen a teacher and students able to work quite happily crammed into a chemistry lab with only stools to sit on. The teacher was very content with the coloured chalks she found near the blackboard and the students delighted to have sinks to wash their hands at before they settled down to work. I've also seen a teacher and students frustrated despite the fact they were in a large, light, purpose-built classroom with overhead projector, radio, cassette and video apparatus. They were frustrated because the automatic curtains had got stuck six inches farther in than was normal, thus blocking a tiny fraction of the splendid view normally visible through the massive windows.

Three particular sources of anxiety in under-resourced settings can be the seating, boards and display surfaces, and individual student materials. I'll consider each of these below.

Practical principles for working with under-resourced classes

Seating

A particular problem here can be when the chairs and tables are fixed to each other and screwed to the floor in long rows. It means that students only see the back of each other's heads, and aren't able to move or work with more than one other student. A helpful book to look at here is Nolasco and Arthur (1988). These authors have a range of suggestions about what to do in this sort of situation. Here are a couple of ideas:

- Don't take the present arrangement for granted. Study the space and the placing of the seats and display surfaces and see if you can improve on the layout of the room. If you can improve on it but you have colleagues who prefer it the way it is, work out the swiftest way of moving things where you want them, and then get students into a quiet routine of moving things at the start and finish of each lesson.
- If moving seats and boards is not possible, for example, in a raked lecture auditorium, look at the different possible configurations of students and get them used to turning round, passing things up rows, etc.

Boards and display surfaces

There may be no boards or display surfaces at all, or they may be too small, in the wrong place or not the type you like. Here are some possible solutions:

- You can make and/or bring in your own, made of the reverse side of wallpaper, poster paper or cloth.
- In a small class you can simply write on paper and gather people close enough so that they can see what you've written.
- You can use individual handouts and reusable packs of materials, and use dictation activities so that students themselves write down the things they need to have on record.

(See also Dobbs forthcoming.)

Individual student materials

There may not be enough books or copying facilities available. Here are a few helpful solutions:

- You can ask students to share materials, but if they share a mother tongue too, make sure you teach them how to say things like 'Can I share?' and 'What page is it?' otherwise you'll be encouraging students to lapse into their own language.

- As suggested above, you can make more use of dictation and laminated, reusable activity packs.
- You can use the central display surface for writing up questions and tasks as well as for 'Mask and reveal' and 'Change the order' activities, and for student writing.
- You can ask students to bring in materials such as pictures and objects. Also ask them to generate materials of their own in class by drawing, making work displays, writing out role cards, etc. See Deller (1990) for ideas in this vein and also Marsland (1998).

So far in this chapter, I've mentioned organisational culture and have looked at different types of classes to see what their attractions and disadvantages are and how best to meet these pluses and minuses in planning and in practice. Next, I'd like to turn to a different way of considering types of classes – by group atmosphere. It's often not a particular type of class, in the sense of a big class or a small class or a very mixed class, that is difficult to teach, but one that has a strange or problematic atmosphere. So I'll look at this particular type of challenge next.

8.4 The unpredictability of working with people

We can do all the planning and preparation in the world for our classes but it won't stop reality from happening! Sometimes ... often, in fact, things don't go the way we thought they might. This can be a great relief if, for example, the quality and quantity of student participation in class is greater than the material deserves! But there are other times when unpredictability is more of a problem.

We could look at a scale here starting at one end with a lesson that goes pretty much as the teacher and students planned and expected it to (which is, very broadly, what I have assumed in the earlier part of the book). Next along the scale is the class with students who just do not seem to like each other. Next might be the undisciplined class, and finally the class where something really surprising happens. I'll look first of all at what you can do when students just don't get along.

Classes with students who don't get on

Any experienced teacher knows that you can have two classes that are objectively pretty much the same in level, size and composition and yet in terms of atmosphere are totally different. One might be good fun with students who are supportive of each other, while the other feels difficult. Walking in to the first group is like walking in to meet your friends. They are lively and cheerful or whatever it is that you like in your classes. The learning seems to go swiftly and easily and you all come out at the end of the lesson feeling even better than when you went in. Let's say you meet your next group after the break. This time you walk in to a funny atmosphere. The students won't listen to each other. They don't seem to like each other. There are sighs and groans and after 90 minutes with them you come out feeling as if things haven't gone well even though you've used virtually the same material that went down so well with the first crowd. Groups all have their own personality or atmosphere no matter how objectively similar they may be in terms of size, level or background. They may also not get on well. Here are some practical principles for consideration based on Woodward 1995.

Practical principles for working with classes who don't get on

Avoidance

This is a short term solution but does ensure a modicum of peace for a while.

- Avoid sitting people close to each other who hate each other.
- Avoid topics likely to cause friction, e.g. sports, politics, culture, opinions. You end up of course with topics as trivial as 'The advantages and disadvantages of long-haired beige carpets' and if someone really wants to pick a fight, they'll even manage it with this topic!
- Avoid people talking to each other. You can act as the broker for all conversation, i.e. all exchanges in the classroom are either indicated by or directed to you. This gives you the power to control any outbreaks of sniping but makes the class totally teacher-centred.
- Avoid argumentative people. You can ignore the main angry people by not speaking to them and by lack of eye contact. If you do this, the rest of the class may, almost unconsciously, do this too. This will probably make the ignored people go quiet and work for a while. Being 'sent to Coventry' has a powerful effect.
- Avoid certain types of exercises such as role play, debates and competitions as these have a naturally stirring effect on people.

Confrontation

- You can have private talks with difficult individuals to discuss their behaviour with them or a group discussion of what is going wrong and why. This will sometimes fix things. (See Hadfield 1992 p. 158 for useful strategies if you decide to take this route.)

- You can take disciplinary action as agreed and laid down by the school in negotiation with teachers, student councils, parents, governors, etc.

Separate development

You can treat the class as separate individuals in a number of ways.

- Institute 'flexi-time' so that people come to class and leave at slightly different times from each other. This will avoid people having fights on their way into and out of class.
- Students can work on separate or different materials or tasks. This takes more teacher preparation time but has the advantage of minimising harsh student-to-student correction or competition. If students don't know what other students are working on, they can't attack each other for being wrong.
- Dialogue journals, fully explained on pages 67–8, involve frequent confidential written conversations between each individual student and you, the teacher. This gives you a one-to-one direct line to students and can help you to understand or resolve conflicts.

Cooperation

- Ideas taken from cooperative language learning (see Johnson et al 1993) are very useful in difficult classes. An example here is asking students to paraphrase what another student has said before going on to make their own comment on a subject. This forces students to listen to one another and often uses up the energy that would go into criticising the other student's language by encouraging instead a neat paraphrase.

Undisciplined classes

Classes can be difficult for reasons other than the fact the students don't like each other. The group may have very low motivation and concentration. They may arrive late, talk to each other a lot, wander around, display dislike of the teacher, push for confrontation, eat, shirk, shout or ignore you.

The first class I ever had was in a college of further education in north London and filled with young day-release postmen. They'd left school early because they hated it. They'd joined the postal service mostly because it enabled them to burn around London on motorbikes all day. As they were only 15 years old, they were forced by law to attend college one day a week and they met me for Sociology and English. I was completely untrained, young, female, part-time, didn't plan my lessons very carefully and didn't have a reputation or a college-wide system of sanctions to help me.

The only peaceful evening I had at home in those days was the Friday evening after I had taught them. The rest of the week was a slow-building terror of having to meet them again on the Friday morning. What did they do that was so terrifying? They lay across my desk. They levered tiles from the floor. They threatened to throw chairs through the windows. But in between the swearing they were sometimes quite nice.

As you can tell from the anecdote above, I don't tout myself as a miracle worker when it comes to difficult classes. I *have* got a bit more skilled as I've got more experienced and older. I've also asked around and done some very fruitful reading. (See especially Appel 1995 Ch. 2, Blum 1998, Grinder 1991, Hadfield 1992, Malamah-Thomas 1987, Ur 1996 and Wragg 1993.) From these and other sources, I offer the following practical principles.

Practical principles for dealing with undisciplined classes

Before class

- Be clear about national and local rules concerning, for example, parental rights and corporal punishment.
- Find out what other teachers in your school do in terms of rules and relationships.
- Become clear in your own mind about what you'd like to see in your classes in the categories of movement, talking, safety, materials, social behaviour, clothing, and so on.
- Plan lessons carefully to involve students in productive, interesting work that moves at a reasonable pace and involves a variety of different stimuli such as pictures, students' own experience, etc.
- Think ahead to the rewards and admonishment strategies you'll use (see below).

In class

- Learn students' names as fast as possible so that you can relate to them individually.
- Be clear to students from the start about what you expect, even if you do this only partially and in negotiation with the students.
- Don't judge students by their appearance. The one with the shaved head and nose ring may be an absolute sweetheart while the one with the straight haircut may be a demon. Or vice versa.
- Establish some routines especially at the start and end of lessons (see Chapter 2).
- Reward good behaviour quickly, clearly and systematically with, for example, nods, attention and interest as well as good grades, smiley stamps or work displays.
- Reward good behaviour much much more than you admonish bad behaviour.
- Be realistic in your demands, taking into account the time of day, energy levels, etc.
- Use pupil territory, walk about and don't get penned or hemmed in one place.
- Behave as if you're in control, i.e. keep breathing calmly and moving and have good eye contact with individuals.
- Develop eyes and ears in the back of your head so that you can spot boredom, fatigue or bad behaviour very early on.
- If a couple of students are particularly vocal or difficult, don't assume that they represent the whole group. The rest of the students may be quite happy with the class and may resent the individuals making the fuss.

Prevention is far far better than attempting a cure once things have started to go wrong. Many of the measures above can be planned and practised quite deliberately. Once trouble starts, however, you're going to have to take rapid, almost intuitive decisions fast. You won't have time to read and consider the ideas below! I doubt too if, in the heat of the moment, you'll even be able to remember them! But if you do have a tough time in class, you may like to think about the way you handled it and either pick up some ideas below or add your ideas to them for a discussion with colleagues.

- When you spot something naughty, observe the people concerned until you're pretty sure your suspicion is well founded and then act quickly.
- Discipline according to what the students need and in proportion to the deed and not according to the depth of your irritation! (This can be hard advice to follow!)

- Try to admonish individuals quickly and quietly rather than across a class.
- Vary your methods of intervening in a disruption by using visual, auditory, kinaesthetic or other methods. So sometimes stare, sometimes make a humorous remark, sometimes gesture, and sometimes withhold attention.
- If using verbal admonishment, keep your voice polite and at normal volume and use positives rather than negatives. Rather than 'Don't talk' or 'Stop yelling!', try 'There's too much loud talking. I want you to listen to each other and talk quietly.' Also, give students time to carry out your request before repeating it.
- Avoid getting into a confrontation. Switch tasks, tell a joke, suggest a talk at a later time convenient to you, anything rather than getting locked in with adrenalin running high on both sides.
- If you have to use some kind of sanction, use one or threaten one that is unproblematic for yourself and others.
- The SECOND the student(s) stop disrupting the flow of the lesson, resume your normal breathing and body movement. Remember the other students who want to get on with the lesson and get right back to the work in hand. Let the conflict go.
- Be consistent. Treat everyone equally and with respect and do what you say you're going to do unless there's a complete hijack (see below).

After and between lessons

- If you've had a bit of a rough time in class, and are feeling upset, don't flay yourself thinking, 'I should have done this' and 'If only I'd done that.' Maybe talk to a colleague about things. They'll help you to put the lesson in proportion and perhaps give you some useful practical advice. Remember that there's always next lesson to get improvements in.
- Reward well-behaved students by, for example, writing to their parents or sponsors to let them know how well they're doing.
- Take a personal interest in all students even the ones who give you trouble (when they're not giving you trouble!).
- If the normal methods above haven't worked for you, do some research into some more unusual ones such as those from Neuro-Linguistic Programming (e.g. adopting a particular spot from which to do your disciplining, and learning when is the best time to break the physiological stand-off that's usually involved in bad behaviour (see Grinder 1991).
- Involve other teachers in creating a patterned system of positive behaviour management (see Blum 1998).

- If other staff aren't particularly interested, or you can't build a school-wide system, build your own system and stick to it in your classes. Word will get around and students will come into your class expecting to behave. Over time you WILL be able to build a better atmosphere. It will take time and it won't be easy but I know from experience that it WILL happen!

Hijacks: Pleasant and unpleasant surprises

I'll now go on to discuss not just the natural negotiation that is part of every lesson or the grumpiness and indiscipline of a particular group, but something a bit more dramatic or unexpected which I call a 'hijack'! This is when something happens that makes it virtually impossible for you to do what you planned. Here's an example from my own experience.

 I was once in the middle of a grammar presentation in a tiny attic room when Camilo from South America spotted strange white stuff coming out of the sky. 'Esnow!' he cried. 'Esnow!' I looked at the utter absorption on his face as he stared delightedly and for the first time ever at the drifting flakes. We all went to the window.

(See Bailey and Nunan 1996 for more examples of surprising events.)

Not all lesson surprises are as pleasant as the above. I've also known lessons disrupted by small children being sick, an ill-tempered janitor who regularly threw us all out on the street early, perverts waving their underwear, schizophrenic 16 year olds talking to their guardian angels, and the very occasional extremely unpleasant individual who upset everyone else immediately ... These are things I call 'hijacks'. You absolutely cannot plan for them and no amount of nicely established routines will win the day here!

There are long-term ways of getting better at 'going with the flow' or accepting real life flexibly and creatively. You can develop a repertoire of optional in-class behaviours and learn when and when not to use them (see Stevick 1986). You can work with 'Decisive incident reading mazes' (see Kennedy 1995 and 1999 and Tripp 1993). You can also work with case studies or vignettes of classroom events in writing, on slides, video or sound tape and have discussions with others on what you see as the reasoning behind the teacher decisions in the material. There's even a 'snakes and ladders' game designed to help you get better at dealing with surprises (see Tanner and Green 1998). But in the meantime here are some practical principles to bear in mind if you have a sudden interruption.

Practical principles for dealing with surprises and hijacks

Some of the advice given earlier under the practical principles for dealing with undisciplined classes will stand you in good stead here, for example, being generally observant.

- Watch and listen to your students and fellow staff a lot. Find out the way they're thinking and feeling. That way you'll know what 'normal' is for them.

When something unexpected happens, allow the interruption on any of the following grounds:

- You have no choice.
- It involves true communication in the target language.
- Students are trying to tell you something they feel is important.
- The hijack is actually more useful and interesting than what you had planned or takes what you'd planned deeper or further in some way.
- It allows you to cash in on a teachable moment.
- The majority of the students state clearly that they like the interruption and it's for their good.
- It doesn't take long and makes one or two people very happy by, for example, accommodating their learning style.

When something unexpected happens, try to disallow it when:

- It's a case of one or two students dominating the air space for too long.
- After checking, you find that all the other students are bored or upset by the interruption.
- You haven't got the emotional stamina or skill to deal with the hijack.

Whether you allow or disallow a hijack, try to do so after you have considered quickly and carefully. State your reasons and decision as calmly and clearly as possible to the group. Remember these points:

- In many groups of teens and older the group itself will often deal with the hijack or help you to. You won't normally be on your own.
- Don't be afraid to call on group members, teachers in adjoining classrooms, the director of studies, etc. if you feel absolutely stuck.
- It's often AFTER the event that you feel most shaken, so indulge yourself by taking time to calm down, go for a walk, talk things over with a colleague or with the person things went wrong with, or whatever you need to feel better and learn from the experience.

It's hard to give advice about hijacks since they are all by definition unpredictable. There is some interesting reading in the area of group dynamics, however, in Houston (1984) and Hadfield (1992).

8.5 The internal variable: Ourselves

So far I've mentioned external factors that can affect the lesson and course planning and teaching you do. 'Internal' factors are very important too. By this I mean that because of our own personalities and habits, we go about our work in our own ways. At times we can be strait-jacketed by ourselves! I'll explain what I mean.

All teachers engage in similar activities such as beginning and ending classes. But the way we carry out these activities can vary enormously, creating distinctly different learning environments for our students and different feelings in ourselves. We could call this personal style or teacher style. It results partly from voice and gesture, gaze and clothing and partly from the proportion and frequency of the various types of content and process in our teaching. Although we may be able to recognise other people's personal style, we may find it next to impossible to put a finger on just what style we have ourselves. I guess this is what good friends are for! We can ask them to pop into our classrooms for half an hour or listen to us talking about our planning or our classes and to tell us what they think.

It's not just our voice, dress, gesture or the proportions of activities we habitually choose and the patterns into which they're arranged that constitute our personal style in teaching. There's also the way we relate to ourselves (do we give ourselves a hard time over a bad lesson or forgive ourselves easily?), to other staff (can we give and take ideas or are we quiet about our teaching?), and to our students (do we need them to love us or does it irritate us when they get too close?). Personal style and relationships in teaching are important since we don't just teach a subject, we also teach ourselves (Dufeu 1994).

Practical principles for dealing with strengths and weaknesses in ourselves

Just as with all the other factors mentioned so far, there are advantages and disadvantages to the way we personally work. It's tempting to think that we are what we are and can't change, or that if we want to change we have to get involved in psychotherapy and other scary stuff. There IS a halfway house in my view.

Finding out about ourselves

We can try to become more aware of our personal style and the effect we have on other people and can then try to build on our strengths and minimise our weaknesses. We can find out in a number of ways:

- We can get as much feedback from students as possible. (See *'Teacher style'* on page 38, *'Dialogue journals'*, on page 67, *'Classes and people'* on page 74, *'Topics and themes'* on page 97, *'Group landscape'* on page 136, and the *'Mapping the lesson'* on page 136.)
- We can have lots of private ponders. (The buzz word for this is 'reflection'!)
- We can read useful books, and team up with a study buddy, critical friend or mentor for discussion and peer observation. There is even a feedback card game out now for the very brave and honest! (See Gerrickens 1999.)

Once we've gained some information on how others see us and how we see ourselves, we can then try to make maximum use of our strengths and minimise our weaknesses. I'll take the weaknesses first!

Working on our weaknesses

There is an activity called 'Headache and aspirin' (Woodward 1992) which I learned from Natalie Hess. First of all you find someone you enjoy working with and take it in turns to be 'Headache' and 'Aspirin'. 'Headache' starts by stating their problem or puzzle. 'Aspirin' just listens as carefully as possible. Then 'Aspirin' offers possible solutions or ideas to the problem. No judgemental comments are allowed. Then 'Headache' and 'Aspirin' swap roles. It's important that both of you get equal amounts of time to talk about your puzzles.

Working on our strengths

I know lots of teachers who feel that their strengths and real enthusiasms lie outside work. They love working with colour, for example, but don't work with it in class. They play sport but feel rather cooped up physically in their classroom. They have a splendid sense of humour but go deadly serious the minute they cross the threshold of their classroom. I'm not quite sure why this happens. Perhaps it stems from a desire to keep work and home, or work and leisure (or pleasure!) separate. Maybe we teachers feel that somehow we can't be ourselves at work, that the institution we work for somehow wouldn't like it.

The wonderful thing about teaching though is that, whatever sort of group you have, however unpredictable they are being, or however routinised and uninspired you may feel, you always have at least a LITTLE leeway in either what, how, when or why you do things, once the door to your classroom is shut.

I had a friend who was locked into a kind of teaching she did not enjoy. She had small groups of students preparing for a reading exam. They insisted on always dealing with short texts and always with the activities in the same order: pre-vocabulary, reading aloud, reading silently, comprehension questions. They were an exam class with an extreme case of exam mentality. They simply refused to work any other way. My friend loved horses. She rode them, trained them and taught riding. One night when I was waiting for her in the corridor outside her room, I could hear her voice. She was reading aloud from a text and, considering she was in a classroom, sounded unusually absorbed and dramatic! She read, '... As the smoke started to curl into the air, the horses one by one lifted their heads. A couple of horses snorted sharply as they smelt the smoke. Old Sam was the first to call out. He neighed loudly and walked nervously around his stable.'

My friend had found her way to survive in a tight situation. She had injected content that was interesting to her into a prescribed lesson structure that she did not like.

In a similar way, I have known other colleagues use the topic or content of texts, tapes, stories and letters to bring in the subjects they are most interested in. Other colleagues use objects or materials that they like, such as textiles, pictures, rods, masks, newspapers and poems. Using materials and content that keep you feeling relaxed or interested, even if it's just for five minutes a day, can greatly contribute to a feeling of freedom in an otherwise tightly prescribed situation.

Other teachers use activities that they particularly like as a way of surviving happily in class. Joachim Appel (1995) has used choral recitation at the start of class to establish a rhythm of interaction. By leading the class in a recitation of, say, a favourite piece of Dickens, he found that, as well as helping with pronunciation and review, it provided a kind of calming social routine that settled the class.

Here we have an example of the kind of skilful navigation through tides and currents that a practised professional teacher can manage and enjoy. We have an example of the 'design' model of planning and teaching that I mentioned in Chapter 7.

8.6 Conclusion

We've seen how teachers can select from a range of topics, materials and activities to make the best of their situation and themselves. It wasn't until I had the privilege of seeing lots of teachers at work in their own classrooms, however, that I realised that, of course, *every* teacher has something they do, or something they are, that is unique to them. It's their own special flair. Thinking of my own colleagues now, I know one who makes handouts which are attractive and instantly recognisable as his because of the hand-drawn artwork. Another colleague works with students to create video projects on an ambitious scale. Another manages to get all the students interested in singing English songs. One colleague is a grand story teller. One wakes students up intellectually. Another bonds with the rather more isolated students in the school who could be so lost without this contact. Every teacher I think of has something special, unconscious and uncontrived that they bring to their job. Perhaps this is the greatest freedom of all, the freedom to express our special gifts.

In terms of the gardening metaphor that I've threaded throughout this book, this chapter has been about the special conditions of your particular garden. Perhaps it's near the sea and thus suffers salty breezes or is in an area of heavy clay soil, perhaps it's enormous or perhaps tiny. The chapter has also been about the way you work as the head gardener, what you're good and bad at and what flair you can bring personally to your garden.

If you're not satisfied with your own small town patio, it's not terribly helpful to look at magazine pictures of enormous country gardens. Pining and longing don't make a good garden. In my view, a good gardener is one who can create something pleasant pretty well anywhere they go, by working with what they've got. By working within limitations and building on strengths and unusual features, we can try to make a good garden anywhere. My personal definition of a good garden is one that suits the people who are in it most. It's one that inspires them, teaches them and makes them feel good about being in gardens generally.

CHAPTER 8: WHAT ARE OUR FREEDOMS AND CONSTRAINTS?

Bibliography

Agosta, J. (1988) *Changing Energies*, Canterbury: Pilgrims.
Anderson, G., Boud, D. and Sampson, J. (1996) *Learning Contracts*, London: Kogan Page.
Appel, J. (1995) *Diary of a Language Teacher*, Oxford: Heinemann.
Bailey, K. and Nunan, D. (1996) *Voices from the Language Classroom,* Cambridge: Cambridge University Press.
Bassnett, S. and Grundy, P. (1993) *Language through Literature*, Harlow: Longman.
Bell, J. (1994) *Teaching Multilevel Classes in ESL*, Markham, Ontario: Pippin.
Blum, P. (1998) *Surviving and Succeeding in Difficult Classrooms*, London: Routledge.
Blundell, J., Higgens, J. and Middlemiss, N. (1982) *Teaching Functions*, Oxford: Oxford University Press.
Boak, G. (1998) *A Complete Guide to Learning Contracts*, Aldershot: Gower.
Bress, P. (1996) 'Review circles' in Woodward, T. 'Warm ups, breaks and fillers,' *ETAS Newsletter*, 13, 2, 43.
Buzan, T. (1995a) *The Mind Map Book*, London: BBC Publications.
Buzan, T. (1995b) *Use Your Head*, London: BBC Publications.
Cambridge International Dictionary of English (1995) Cambridge: Cambridge University Press.
Campbell, C. and Kryszewska, H. (1992) *Learner-based Teaching*, Oxford: Oxford University Press.
Celce-Murcia, M., Brinton, D. and Goodwin, J. (1996) *Teaching Pronunciation,* Cambridge: Cambridge University Press.
Chapman, B. and Fisher, S. (1995) *Conducting tracer studies in adult language and literacy programs*, Teacher Resource Series No. 6. NCELTR Sidney: MacQuarie University Press.
Claxton, G. (1998) *Hare Brain Tortoise Mind*, London: Fourth Estate.
Cohen, L. and Manion, L. (1989) *A Guide to Teaching Practice*, London: Routledge.
Collie, J. and Slater, S. (1987) *Literature in the Language Classroom,* Cambridge: Cambridge University Press.
Collins COBUILD English Grammar (1990) London: HarperCollins.
Collins COBUILD English Dictionary (1995) London: HarperCollins.
Concise Oxford Dictionary (1999) Oxford: Oxford University Press.
Cook, G. (1989) *Discourse*, Oxford: Oxford University Press.
Cross, D. (1995) *Large Classes in Action*, Hemel Hempstead: Prentice Hall.

Davis, P., Garside, B. and Rinvolucri, M. (1998) *Ways of Doing*, Cambridge: Cambridge University Press.

Deller, S. (1990) *Lessons from the Learner*, Harlow: Longman.

Dobbs, J. (forthcoming) *The Writing on the Wall*, Cambridge: Cambridge University Press.

Douglas Brown, H., Cohen, D. and O'Day, J. (1991) *Challenges*, New Jersey: Prentice Hall.

Doyé, P. (1999) *The Intercultural Dimension of Foreign Language Teaching*, Berlin: Cornielsen.

Dufeu, B. (1994) *Teaching Myself*, Oxford: Oxford University Press.

Ellis, G. and Sinclair, B. (1989) *Learning to Learn English*, Cambridge: Cambridge University Press.

Estaire, S. and Zanon, J. (1994) *Planning Classwork: A Task-Based Approach*, Oxford: Heinemann.

Frank, C. and Rinvolucri, M. (1983) *Grammar in Action*, Oxford: Pergamon.

Gairns, R. and Redman, S. (1986) *Working with Words* Cambridge: Cambridge University Press.

Gerrickens, P. (1999) *The Feedback Game*, Aldershot: Gower.

Grange, C. (1993) *Play Games with English 1,2,3*. Oxford: Heinemann.

Graves, K. (2000) *Designing Language Courses*, Boston MA: Heinle and Heinle Publishers.

Grinder, M. (1991) *Righting the Educational Conveyor Belt*, Portland: Metamorphous Press.

Grundy, P. (1989) 'When will they ever learn?' *The Teacher Trainer*, 3, 3, 4–11.

Hadfield, J. (1984) *Communication Games*, London: Harrap.

Hadfield, J. (1992) *Classroom Dynamics*, Oxford: Oxford University Press.

Hadfield, J. and Hadfield, C. (1995) *Reading games*, Walton-on-Thames: Nelson.

Hancock, M. (1995) *Pronunciation Games*, Cambridge: Cambridge University Press.

Hedge, T. (1988) *The Skill of Writing,* Oxford: Oxford University Press.

Hess, N. (1998) 'Voices of TESOL', *TESOL Matters*, 8, 4.

Horn, V. (1977) *Composition Steps,* Rowley, Mass.: Newbury House.

Houston, G. (1984) *The Red Book of Groups,* London: Gaie Houston.

Jeanrenaud, P. and Woodward,T. (1997) 'Effective tutorials', *Modern English Teacher 6*, 2,58–59.

Johnson, D., Johnson, R. and Holubec, E. (1993) *Circles of Learning*, Edina: Interaction Book Co.

Johnstone, K. (1981) *Impro*, London: Methuen.

Jordan, R. (1997) *English for Academic Purposes,* Cambridge: Cambridge University Press.

Joyce, B., Calhoun, E. and Hopkins, D. (1997) *Models of Learning – Tools for Teaching*, Milton Keynes: Open University Press.

Kay, S. (1994, 1995, 1996): *Reward Resource Pack: Communicative Activities for Students of English* (Pre-intermediate 1994, Intermediate 1995, Upper-intermediate 1996), Oxford: Heinemann.

Kennedy, J. (1995) 'Getting to the heart of the matter – the marginal teacher', *The Teacher Trainer, 9,* 1,10–14.

Kennedy, J. (1999) 'Using mazes in teacher education', *ELT Journal,* 53, 2, 107–113.

Klippel, F. (1984) *Keep Talking,* Cambridge: Cambridge University Press.

Kramsch, C. (1993) *Context and Culture in Language Teaching,* Oxford: Oxford University Press.

Langsch-Brown, B. (1998) 'Maintaining control through lesson planning', *ETAS Newsletter,* 15, 3, 37.

Laroy, C. (1992) *Musical Openings,* Harlow: Longman.

Laufer, B. and Shmueli, K. (1997) 'Memorizing new words: does teaching have anything to do with it?' *RELC Journal,* 28, 1, 89–108.

Lewis, M. (1993) *The Lexical Approach,* Hove: Language Teaching Publications.

Lindstromberg, S. (1990) *The Recipe Book,* Harlow: Longman.

Lindstromberg, S. (1997) *The Standby Book,* Cambridge: Cambridge University Press.

Longman Dictionary of English Language and Culture (1992) Harlow: Longman.

Longman Language Activator (1993) Harlow: Longman.

Maclennan, S. (1987) 'Integrating lesson planning and class management', *ELT Journal,* 41, 3, 193–7.

Malamah-Thomas, A. (1987) *Classroom interaction,* Oxford: Oxford University Press.

Maley, A. (1995) *Short and Sweet,* London: Penguin.

Marsland, B. (1998) *Lessons From Nothing,* Cambridge: Cambridge University Press.

May, P. (1996) *Exam Classes,* Oxford: Oxford University Press.

Murphey, T, (1991) *Teaching One to One,* Harlow: Longman.

Murphey, T. and Woo, L. (1998) 'Using student feedback for emerging lesson plans', *ETAS Newsletter,* 15, 3, 27–29.

Nattinger, J. and De Carrico, J. (1992) *Lexical Phrases,* Oxford: Oxford University Press.

Nolasco, R. and Arthur, L. (1988) *Large Classes,* London: Macmillan.

Nunan, D. and Lamb, C. (1996) *The Self-Directed Teacher,* Cambridge: Cambridge University Press.

Nuttall, C. (1996) *Teaching Reading Skills in a Foreign Language,* Oxford: Heinemann.

Oxford Photo Dictionary (1991) Oxford: Oxford University Press.

Oxford Elementary Learner's Dictionary (1994) Oxford: Oxford University Press.

Peyton, J. K. and Reed, L. (1990) *Dialogue Journal Writing and Non-native English Speakers: A Handbook for Teachers,* Alexandria: TESOL.

Peyton, J. and Staton, J. (eds.) (1991) *Writing Our Lives,* New Jersey: Prentice Hall Regents.

Pincas, A. (1982) *Writing in English,* London: Macmillan.

Porter Ladousse, G. (1983) *Speaking Personally*, Cambridge: Cambridge University Press.

Prodromou, L. (1992) *Mixed Ability Classes*, London: MEP Macmillan.

Prodromou, L. (1995) 'The backwash effect: from testing to teaching', *ELT Journal*, **49**, 1, 13–25.

Richard, R. (1994) 'Dear Norman' in '*The Independent* Story of the Year 2', June 1994.

Rinvolucri, M. (1998a) 'Dancing letters', *English Teaching Professional*, **8**, 12.

Rinvolucri, M. (1998b) 'The host family: A major learning resource', *Arena 21*, ARELS.

Rost, M. (1991) *Listening in Action: Activities for developing listening in language education*, Hemel Hempstead: Prentice Hall.

Scharle, A. and Szabo, A. (2000) *Learner Autonomy*, Cambridge: Cambridge University Press.

Stevick, E. (1980) *A Way and Ways*, Cambridge, Mass: Newbury House.

Stevick, E. (1986) *Images and Options in the Language Classroom*, Cambridge: Cambridge University Press.

Stricherz, G. (1982) *Before the Bell Rings*, New Jersey: Alemany Press, Regents Prentice Hall.

Swan, M. (1995) *Practical English Usage*, Oxford: Oxford University Press.

Swan, M. and Smith, B. (1987) *Learner English*, Cambridge: Cambridge University Press.

Tanner, R. and Green, C. (1998) *Tasks for Teacher Education*, London: Routledge.

Thornbury, S. (1997) 'Reformulation and reconstruction: tasks that promote "noticing"', *ELT Journal*, **5**, 4, 326–335.

Tripp, D. (1993) *Critical Incidents in Teaching*, London: Routledge.

Trompenaars, F. (1993) *Riding the Waves of Culture*, London: Nicholas Brealey.

Underhill, A. (1980) *Use Your Dictionary*, Oxford: Oxford University Press.

Ur, P. (1987) 'Teaching heterogeneous classes part two', *The Teacher Trainer*, **2**, 1,10–13.

Ur, P. (1996) *A Course in Language Teaching*, Cambridge: Cambridge University Press.

Ur, P. and Wright, A. (1992) *Five-Minute Activities*, Cambridge: Cambridge University Press.

Valdes, J. M. (ed.) (1986) *Culture Bound*, Cambridge: Cambridge University Press.

Van Ek, J.A. (1990) *The Threshold Level in a European Unit-Credit System for Modern Language Learning by Adults*, Strasbourg: Council of Europe.

Vogel, J. (1998) 'How far ahead do you plan? Instant and constant preparation', *ETAS Newsletter*, **15**, 3, 30.

Watcyn-Jones P. (1993) *Vocabulary Games and Activities*, London: Penguin.

Watcyn-Jones, P. (1995) *Grammar Games and Activities*, London: Penguin.

Weintraub, E. (1989) 'An interview with Ephraim Weintraub', *The Teacher Trainer*, 3, 1, 1.

Wilberg, P. (1987) *One to One*, Hove: Language Teaching Publications.

Williams, M. and Burden, R. (1997) *Psychology for Language Teachers,* Cambridge: Cambridge University Press.

Willis, J. (1994) 'Preaching what we practise – training what we teach: TBL as an alternative to PPP', *The Teacher Trainer,* 8, 1, 17–20.

Woo, L. and Murphey, T. (1999) 'Metacognition with action logs', *The Language Teacher*, May issue.

Woods, D. (1996) *Teacher Cognition in Language Teaching,* Cambridge: Cambridge University Press.

Woodward, T. (1991) *Models and metaphors in language teacher training*, Cambridge: Cambridge University Press.

Woodward, T. (1992) *Ways of Training*, Harlow: Longman.

Woodward, T. (1995) 'It made me think . . . about challenging classes', *Modern English Teacher*, 4, 2, 66–9.

Woodward, T. and Lindstromberg, S. (1995) *Planning from Lesson to Lesson,* Harlow: Longman.

Wragg, E. C. (1993) *Class Management*, London: Routledge.

Yorkey, R. (1970) *Study Skills for Students of ESL*, New York: McGraw Hill.

Index